GLENN MAXWELL

with Adam Collins

The Showman

GLENN MAXWELL

with Adam Collins

The Showman

**SIMON &
SCHUSTER**

London · New York · Sydney · Toronto · New Delhi

THE SHOWMAN
First published in Australia in 2024 by
Simon & Schuster (Australia) Pty Limited
Level 4, 32 York Street, Sydney, NSW 2000

10 9 8 7 6 5 4 3 2 1

Simon & Schuster: Celebrating 100 Years of Publishing in 2024
Sydney New York London Toronto New Delhi
Visit our website at www.simonandschuster.com.au

 A catalogue record for this
book is available from the
National Library of Australia

ISBN: 9781761428203

Cover design: George Saad
Front cover photography: Robert Cianflone/Getty images
Back cover photography: Robert Cianflone/Getty images
Edited by Geoff Lemon
Co-authored by Adam Collins
Typeset by Midland Typesetters, Australia
Printed and bound in Australia by Griffin Press

The paper this book is printed on is certified against the
Forest Stewardship Council® Standards. Griffin Press holds
chain of custody certification SCS–COC-001185. FSC®
promotes environmentally responsible, socially beneficial
and economically viable management of the world's forests.

For Vini, who I never want to do life without

And for Logan – I can't wait for you to read this someday

Contents

Foreword

Pat Cummins

I remember the exact moment Glenn Maxwell came into my life. He was on a television screen, batting for Victoria in a one-day match. He hit a massive six one ball, and smacked a catch high in the air the next. 'Classic Maxi,' laughed Sean Abbott, sitting next to me. They had just been at the Academy in Brisbane together, and Sean told me this fella wanted to hit every ball he faced onto the moon. He sounded like somebody I should be keeping an eye on.

We would be in the same Australian squad not long after, touring the UAE when Maxi made his international debut. We were all worried about Saeed Ajmal in the Pakistan attack, dominating with his ability to spin the ball both ways. Maxi rolled up to our analyst to ask for a replay of a delivery we'd just been shown. Next time we were all waiting to bat, he declared, 'All good, I can pick his doosra no worries!' When it was his turn, he reversed Ajmal first ball – he'd picked the doosra, no worries.

That's an encapsulation of the next 12 years we've spent playing for Australia. His endless confidence in doing things his way is something to behold.

In those early T20 days, you rarely saw batters risk getting out in ways that might be criticised as stupid. Even more so playing for their countries. Maxi was never saddled with that baggage, turning risk into his signature. Sometimes that made him hard to watch, especially when I was next in. But his way was never without calculation. He worked out half a decade before almost anyone how to be the ultimate matchwinner.

By the time I was leading Aussie teams, Maxi's career had proved there was no gain in trying to curtail him. In a way, it's easy to captain Maxi: you just get out of the way. Give space to his potential, put him into a position to shine. Remove inhibitions. He's the player we are happy to shift the whole team around, placing him as perfectly as we can in a game. Because more than anyone, he can win games by himself.

Our conversations seldom go further than encouraging him to trust his instincts, because those instincts create chaos for fielding teams while boosting our guys. Maxi getting off the leash in white-ball cricket is like Steve Smith grinding a Test team into the dirt. The opposition reaction is the same – frustration turning to despair, and soon there's no way back.

Of course, it doesn't always work. Any approach has rough edges. But as a team, plenty of us are picked to play percentages and aim for consistency. Eyes wide open, we ask the opposite of Maxi.

There will never be a better example than his 2023 World Cup. I had the best view of the 40-ball ton against the Dutch, but the next time I was at the non-striker's end was so different. Against Afghanistan, at 7 for 91, batting was as difficult as I've experienced in one-day cricket. The ball was swinging then turning square. I was hanging in there like day five of a Test. Down the other end, his body shutting down one limb at a time, he was hitting some of the most absurd shots imaginable.

Our personalities were well balanced for that partnership. As he will tell you, we laughed a lot and tried to live in each moment. There were so many of them: reviews, drops, half chances, beaten edges, nicks, boundaries, maidens, Maxi lying flat on the turf.

He leaves nothing in reserve, and didn't that night. On the line between crazy and genius, I know which side he falls on. At the end of one over, a long way from the target, he said, 'You just block out maidens, I'll get all the runs.' From anyone else, that sounds mad. But out of his mouth, it sounded plausible. It gave me the confidence that I could do my bit.

When history assesses his 201 not out, I firmly believe it deserves even more credit. It's undoubtedly the best one-day innings I've ever seen, and has to be the best ever played. It was the night his greatness had the space it needed to flourish to its fullest, and it was there for the world to see and respect.

That win gave the last burst of confidence our group needed that we could do whatever was necessary to win that World Cup.

I already thought that Maxi's ceiling was higher than any player I've taken the field with. That innings had us all believing it was higher again. It was fitting that he would go on to hit the winning runs in the final.

Maxi will say he's changed a lot from the brash young bloke I described. It's been special to become fathers around the same time, and to see what a great dad he is to Logan and the team he makes with Vini. All the parents in the Aussie side share that. But he's still the guy who insists he can pick any bowler and hit them anywhere he wants. The bravado has never dimmed. And when his plans don't come off, instead of regrets, his first thought is always that he can't fathom how he didn't nail it, and that he definitely will the next time. That's a wonderful trait, in our game or in life.

After that World Cup, there was naturally a point of wondering what's next for a guy who has done all one can in a gold Australian shirt. I know his appetite is vast and he will continue to push for selection in every national team, and I assure you that his name comes up in every one of those discussions. I suspect it will continue to well after he's retired. That's because he will always be the guy capable of anything, with his belief that he can win any game, from anywhere, at any time.

Foreword
Virat Kohli

Sit down for an interview with Glenn Maxwell? During an Indian tour to Australia in 2016, it was an interesting request. My management passed on the information, and it sounded unusual, but I cautiously agreed.

Of course, I was familiar with his work. Maxi arrived in the IPL in 2012 and there had been a lot of cricket between Australia and India since. His talent was obvious: a guy who had every shot that existed and invented some that didn't. I would see flashes of this ridiculous ability. But we didn't know each other beyond the back and forth on the field.

This video interview was part of a series he was doing with Cricket Australia, and our chat had the questions you might expect: my enjoyment of being anonymous in Australia, playing alongside Sachin Tendulkar, my fiery streak on the field. We were done in ten minutes.

After filming, though, when he was less nervous, we moved on to what he really wanted to speak about. It was the first time we'd spoken properly, and my impression was of a guy who wanted to take his game to the next level, and was soaking up everything he could from my experience. He asked loads of questions about my preparation and dealing with a public profile. You know when someone is really listening, wanting to learn, and Maxi was.

I marked it off as a nice experience, wished him well, and left knowing we would see each other on the field. As it turned out, in one of those games, the occasion got the better of us. I'm sure that story features in this book, and the result was a distance between us. I had a rapport with some Aussies like Steve Smith, with a rivalry underpinned by respect, but Maxi and I were competitors only. We were both at our most intense, struggling to find balance.

Deeper into my career, I realised that our world view as younger men wasn't the only way to succeed. Forever combative, always on the edge, can lend you energy for a time but can ultimately be exhausting. Maxi and I have spoken since about feeling this way, where offence was easily taken and tempers frayed. He had a smile on his face more than I did, always a joker, but we were both part of a wider culture.

In time, the IPL can help sort out this balance for some players, and the timing of reaching this understanding helped me and Maxi. Our interview returned to mind, helping reorient my thinking towards what he might be able to do at Bangalore in 2021. Watching him play made me think he would enjoy our environment. I put this to AB de Villiers, my trusted offsider in that dressing room, and he immediately agreed.

Not only did we think that Maxi would be a great fit in our middle order, we also thought he would be grateful for the chance to stop being the centre of attention, given there was already a spotlight on me and AB. We thought that might get out the best out of him. Since his Kings XI campaign in 2014 he had been searching for his best, and we all knew he was too good not to find it eventually.

It was a thrill seeing that come to pass, and at the same time having his huge cricket intelligence engaged for us. He was a dream recruit. It lives as a frustration for both of us that we weren't able to win the trophy in that first season.

It didn't take long for us to develop a closeness beyond the dressing room, as it became obvious that Maxi is about genuine care and connection. There's so much more than meets the eye. He's an easy person to be open with, and that goes both ways. I never knew how sensitive he is as a person, and I mean that in a positive way. Our friendship expanded to our families, as we navigate our journey as fathers. We text constantly, silly things that will make the other laugh. It's natural, like we've been mates forever.

When he had the night of his life in Mumbai against Afghanistan, I was thrilled for him on a personal level. I knew it would also make life more difficult for my Indian team, with Australia believing they could win from anywhere, but I was able to keep those thoughts separate while watching from Bangalore.

I missed some of the innings after Australia went four down. The game was moving so quickly in Afghanistan's direction, and knowing their spinners, it would get no easier. Checking in as he and Pat Cummins rebuilt, I said half seriously that with Maxi there, anything could happen.

By the time he reached his century, I genuinely thought he was going to win it. I've seen what it's like when Maxi gets hold of a team, and it felt like this was one of those nights. Yet to think he would end up with a double century was another layer of unbelievable.

The whole cricket world was glued to those final stages, as he kept bombing sixes on one leg, without a helmet too. Going down time and again with cramp, limping for singles – it was compelling drama, and so Maxi.

When it was over, I texted him along those lines: that he is a freak and a madman. In my view, he is the only player in the world capable of doing what he did. Concluding with such a milestone was perfect, capping an unparalleled knock.

Twelve days later, in the final, when Maxi threw a ball back in, I instinctively stuck up a hand and blocked it. Earlier in our careers, with so much on the line, you can guarantee there would have been an altercation. But now? We pretended to fight for a second, before both starting to laugh.

That's exactly as it should be – competitive but respectful. When someone can make friends along the way, from unexpected beginnings like Maxi and me, we're all the better for it. That's special, and a bond I know will be lifelong.

Co-author's note
Adam Collins

The bloke remembers everything.

Of all the cricketers I've interviewed, none have enjoyed powers of recall like Maxi. It's because of this that we realised early on, years before getting our act together to write a book, that any project on his life could be much more than a bog-standard tour diary.

When his leg snapped in late 2022, it felt like that was the end of the story. There might not be any more career to document. Little did anyone know what Glenn's 2023 would morph into when he made it back for the World Cup.

In reading this, think of us as charting time in two directions, x-axis and y-axis. One path goes through the most dramatic year of his life. The other ranges further, weaving in relevance from all the years before it. This means some chapters bounce around wildly, but then, so can Maxi. Like all things with him, it's about holding on and going for the ride.

In many ways, he has lived his career as an outlier, but he's also someone who has helped shape the modern game so that his way is more the norm. Behind the image of the cricketer, the person is vulnerable, sincere, and so much fun. Enjoy a guy who is happy to share all of this with you in such an unguarded way. He's worth it.

Prologue

There are 34 steps from the field of Wankhede Stadium to the dressing room. I stood at the bottom of them without a clue how I was going to get to the top. I had cramps stabbing through both hamstrings, with exhaustion having set in long before.

Still in my pads, with my bat in one hand and my cap on backwards, I stood still in the Mumbai night and took it in. The scoreboard still showed my name next to 201 not out. It still read 'Australia wins by three wickets'. Even so soon, I understood what this innings meant, and I knew it was ridiculous.

From where we were a couple of hours earlier to where we were now – it was a lot.

I knew that this would be big when Australia woke up. Not to the extent that I could predict there would be a pub in Melbourne where the chef would decorate his meals with 'Maxi 201' on every plate. But I've been around long enough to expect some response.

Yet what came back to me most strongly right at that moment was how close this came to never actually happening. How near I was to losing cricket altogether. It was not quite a year since November the 12th, 2022, when my left leg snapped in two – a gruesome injury from a terrible accident.

When I finally drew a breath and tackled those stairs from the field, each step was a symbol for every step I had taken in the previous 360 days, both as a cricketer and a human being. On both fronts, I'd never been prouder.

———

There have been opportunities for me to write a book across the 12 years I've been playing international cricket and the Indian Premier League, but I resisted. I always thought that it could wait, that I would rather reflect on things at the end of my career.

But this story, from that broken leg to hitting the winning runs in the 2023 World Cup, and becoming a father along the way, finally felt like one that deserved telling.

What follows in these pages is the tale of those months in depth – a year of my life, on the page.

But I also knew that just banging together a retrospective diary wouldn't be the right book, because my whole life to that point, in and out of cricket, had shaped what happened in that year and the way I was able to make it back on the field.

To know me is to understand how far away I was from having a professional career at all, and how close I was to leaving the game behind before I'd turned 20 years old.

It's to know my want to be a father, and why the obstacles along the way hurt so much. It's to know how integral being a family man is to me, and how that stems from how I was raised.

It's to recognise in these pages the grown-up I've become (at least most of the time) and to see how far I had to go before getting my act together with my wife Vini.

It's to understand that dealing with mental health is a part of who I am.

This is the journey you are about to go on with me, one that takes all this in. It's daunting, but when I decide to do something, I've always been the type to throw myself into it. So that's my attitude to sharing my story with you.

Ideally, I want you to feel like I'm sitting opposite you at the pub, telling these stories on a long afternoon. Because of that, they will bounce around into the corners of my unusual, lucky existence. But the diversions will get back to the centre, the tale of a year more eventful and volatile than any I've had. I hope you enjoy the ups, the downs, and the place we end up.

This is something I couldn't have committed to before. I'm glad I have now.

1

Snap

Snap. Typically, that's a word with great connotations for me: people talk about the way my wrists snap through the cricket ball when I send it through cover or over the leg side. But on the night of November the 12th, 2022, it meant something very different as my left leg slipped from underneath me, and a hundred kegs of former fast bowler fell squarely onto it.

Try to imagine grabbing a fistful of Paddle Pop sticks and bending them to breaking point – when I think back to that night, it's this visceral sound that haunts me. I had broken bones before, it's an occupational hazard as a sportsman, but this one was different. It was the most painful experience of my life. My screams were loud and desperate. My leg was in bits, my ankle destroyed, bad enough that doctors were quietly bracing my wife for the even more traumatic possibility that my left foot would need to be amputated.

———

The funny thing is, I can't begin to tell you what a wonderful day and night it had been.

It was only a week after we had been knocked out of our home T20 World Cup at the group stage on the basis of net run rate. In our final game in Adelaide, I won player of the match for a quick half-century before we held off Afghanistan with the ball. But the win wasn't enough – we were too far behind on run rate after New Zealand had thrashed us in our opening match.

I was as angry as anyone at not being able to defend our title, one that a congested calendar only gave us a year to enjoy after winning in Dubai in 2021. Speaking to the media, I tried to explain that as a modern professional, you couldn't afford to lie around licking your wounds. The comments were misrepresented by people who wanted to say that I didn't care, but the simple fact is that in cricket at this level, there's always something else around the corner that demands diligence and focus. This time we had a one-day series against England. It didn't have much riding on it, sure, but an international is an international, and I was preparing the right way on that fateful Saturday.

Because we hadn't made it to the business end of the World Cup, I was able to get a rare bit of downtime. And because I'm a cricket nut at heart, that included taking myself off to the Junction Oval to watch the Melbourne Stars play their Women's Big Bash match that afternoon. Having played for the men's team for so long, I've done a fair bit of coaching some of the women behind the scenes, and the longer I hang around the game, the more pride I take in seeing people I've worked with making their own way. Tess Flintoff is one of them, who barely a week earlier had smashed the fastest WBBL fifty off 16 balls, so it was a great time to catch up with her parents.

I had a chat on TV with an old teammate, Brad Hodge, and otherwise kicked back to watch the game. It was a gorgeous late spring afternoon, and it finally felt like all was coming good in my world as we entered the last months of 2022. It had been a capricious cricketing year, which is par for the course when your role is as heavily reliant on risk and reward as mine, and it had been a tough year personally, which I'll tell you more about later in the book.

So it was balm for the soul to know that I was going to be able to attend Chris Reidy's 50th birthday party that night at his home in Bayswater. When so much of life is spent in the playing bubble, I savour the rare opportunities that arise to be at home with the people who knew me before the world did. These are the friends who make a point of keeping my feet on the ground, usually by ripping the shit out of me, but always with love. It's such a relief to really be ourselves, picking up conversations from where they left off no matter how long it has been since we last had the chance.

The birthday boy had a big hand in my cricket as a teenager, as did a number of the dozen or so people at this gathering of tight friends. Chris had helped enable my first trip to England as a teenager from club cricket, and had also taught me in my first year of TAFE.

Out of school, far from sure that I was going to be a professional player, I was an inaugural member of Cricket Victoria's Sports Development course – 16 guinea pigs who just wanted to find a way to combine sport and further education. Chris understood me, we got on really well, and it just so happened that he coached Fitzroy-Doncaster.

It wasn't clear what sort of player I was going to be. I was on Victoria's radar through age-group cricket, and they liked me as a middle order batter who bowled off-spin. My club, Richmond, thought I was going to be an opener who bowled medium pace. I could see this tension costing me opportunities to advance to the next stage, and Chris, in a canny play, saw a chance to recruit me from the classroom to his club. I remain a proud member of the Lions more than 15 years later.

On an occasion like his birthday, I'd normally have a few beers, but with the England one-dayers starting that Thursday I decided to drive instead. The night played out as so many others have – a handful of pals, wives and partners, a couple of kids floating around. Chris's son Lachy had bought him a beer pong set as a gift, so we were throwing table tennis balls around and generally talking a lot of shit.

I'm stressing this family-friendly vibe when introducing Ben Waterman to the story. For a long while I've been reluctant to put his name into print, but if we're telling the story then we have to do it properly. I had known Ben nearly as long as I had Chris – Ben was also a teacher of mine in my second year of TAFE. And he was also a teammate; a big fast bowler at Fitzroy-Doncaster who I played alongside plenty of times. On the subject of keeping me humble, nobody does it better. I'm sure to Ben I'll always be an annoying 19-year-old, so I can't help setting out to play the role, and he fires right back.

Truthfully, I can't even remember the details of our volley of barbs this Saturday night, but whatever was said I decided to chase after him. It wasn't a thought-out plan but it probably would have ended in a wrestle and some foolishness. Ben took off, I was in hot pursuit, and as I reached him he turned back to track my progress and slipped.

We weren't sprinting on a tennis court, as per some reports, we'd just stepped onto some synthetic grass. Because I was so close to him and running, my foot skidded out as well. His tumble took him across my left leg. Fast bowlers can end up as big lads after giving the game away, and this is the case for Ben. Any pleasure I ever took in telling him so, karma paid it back in spades.

Under his frame, my leg snapped. I shrieked. 'I've broken my leg!' I said, and knew without a doubt that it was true. 'Please tell me you're taking the piss?' said Ben, my poor friend already full of panic as he found his feet. If only. I'm glad Vini was around the other side of the house with everybody else and didn't see the first moments, but she certainly heard the aftermath and came straight over. I asked for an ambulance; it was panic stations.

Clearly, everyone at that party knew that as much as this would have been awful for anyone, it carried the added weight that my body in perfect shape was my living. There were a lot of tears. Ben was devastated; he could barely look at me. I was laid out on the ground with my foot propped up. From then, things came to a standstill.

It turns out that 9:30pm on a Saturday is not a good time to get yourself injured, because that tends to be when everyone else is doing it too. There wasn't going to be an ambulance swinging by to rescue me in the outer eastern suburbs of Melbourne – the 000 operator said it could be 90 minutes away. Rain had arrived, every cricketer's nemesis – my friends had to put up a small marquee on top of me. It was grim. My trouser leg was tighter by the second as the ankle and foot swelled in a way I'd never seen before.

In no state to do it myself, I asked Vini to start calling around. We couldn't reach the Australian team doctor, not unreasonably on a Saturday night, but we did get onto Trefor James, the former team doctor at Victoria. After explaining that we had no bead on an ambulance and that by now my foot had practically exploded out of the shoe, he was keen for us to take charge of matters ourselves. He arranged for us to be taken in at the Epworth in Richmond, about 45 minutes from Bayswater, and said that Vini should drive me there.

In the meantime she had to call my mum, Joy. She's my biggest fan and rides the bumps with me, and still keeps a scrapbook of news clippings from my good days. We were able to reassure her that I was being taken care of, would be at hospital soon, and it was going to be fine. Except I didn't have much faith in that myself.

Somehow my mates carried me to the car and manoeuvred me into the back seat. We got to hospital far earlier than we would have otherwise, but the trade-off was acute pain flashing through the break with every bump and turn. Three quarters of an hour felt an eternity with my foot dangling from the leg.

We're able to laugh about it now, but Vini was mortified when the full extent of the damage became known. That's because she spent most of the trip calling me a sook and suggesting that I probably just had a sprain. I can't blame her for thinking that I was a diva given how pampered we are on the playing circuit.

At the hospital I didn't jump the queue because I'm a cricketer, but the level of pain got me seen right away. It wasn't long before we had a look at an X-ray that confirmed what I knew, even if Vini didn't. I had done a good job of destroying my lower leg, not just snapping one bone but shattering pieces of it in the process, while chipping the other. As for my foot, well, it was a circus, busting all the ligaments plus the syndesmosis joint that keeps the whole show together down there.

As the doctor was explaining this, the penny truly dropped. I remember as a teenager when Nathan Brown broke his leg playing footy for Richmond – it was sickening at the time, but even worse later as it kept him away from the game for so long and led to his premature retirement. He was never the same player. I now had an overnight wait to think about this before an operation.

Funnily enough, faced with possible disaster, my brain went into overdrive in the other direction, trying to locate any positive I could find. Blame it on the painkillers that had finally been pumped into me. I switched to thinking about footballers who made it back inside a couple of months, and how that would be me after they popped in the pins and got me into rehab. In this dream sequence, I'd get back for the second half of the Big Bash League, demonstrate that I was good to go, get picked for the Indian Test tour, and never think about the leg again. All after a nice little mental health hiatus – maybe this was the best thing that could have happened!

Of course, this was wildly wrong and ridiculous. With that Test opportunity, the idea was that the summer of 2022–23 would lay the foundation for getting me back into the team. There was an Australia A outing against the South Africans in the offing, and more Shield cricket than was usually possible. Nothing was certain, but after the profound disappointment of not quite getting to use my baggy green earlier that year, this was where a lot of my attention was. I didn't accept that any chance I had of turning out in those Tests against India was scuppered the moment my leg broke.

It had been in Sri Lanka in July 2022 where my dream became close again, after so much false hope. During the one-day series before the Tests, I was at a function with Aaron Finch, my former housemate and current captain for Australia's white-ball teams. I wasn't in the Test squad but there was open-ended language in the announcement that gave them flexibility to expand the group using limited-overs players, and I had started the trip with 80 not out from 51 balls to get the job done in an exciting chase.

As I wondered aloud to Finchy, he kept it simple, as he has throughout our friendship. Gesturing to our coach, Andrew

McDonald, he said, 'Ronnie's over there. Why don't you go and ask him?'

So I did. I framed it by asking what the chance was that I would be one of those additions to the Test squad. He replied, 'Probably 98 per cent.' I couldn't believe it, and before I knew it I was breaking down in tears. He asked whether they were happy tears, and they were. It had been a long time coming. I had accepted that my Test dreams might be done. To have that revived meant the world to me, and it showed our team's evolution that they could see a way for me to contribute despite so few recent chances to play red-ball cricket.

I'll never forget those first few days back at Test training. It was my first time since 2018, and I loved every second of it with the wickets spinning and rolling at Galle. At no stage did I have to think about power hitting, instead working on problem solving and survival, finding a way to score. This is why I've never considered myself a white-ball specialist – the challenge of red-ball cricket is just too compelling. Even getting under the lid for bat-pad catching practice was a thrill. I would have given anything to play that fortnight.

The day before each Test in Sri Lanka, I looked a decent chance. The day of both, the chance disappeared. It was painful to get so close, a pain I mostly took out on the golf simulator in the team room. But it did give me belief that it was within touching distance for our next overseas assignment in India, the cricketing landscape I know better than anywhere in the world. That pathway back to Test cricket was so important to me that, in the middle of this traumatic episode, I just couldn't imagine that it was closed.

I didn't sleep a wink that night. By the time I got into a hospital bed it was 1am, and it would be past lunchtime the next day before I was put under for surgery. My mind was wandering between that outlandish positive thinking and the throbbing pain in my foot. It was getting bigger by the minute, and there is only so much that painkillers can do. Those hours on my own, sitting and enduring, were the longest imaginable, and I was no chance of sleep.

When morning came, it was time to make use of the waiting with a few phone calls. I've been around long enough to know how breaking a leg on a Saturday night can look, especially given I had a not unreasonable reputation as someone who has enjoyed a few evenings out across the journey. First call was to Australia's chief selector, George Bailey. We've enjoyed a terrific relationship since playing for our country together, especially under his leadership. Bails trusts me and treats me like an adult. After the inevitable prognosis, I pretended to be blasé to lighten the mood: 'So mate, you might need to find a replacement for me for these one-dayers.'

George was as collected as ever. It was a similar conversation with Ronnie, another former teammate. He was a fixture for Victoria across formats when I started in 2010, and we batted together in his last Shield match for the Vics in 2014. He went on to coach me in that side before getting the national job. He was someone else with a lot of trust in our relationship, and it was important to me that they knew the full story, especially the fact that alcohol wasn't involved. Cricket Australia would soon release a public statement that was carefully written to make the same point.

When the time finally came to get the leg sorted out, I convinced myself that it had been done. Initial feedback was that the operation had gone well, and that after a few days I could be released to get home and take care of myself. Getting this done ended up being ridiculous, with my manager, Ben Tippett, having to sneak me out the back door of the hospital to avoid the chance of media attention.

So the world knew. My circle of friends is a big one, and the flood of messages coming in made it clear people were upset. I know how many are on this ride with me, and my positive thinking in that initial 24 hours had been as much about convincing myself that I'd be okay for them. But it was never likely to work that smoothly.

In the days following surgery, there's meant to be a natural improvement with the leg in a cast. But the existing swelling meant that didn't happen. I couldn't get comfortable no matter what I tried. It turned out the swelling hadn't stopped and was pushing against the confines of the cast, so the pain was out of control. They had to go back in and cut the cast to shove ice packs down both sides. My daydreams of getting back on my feet within a couple of weeks, wandering around the house to work on my putting and my short game, disappeared.

This was when Vini was told to start preparing for all eventualities. The doctors thankfully didn't share this with me yet, as

I would have freaked out. But the swelling was at risk of escalating into compartment syndrome. This means that intense pressure on the muscles can lead to infection and necrosis. If they couldn't get it under control in the very short term, the risks for the limb were existential. I might never walk properly again. I might never play cricket again. I might, if everything went wrong, lose the foot entirely.

2

Back to Reality

Spoiler alert: the doctors didn't cut my foot off. But, fuck me, there were moments – irrational, crazed, middle-of-the-night moments – when I thought we may as well be done with it. A tip for anyone unlucky enough to shatter a limb at some stage in their lives: do not mistake the comfortable numbness of a cocktail of painkillers in hospital as proof that you're ready to go home.

Of course, that's exactly what I did – discharged five days after going under the knife. To that point the doctors had been giving me the maximum acceptable amount of prescription opioids and I was also on a ketamine drip. In simple terms, I was out of it, which helped them manage the situation of getting the swelling down. Stuck in a bed with a conveyer-belt of icepacks being applied, the treatment eventually made sure that we avoided the drastic result they had been worried about in the first 24 hours.

In a situation like that, getting all the care in the world, it made my desire to get home as soon as possible all the sillier, but it gives another insight to my altered mindset. My outlook went in waves, but there was a prevailing positivity with my questions geared around when I'd be able to start walking, begin rehab, and get back on the field. It turned out I was way off the mark.

So I convinced them to send me home on the Friday because, let's be honest, I was bored. What the hell was I thinking? This proved a horrific idea, which became apparent across that weekend. So much had happened in the short time since the accident, but I wasn't prepared for the next round of pain to be just as severe.

On crutches with a moon boot, which had replaced the cast to allow for swelling, the name of the game is to keep all weight off the foot. But for a bloke who makes his living being physically coordinated, do you think I could successfully follow such instructions? Every tiny slip, every glancing knock to any part of my leg, and the searing agony returned, even from areas a long way from the damage. It turns out the song is right, everything in the body is connected. I was a total mess, constant tears, the works.

Thankfully Vini is a pharmacist, so there was nobody better to have on hand. One of the issues was that outside the hospital walls, the doses of my painkillers were lowered dramatically, so they weren't touching the sides and couldn't make me drowsy enough to sleep. I was knackered, always awake, and often panicking. There's no way back to hospital at that point, and clearly I should never have left.

A privilege of being a professional athlete is having medical support on hand, and I was not too proud to call on Cricket Australia. It was an important turning point, as the drugs were restored to a level where they had some effect, and I could finally get some sleep before getting back into the anti-swelling cycle with both sides of my foot draped in plastic bags full of ice packs. Talk about sophisticated.

As a classic extrovert, I'm fuelled by other people. By this point I was missing that stimulation. I was fielding plenty of texts and calls, but there is a difference between that and talking shit with my teammates. The doctors were checking in regularly and I was peppering them with questions about what my short-term goals could be. At that stage I just needed something.

A big moment came nearly three weeks later, when I was able to prop myself up on an exercise bike to very gently go through the motions. Physically, this was next to nothing, but psychologically it was huge: the forward momentum of the pedals was a tangible symbol that the process of recovery was finally under way.

I've always tried to be an open book with the media. Honestly, what's the point in any other approach? The people who write about the game have a job to do like anyone else in the community. Getting annoyed by stories that don't break your way is natural, but getting fixated on it achieves nothing. With this in mind, I knew it was important to sit down for an interview to give some detail about what had happened on that night and a sense of how I was going.

That was recorded for Cricket Australia's platform, and I felt a lot better once it was all said and done. Giving a detailed account was always going to lead to further stories about it, but better my words being quoted than online conspiracy theories. That's another part of life in the public eye that I've had to condition myself to over the years and not get emotionally involved in.

Rehab also meant that inside a month of the break, I was back to work at the Junction Oval. Not the work I wanted to be doing, but it was time to begin the really hard yards as I prepared to get out of the moon boot. Patiently overseen by Nick Adcock and Adrian Mott from Cricket Victoria and Andrew Oppy, who took over my case, the early stages involved pool work to control the weight I was putting onto the foot. Even something as basic as completing a set of calf raises gave me more confidence in everyday life, which improved again getting into the gym.

I appreciate that none of this is riveting, but it's an experience shared by almost anyone in sport. Being ruled out by long-term injury, it's easy to lose your sense of self, so having a plan was satisfying, even if it had to evolve and adapt to my ongoing pain. Being at my home ground was important too, able to catch up with teammates and be part of off-field conversations and planning.

Between phone calls with Cricket Australia to check on my progress, there was plenty of alone time and that was well spent. There are so many moving parts to a career like mine that it isn't often that you get a chance to reflect. In patches, Covid had been like that for all of us, but this was different as the pause was mine alone.

I remember drifting off thinking about my childhood and how dominated by sport it was. Playing with my brother, Daniel, with a set of lego for stumps – how we would roll around laughing every time one of us was bowled before building it back up again. In that same living room when we were a bit older, constantly flicking a cricket ball when the other least expected it – right over the top of a glass table, of course. Mum would often be stuck sitting between us for this. Resigned to the fact that she couldn't stop us, she would lament that we were going to break the table one day. But we never did – it's a point of pride even now.

Outside, everywhere was a cricket ground. South Belgrave, where my parents still live, is about 45 kilometres from the middle of Melbourne, so it means plenty of space. Our backyard had a slope back towards the house, which might, if studied, suggest something about the unusual areas where I still hit the ball. My strongest recollections involve a tennis racquet rather than a cricket bat, as a bratty 10-year-old me collected plums from our tree and thumped them as far as I could over the house towards the road. That was my first T20 range hitting.

The toughest battles in childhood were saved for my best mate, Rob Cockerell. Mum would drop me at his house every morning before school, and get me much later in the afternoon when she finished work. At any available time when the sun was out, we were going at each other in his backyard.

It was a steep downhill run to the bowling crease along a thin brick path, at the end of which we would try to knock each other's block off. This wasn't hard with that angle, which would continue down the pitch until a flat section where we would bat, so even on a good length, you were often sniffing the ball. But it was important to get something in the way, because the kitchen window was directly behind the stumps. It was fast and furious, influencing how I went about things when playing on a Saturday.

Rob was a skilled sportsman, and it was of some satisfaction to him that in our final year as juniors at South Belgrave Cricket Club he was named the team's best all-round performer. I got one back on him in winter, though – despite him being the better footy player, I snaffled the Best and Fairest in our Under 18 year, the final season where I was able to combine playing both sports. Sure enough, he was best man at my wedding and I was best man at his. Some bonds last forever.

Those who know me from South Belgrave days still use my nickname – Aussie. It has nothing to do with ambitions to play for Australia and everything to do with my childhood idol Austinn 'Aussie' Jones, the lightning-fast wingman for my beloved St Kilda Football Club, who would have won the Norm Smith Medal in the 1997 Grand Final if not for Darren Jarman.

My sporting obsession was baked in by the fact that we lived literally across the road from the cricket and footy clubs. The nets were no more than 150 metres from my front door via a bike track, and I gave them a serious workout. So much so that when the club built a fence around the ground when I was a teenager, my dad Neil negotiated that they put the gate directly in our route.

I was such a lucky kid. And in my low moments through the rehab process, of which there were plenty, I was able to connect to that and remind myself that I've been blessed since the very beginning.

Nevertheless, it was tough watching Australia take the field that summer, especially the Test team. Sure, I wasn't going to be playing on Boxing Day – it's one of my great disappointments that I've never had the chance to play a Test at home. But the fact that there had been such a clear path back to wearing my baggy green in India, and the increasingly obvious fact that it had closed, hit hard.

There was, however, another segment of the Indian tour: a one-day series directly after the Test matches. Given the 50-over World Cup would be played in India some six months later, Bails and Ronnie saw this earlier series as effectively the start of our campaign. In the ordinary run of things, staying on the safe side by missing a bilateral trip would probably be the course, but in a World Cup year? I had a new goal: India in March.

It was pushing that bit harder than I might have otherwise that gave me a reality check. Bails never said explicitly that I would need to play a state game before being considered for India, but reading between the lines it was only fair. Our training is so closely monitored that they have access to everything, and by early February I was making quick progress with my running. The Big Bash had been and gone but there were Shield games coming.

The frustration of having never played a Test at home extends to how little I've been able to turn out for the Vics in four-day cricket as my career has gone on. Look at my first-class stats in late 2024, and it was only 10 games ago that I hit 278 against New South Wales at the Junction Oval. But my problem is that 10 games takes us all the way back to November 2017. Being on duty for every Australian white-ball game that I'm fit to play means they routinely clash with the Shield, which is played at the shoulders of cricket season thanks to the Big Bash in the middle.

So the fact that I was going to make my comeback in a first-class game was so unlikely that I was able to have a quiet chuckle to myself. I had been in touch with the coach, Chris Rogers, throughout my recovery and he knew there was this window to play back-to-back games, with South Australia in the final week of February followed by New South Wales at Albury. I got the news that I was picked. It was on.

It was a tantalising prospect, not just returning to the field, but having the chance to turn it on in my first red-ball game for nearly four years. How different the world, and my life, had been back in October 2019 when turning out at the WACA. The current game was also a crucial one, with the Vics needing to win to stay in the hunt for a final berth.

As you climb up the sporting pyramid, the difference between levels becomes more distinct. I had played a game for Fitzroy-Doncaster on the way back to this Shield fixture, but I was so far within myself that I can barely remember it. Imagine saying that to the teenager who, in his second game of District Cricket, was up against Shane Warne, who naturally enough rattled off a ton and got me out. That is to say, this wasn't my first game of cricket back, but it was the first where my body would be under full duress. And didn't it show.

Walking back into that dressing room, it struck me how fortunate I was that this was happening now and not when I first rocked up as a 20-year-old. Under the guidance of Bucky Rogers, and the on-field leadership of Pete Handscomb and Will Sutherland, the Victorian team is a work in progress but the dressing room is an emotionally healthy place. There's an understanding that people are different, and a will to embrace and nurture that. It's a nice place to be.

I wouldn't change much about the exhilarating time I've had in the game, but I wouldn't want to relive my earliest days as a Victorian player. Despite being a juggernaut, with a current or former Australian player in practically every seat, it was rugged. Riven by internal rivalries and worse over many years, I was totally out of my depth as a kid who just wanted to play well and do it with a smile.

I was well looked after by people like Ronnie, Bobby Quiney, Clint McKay, Brad Hodge, and David Hussey – senior players who'd seen plenty – but it took me years to feel at ease. Way too long, now I'm thinking back to it. It wasn't a place where I could be myself and love the game. I'm so pleased with how it has improved.

I was also very grateful to have the chance to give something back. Spending so much time around the state team in recent years but not actually playing is a strange dynamic at times. With Sutherland in charge that week, a young captain, I was excited and nervous, just as I had been as a rookie finding my way.

That was until the game started. I know that getting a close leg-before decision is part of the game, as I did early when we batted. I'm far less comfortable with feeling like an old-age pensioner in the field, which was how it played out when we bowled. There was nothing wrong with how the game was going, well ahead and rolling through them, but the experience of being in the middle was so different to the straight line and agility drills that had been my bread and butter over the last couple of months.

Reacting to live in-play moments, in a mix of jerkiness and impulse, is second nature when your body is right. It was a different story here. I take pride in people saying that I'm one of the best fielders of my generation, because I've worked so bloody hard on it. Over these few days, instead of being a chance to show everyone I was fit and firing, it only served to demonstrate how far away I was.

So deflated from that run-around in the field, I was on a hiding to nothing the second time I batted. I wasn't in the right mindset to go out and find the rhythm I craved, let alone to follow my way of putting pressure on the fielding team. Getting knocked over second ball felt about right.

Conditioned to the T20 circuit, I've learned how to respond with balance to poor performances. The positive was that we had won the game comfortably, and the bigger picture was that I hadn't reinjured myself. I'd be better for it next week in Albury.

Between games, I was down for a running session at training. Way back in the first season of the Big Bash League in 2011, playing for the Renegades, I had a grade two tear in the posterior cruciate ligament of my right knee. It was a big deal at the time but I recovered quickly and it was never really spoken about again. However, it has always been with me, manifesting more recently as patella tendinitis. Not major, but bloody annoying.

In my positive-energy mode after my recent accident, I thought that one of the unintended benefits of busting my left leg would be that my right knee would get a better kind of break. During recovery on crutches, only able to use the right leg in any meaningful way, I would think about how much strength I was building in that knee, especially when lowering myself into bed each night.

Well, what do you know – I was wrong. The sprints started well. Two days out from Albury, I'd convinced myself I was turning the corner and all would be right in my second start. Just as that thought entered my mind, 10 metres into a new sprint, the right knee collapsed from beneath me and I went down like a sack of shit. I sat on the turf and roared, 'You have got to be fucking kidding me?!' Had I done my knee again? Was it back to square one?

Thankfully, my worst fears weren't realised. There would be no trip to Albury, but the knee was alright, it was a flare-up of the tendonitis. My Australian season was done: one game, no overs, five runs and a duck. It didn't matter, though – they picked me anyway. I was off to India.

3

Heartbeats

It started with a barely detectable line. To me, at least. Vini
had been doing pregnancy tests for months by this stage, and
having done what felt like a million Covid tests over the previous
couple of years, I fancied myself an expert in interpreting what
a stick says. To me, the line was too faint to be real. After the
heartache to this point, that was how I was going to protect
myself.

———

We never knew for certain that we would be able to have kids.
Not that anyone can be sure at the start, but we went in with our
eyes open that Vini had been told she might never fall pregnant
without some medical intervention. It's not the sort of information you can dwell on, trying to focus on the positive side of
the equation, but it did lodge in a place in my mind.

Then we got pregnant anyway. It was the Indian Premier League, the southern autumn of 2022. To give the tournament the best chance of going ahead, having been stopped in its tracks by the pandemic a year earlier, we were still in a tight bubble some two years into the Covid saga.

The timing was unbelievable. Just before coming over, we'd had two weddings within 10 days in Melbourne and the Yarra Valley, one the conventional Western style and the other our elaborate Hindu ceremony. I've been lucky to travel the world, but for a boy from the outer suburbs, this was a remarkable and joyous experience to be in the middle of. What a ride.

Our general intention was that we would try and have a baby after the wedding, but it wasn't something we were banking on. We anticipated challenges, even if we didn't necessarily voice them. Then one day in Mumbai, as I was heading off to play golf, I got a call from Vini to come straight back to our hotel room. I was worried but I needn't have been – it was the best possible news. I remember seeing her tears upon opening the door. It was one of the best moments of my life.

Perhaps because we were so pleasantly surprised by our immediate success, I ignored the convention of waiting for 12 weeks and instead told . . . well, everyone. Initially my brother Daniel and his wife Hayley, who had come out to join us at the IPL – they were the first to find out. But in an environment like that, we were naturally spreading the good news.

We thought the best thing for Vini would be to get home to Melbourne, and within a couple of weeks we had bought a house. We knew what we wanted and it all lined up. It was only six weeks in, but we wanted to get everything right.

Suddenly it wasn't. A couple of weeks after she went home, we had a routine scan booked, and I was able to be there in the handful of days between the IPL and my next Australian commitment in Sri Lanka. I was so glad it lined up. Until the scan showed no heartbeat. There hadn't been for about a week, we were told. Vini by some intuition had felt that something might not be right, but to hear that silence and see that screen confirming it was a lot.

Two days later came the miscarriage operation, a dreadful thing. Objectively you know this is very normal and common, but when it was overlaid with the knowledge of how hard it had been to get pregnant in the first place, a sense of dread fell upon us. We had to face the reality that maybe this was our one chance.

What can you do? There is a ruthlessness to the schedule at the top. Two days later I was back on a plane, back on the bike. In Sri Lanka I was all over the place, finding it difficult to concentrate. I made some scores in the series that belied how scattered my brain was – it was hard for me to think about anything else. It helped to open up to some of my teammates, as well as some former ones like Bails and Ronnie. Ashton Agar, younger than me but wise beyond his years, was a perfect sounding board.

Life just moved on. After Sri Lanka, it was England for the inaugural edition of The Hundred where I was playing for the London Spirit. This was sad in an entirely different way – Shane

Warne had recruited me to the club, and a big part of why I wanted to be there was to spend time with him. Warney had always been a huge supporter of mine, and like everyone my age, he was my hero. Then a few months before that season came the news that he had suddenly died. It's never a chore being in London, but instead of hanging out with the great man playing golf or talking about our Saints, I would be noticing his absence.

One of the people I had told about Vini's pregnancy at the very start was Faf du Plessis, my teammate at Royal Challengers Bangalore. With a lot of life experience of his own, he was thrilled for us. Catching up with him at The Hundred, his first question was about how we were getting on and how excited we must be. In the aftermath, I had forgotten to tell him that it hadn't worked out.

For me and Vini through the remainder of our year, our pregnancy tests kept striking out. More negative thoughts started to creep in about whether we had lost our chance, even if we were comforted by the fact that a pregnancy had been possible. We took up some further fertility testing and started to consider IVF options. In hindsight this was an overreaction, but the miscarriage really beat us up.

So we come back to that faint line that I told you about before. It was January 2023, well into my rehabilitation process from the broken leg and trying to imagine what 2024 was going to look like. As the week progressed, the line got stronger, and the year ahead was suddenly looking very different.

Our reaction this time around wasn't the same elation, it was more relief. If anything, we were preparing for more heartache and were guarded. I certainly didn't go around telling everyone again. We really wanted this to be our time, as it had been for so many of our friends. A big part of me felt this urgency of wanting my kid to be old enough to see me play, and to have that last as a memory for them. It was a tense couple of months.

But this time, we came full circle. In the exact same room we had been in the previous time when finding out there was no heartbeat, this time the scan found that pulse of life and showed it to us on the monitor. It was such a profound relief, a feeling that suddenly everything was right in the world. Sure, I still couldn't sit on the floor without my leg aching, but none of that mattered a bit. A building storm cloud of anxiety drifted away in an instant. My year to come as a cricketer might be a great success or might take me to the end of my career, but either way I was going to be a dad at the end of it.

———

Before flying out to India, not just for the Australia one-dayers but straight into several months at the IPL, I had a date with my couch to watch the preceding Test matches – the Border Gavaskar Trophy. There's no point doing that thing cricketers do and pretend I wasn't paying much attention – of course I was. Doubly so because this was meant to be my comeback series.

Watching from home was always going to be deflating, having put in so much work over the summer only to end up a month short of where I needed to be. Of course my mind went to imagining how it would be out in the middle, confronting such intense challenges against the ball on tracks turning miles. Especially at Indore, which had the added difficulty of balls rolling along the ground – working out a way to combat that and succeed is my idea of fun.

The few Tests I had got to play had all been in Asia, as has so much of my career. The Indian attack is one I know better than any. These are guys I've played against in limited-overs cricket for Australia and in the IPL for over a decade. It feels like I've faced Jadeja and Ashwin a hundred times in match conditions, and a lot of those I've come out on top. It's no exaggeration to say that India is my second home.

For these reasons, despite not having played much red-ball cricket in the last five years, I had the evidence that I can put in a serious showing over there. Specifically, the Ranchi Test of 2017, on our previous India tour. I was brought into the side halfway through a ding-dong series, one-all going into the third Test. I was thrilled to be back but shattered for Mitch Marsh getting injured – one of my best mates. It never stops being strange being pitted against each other.

Having been dropped for years at a time after my two previous cracks at it, I was desperate to make this chance count. It goes down as one of the most rewarding moments, scoring my first Test century. I'm aware that I'm known as the guy who can hit a 50-ball ton with the shots for that type of innings, but on this day I showed I had other attributes you need as a Test player. It took me 56 balls to hit a boundary that day and 90 to strike a second – I doubt I've ever played an innings with that sort of breakdown. Ashwin and Jadeja were all over me early, then I was all over them in the final hour before stumps. It was just how you dream of it being.

I remember waking up on 82 not out and feeling that expectation, wanting to do it for all the people who had backed me all the way. With the exception of one square drive on morning two it wasn't the most convincing advance to three figures, but when it came every emotion poured out of me. This continued in the media conference after play, when I was teary again – a bit of a theme at that stage of my career.

For the whole time I was out there, Steve Smith was down the other end. My first memories of Smudge go back to when we were underage state players, him for New South Wales and me for the Vics. He was clearly a gun, already getting a run in the Blues' one-day team and dominating against age-group peers. He was one of the players I benchmarked myself against, wanting to get where he was.

It wasn't long before we were getting picked in Australian squads, him a couple of years before I made my T20 and ODI debuts in 2012. Our interests varied, especially in the years when I was going out a lot more and he was still thinking about cricket in his downtime hours. My enduring memory of those early years is just how highly I regarded what he did.

We were in India together in 2013, my Test debut and the tour when he returned to the side, never to leave it again. It was a wild journey – getting pumped four-nil, Homeworkgate, all the rest. But when Smudge came in for the Mohali Test, smooth as you like hitting 92, there was no doubt in any of our minds that this was the start of something special.

Four years on, a lot had played out. We had won a World Cup together in the March of 2015, him hitting the winning runs to seal a competition where we had both done well. It had been a traumatic summer, starting with losing Phillip Hughes, who was part of our generation at junior level. Hughesy and I had only been playing together for Australia the month before the tragedy; it's still unbelievable a decade on, and I still don't think it's understood how deeply that affected the players, especially those who were there that day like Steve.

That intense summer turned Smudge into Australia's Test captain for the first time, when Michael Clarke got injured. It became permanent later in 2015, with Pup retiring alongside a stack of senior players who had been in that World Cup team – Mitch Johnson, Brad Haddin, Shane Watson. We were very much in transition, but so was Steve's life, when you consider all that had happened.

The ups and downs of Smudge's early days in charge affected me at the end of 2016, after the Test team were rolled for 85 by South Africa in Hobart for five losses on the trot. The Shield round that followed was clearly a Test audition for up to three spots in the top six. There had never been anything like this in my time as a player; everything was on the table.

At the same time, my relationship with Victoria was in an awkward spot. A few months earlier I had caught up with Pat Howard, the high-performance director of the men's national teams. I arrived in Sri Lanka ahead of some T20s, having been left out for an ODI series: my first squad omission since debut.

I asked Pat what I needed to do to be a regular three-format player for Australia. Beyond making lots of runs, was there anything strategically that he thought could help my cause? I was surprised but grateful at a straight answer: he thought I had become too comfortable in Victoria. He suggested that a change of states could show I was keen to better myself.

Of course, I'm a proud Victorian and felt huge loyalty to the state that had nurtured me. But when the key decision-maker in the country speaks straight to a nationally contracted player, I would have been mad to ignore him.

I rattled through a checklist. Queensland and Western Australia, I'd never get a bowl in seamer-friendly conditions. Tassie was much the same at times during a season. If I made runs for South Australia, there was a risk of being seen as seeking out the flattest track in the country.

That left New South Wales. The SCG was never going to be the easiest place to score, and there's more tendency to give spinners a go. Great idea, Pat agreed. He would give me as much help as necessary.

I explained my interest to Moises Henriques, the captain at New South Wales, and he was surprised but keen. I went for coffee with administrators in Sydney and that was that. Paperwork was all that remained.

The next thing I did was sit down with Wadey and Ronnie – the Vic captain and coach – along with Tony Dodemaide and Shaun Graf from Cricket Victoria. It wasn't complicated from my perspective. I'd rather stay a Vic, but I had to do what was best for my Aussie career in all three teams. They weren't thrilled but respected my wishes. In my mind, it was a done deal.

The story got out, as these things do, and there was media interest. But the angle was that the move was going to be denied. What was going on? Only then was I told that there was a transfer deadline each year and all those involved had missed it.

I had followed advice, did what I thought was the right thing, and it had blown up in my face. I sent a message around the Victorian playing group explaining what had happened and that I was fully committed to the team's success, and that if there were any questions, I was happy to talk it through. It was an uncomfortable situation but nobody approached me. It seemed that was that.

Until the eve of our first Shield game of the 2016–17 season, that is. After our final training session before taking on Tasmania, I was tapped on the shoulder to chat with the coach. To talk tactics, I assumed. But Ronnie was there with Wadey and Andrew Lynch, chairman of selectors. Ronnie cut to the chase – I wasn't playing the next day.

What? I had led our batting averages the previous season and been told by Howard I was on the radar for Tests in the summer ahead. Team balance, came the response. I challenged that again. Lynchy, silent to that point, jumped in: 'Well, you shouldn't have fucking tried to go to New South Wales then!' Ohhh. With the quiet part out loud, there was nothing left to say.

The next morning Stoin did a neck injury in the warm-up, but Dan Christian was called up from grade cricket. I would remain twelfth man. Once Pat Howard realised, he got in touch with the powers that be to say that if I wasn't selected for the next game, other arrangements would be made. It wasn't clear what he meant, but I got recalled against Queensland and made 81 in a thumping MCG victory.

With that Queensland game happening while the Test team struggled in Hobart, it made me one of the contenders in the upcoming audition round. A home debut at last, a tantalising prospect. Awkwardly we were playing New South Wales at the SCG. Wadey was also in the frame for a Test recall as the wicket-keeper batting at seven. We weren't competing for spots, but we both wanted to play well. As captain, he decided to slot in ahead of me at five. As it turned out, neither of us made any runs, we won by a mile, and he got named in the Test squad for Adelaide while I didn't.

The batting order prompted a bit of media chat, so at a press conference a couple of weeks later I was asked, in a slightly coded way, about where I thought a wicketkeeper should bat. I responded – too quickly, I soon realised – that it should be seven.

The follow-up question asked how I had felt waiting down the order, and whether that was 'painful'. I made the error of repeating that word, and that became the headline. When asked why we had batted where we did, there was only one truthful answer: 'He chooses the batting order.'

It wasn't my most diplomatic moment, but it wasn't meant to be shots fired. Wadey is a fantastic player and we've enjoyed a lot of success together. It was more that I've always been comfortable answering questions, which means I've been guilty of saying what I would in the pub instead of thinking about how it might be turned into a news report. I thought these were matter-of-fact comments and it's bad practice to suppress athletes giving straight answers. But within minutes I realised what I'd done.

With the Australian team struggling, outlets were looking for negative headlines. This offered up discord between national teammates, a player against a state captain. I understand why it snowballed, but what happened next is the part that still rankles some years later.

First, Smudge went in hard at his own press conference the next day, describing what I'd said as 'very disrespectful'. He really went on with it. 'Everyone was disappointed in his comments, I've expressed that to him myself and spoke to the team. One of our values is respect, having respect for your team-mates, your opposition, your fans, your media.' And one more: 'The leadership group got together and we decided to fine Glenn. We thought that was sufficient punishment, so we've gone down that path.'

This last bit was weird. The leadership group consisted of the four senior New South Wales players: Smudge, Davey Warner, Mitch Starc and Josh Hazlewood. And they did fine me. Ten grand. I assumed that like Cricket Australia sanctions this would be taken out of my wages. No. This was different. I had to supply the money, in cash, on the spot. I still don't know what happened to it. Was that our beer money for the summer? It was a mystery.

I wasn't officially suspended either, but that was the other curiosity, as I rode the bench for all three Chappell–Hadlee matches against New Zealand in early December. There was no reason to miss those games on form, and I can add two and two together. This wasn't my first suspension – I'd once missed a recovery session for Victoria, and had had something similar at Yorkshire when I missed a coach's phone calls – but this one was just weird. While I was running drinks, Victoria were playing Tassie at Bellerive – another first-class game missed.

For all of that, I did my time and returned to the side for the Pakistan one-dayers in January. A month on and it was like it had never happened, to Smudge's credit. And two months from then, we were in the middle at Ranchi. I'm not sure how much he's thought about it since, but it was so special being out there with him, rattling off tons and feeding off each other. I know it's easy to see him as highly strung, but he was playing so well at that moment in time. He was as calm as I've ever seen him with bat in hand, before or since. We were just two guys who had come through together and were doing what we had trained for.

When my milestone came, I leapt into his arms and nearly knocked him over, and he was genuinely thrilled for me. Not long after, I feathered one off Jadeja. On a good batting pitch, it meant that I had left runs out there, so I didn't lock down that spot as my own. I probably also denied Smudge another Test double: he was on 126 when I left and ended up last man standing on 178. It was one more plot point in our occasionally complicated relationship, and part of maturing is accepting our similarities and differences.

Over the years, those memories have found a place for me. There was a time when that innings was so bittersweet – the proof I could do it, the verification of who I was, but having no bearing on my fortunes. As I've matured, I've also considered that getting out for 104 instead of powering on to a big ton in the first innings might have seen us batting on big enough to win the match and the series, instead of having to bat out the fifth day to save it thanks to Pete Handscomb and Shaun Marsh. So no, I don't go back to YouTube watching that innings over and over, and certainly not during the series I was watching in February 2023.

———

There is always an interesting energy when the white-ball boys join the Test squad towards the end of a series. We're proud of the culture that we've built up in that dressing room, with fellow mischievous personalities like Marcus Stoinis and Adam Zampa adding a fresh and welcome dimension. There's a lot of love there, with Mitch Marsh right in the middle of it. The T20 World Cup that we won together in 2021 was proof to many that this was the right way to run a modern dressing room.

When we rolled into India in March 2023, the Test guys were just beginning a long couple of days in the field at Ahmedabad on a pitch that was perfect for my RCB mate Virat Kohli to make a ton for the first time in long while. It had been a hard-fought series and there were a lot of tired boys in the hotel corridors.

Our job in a situation like that is sometimes to keep the energy up, but also to know when to give them space. Truth be told, knowing we had a nice little run-up before our first game, most of us also saw it as a chance to play plenty of golf. I wished the Test team well as we left the hotel at the same time: them onto the team bus, me to get a round in. Have fun, gents. Do let us know how you get on out there!

Let me bring you into the place of golf in cricket, because you might have noticed it's a big part of our lives. Golf was what the medical staff had commissioned me to play to prove that I was able to be on my feet for four hours without needing a break – that's roughly the length of a one-day innings. But that doesn't scratch the surface of how much we play, especially on tour.

I was no more interested in golf than the next cricketer when coming through the ranks, but that changed as I climbed the levels. Having a reputation as half decent, usually with the lowest handicap in the Australian team, has led to a few endorsements, getting me the Callaway sticks that I now take around the world.

I know that on tour, it sometimes looks like we are organising our training schedule around golf. There is a method to this that can be a bit lost. For a lot of us, being on the golf course is almost a meditative experience. Those hours are where I feel most free, disconnected from my phone and any wider pressures. If you played it professionally it would be different, but for us it's recreation with nothing riding on it, like what we did as kids.

So when we talk about players getting the bug for golf, as per my self-diagnosis, you typically have a cricketer who is craving quiet time. Or is this just self-justification for playing the game every waking moment? I'll let you decide. For those wondering who is the best, it's not Ricky Ponting, although he's close. The only cricketer who could have a serious golf career would be Jon Holland – that bloke is a freak. I'm looking forward to playing amateur tournaments one day but I suspect that will be my lot.

The golf test on my fitness didn't tell the full story in India. Much as it was in the Shield game the previous month, my body wasn't up to the rigours of being out in the field in a professional game. After 27 overs I needed to get off and ice my leg. The intensity of a one-day international with all the jolting and jerking had the same result as when I played for Victoria. Having made so much progress through January, to be hitting these roadblocks with my basic agility was really starting to play on my mind.

So it was one and done in India as it had been for the Vics. I wanted to get on as a sub in the remaining two games, but the medical staff were clever enough to deny my competitive instincts.

It was back to the routine – lots of intense stretching, hours in the gym, bucketloads of ice, rinse and repeat.

My next assignment wasn't going to be any less taxing. As soon as we were finished in the Aussie uniforms I was due to switch straight into the red, black and gold of the Royal Challengers Bangalore. It was time for the IPL.

4

Wild Wild West

Cricketers have a strange relationship with time off. On the one hand, you can quickly have too much of it if you aren't getting picked up on the T20 circuit. On the other, if you're busy, those weeks in the diary where you're uncommitted are precious. So when there was a buffer built in between the India series and the IPL, usually I would make that battery-charging time for anything other than picking up a bat and a ball.

Coming into 2023 though, it was so different. Since the T20 World Cup in November, I'd barely played a competitive match. Instead of finding a resort to chill out for a week, I was straight into at my home away from home in Bangalore – my third season at RCB. There was no better place to crack on with the relentless physical work to get my leg to where it needed to be. I couldn't afford a third false start, especially with the one-day World Cup six months away.

As it turned out, those 10 days would lay the foundation for everything that followed. A combination of gym, physio, pool and practice matches – all carefully planned with the big crew of strength and conditioning staff all IPL teams are blessed with – saw me turn a corner. Finally, in the nick of time ahead of the first round, my agility and speed were returning. We built up the intensity rather than letting me be a bull at a gate, so I wouldn't get back into the cycle of intense activity followed by two days battling pain.

I have so much gratitude to the staff at RCB for investing that time into me, especially when it's the fast bowlers who generally need the attention to get through a campaign. A function of being in such a lucrative tournament is you don't want for anything, so being able to draw down on those resources gave me the best chance possible to be me again.

———

The IPL has been a big part of my life for a long time, albeit one that can go under the radar in Australia due to the time of night the matches are on. It's well known that the competition is a huge deal, but in some respects it feels like it happens adjacent to the conversations around the national team. That can be a relief when things aren't going well, and frustrating when you're flying.

I've had plenty of both experiences, going back to when I first turned out for Delhi Daredevils in 2012. I was fast-tracked into that T20 lane despite not actually having played much of the format, which is funny given how it has played out.

As a youngster I was captivated by Test cricket, and that's what I wanted to do as a player. My club career started off with me batting down the list, with my bowling as much of an asset. Then one evening I was popped in as nightwatchman, returned to make a ton the next week, and next thing I became a number four or five instead of batting at seven, with all the expectations that go with batting up the order. When getting into the Victorian system, I was back down the list in that all-rounder spot, picked more for my fielding than anything – the first time I was selected was actually at number eight as a 20-year-old in the One-Day Cup final in early 2010.

I was savvy enough to realise that if I was going to make an impression with the bat so far down the list, I was going to have to find a few tricks. A shift started to take place. This paid dividends, big time, in a televised game down at Bellerive Oval a year on from that first appearance. Tasmania were a really strong team, winning the tournament the year before, and set us a run-a-ball chase with George Bailey and Mark Cosgrove making tons – little did I know what a big part Bails would go on to play in my career.

Under lights, we were nowhere when I walked in at the fall of the sixth wicket with 102 runs needed in 14 overs. Given it was a situation where I just had to go for it, I felt totally at ease from the moment I walked out. In 27 balls I hit 61 to get us the win, including a few hefty sixes. On commentary, Mark Waugh and Damien Fleming were excited, and the headlines confirmed that 19 balls was the fastest half-century in the competition's history, breaking a record that went back to David Hookes.

It's quite something how your stocks can rise at that age. In the space of one innings I went from a bits-and-pieces fifth bowler who threw himself around in the field to being talked up as someone who could slot into the Australian team. A week later against South Australia, in my second Sheffield Shield game, I hit 63 in the first innings followed by 103 not out in quick time. These knocks turned out to be life changing.

My next year for the Vics didn't repeat those highs. I was decent in the Shield, having a consistent campaign without reaching three figures. But I stunk the joint out in the 50-over tournament and fared little better in the Big Bash, which in those days was a very short hit-out. Nevertheless, I was encouraged to have a dart at the IPL auction for the 2012 season – what was the worst that could happen? I had it in me to be a matchwinner, I might get lucky, and there had been whispers I might get picked up late.

In the end, nobody wanted me, and I was fine with that. Off the field, I was into my first year of a Bachelor of Education for primary school teaching at Victoria University. I had a state cricket contract, I was in my early twenties with ample time on my side, and all I knew of the IPL had been seeing Mitch Marsh running around as a teenager a couple of years earlier.

Having missed out, the last thing I expected was a phone call telling me that Delhi wanted to select me as a replacement player at the start of the season. You beauty! A contract worth $50,000 made me feel like the richest man alive, just as it had when Victoria put me on a rookie deal for $16,000. I'd never been more excited about anything, and, as you have probably worked out by now, I can be a pretty excitable character.

Fourteen months on from that night in Hobart, I was on a list with Kevin Pietersen, David Warner, Mahela Jayawardene, Morne Morkel, Ross Taylor . . . it went on and on. My future housemate Finchy was there too. The reason I was called in was that the international schedule was congested that year, and the overseas bench wasn't deep for the first fortnight, with KP being kept back by England. I wasn't just making up the numbers – I was playing right away.

The first night was truly bonkers. The second game of the tournament, with all eyes on every moment, we were up to Eden Gardens to play Kolkata; they had made the finals the previous year, whereas the team I'd joined finished dead last. Even in our warm-up, the ground was heaving with expectation – but then the rain started. And it was heavy, with the whole ground covered in a matter of minutes. In our dressing room, the big dogs like Virender Sehwag had their feet up, expecting the game to be called off at any moment, with water pooling all over the place. But then, with the clock nearing 11pm, in walked Kumar Dharmasena to tell us that we would be getting on for a 12-over game, set to begin in under half an hour.

Fielding first, the 70,000 people in the ground sounded like triple that to me, louder than footy finals at the MCG. The ground was shaking and so were my hands. Two legends in Brendon McCullum and Jacques Kallis faced up. For the only time in my career standing at cover, something that to this point had only happened in state games, I didn't want the ball. Brett Lee hit me for a six in my single over, but I was just relieved to get off the field without having embarrassed myself.

Set 98 for victory, we still had 41 to get when I walked in at number four in the eighth over. First ball to me was a yorker from Marchant de Lange, who back then was genuinely sharp – I looked at the board and the delivery was over 150kph. Thankfully, Irfan Pathan was with me, and after joking that I'd never faced a ball that fast in my life, he basically took care of business. My 3 not out was nothing to write home about, but now I had a taste for the IPL. I've been going back for a dozen years.

Picked for the next game, against RCB at the equally ferocious Chinnaswamy Stadium, I had a decent time in the field picking up my first wicket but was out cheaply to Muttiah Muralitharan. It was still unbelievable to me that I was facing a man with 800 Test wickets to his name – I doubt he thought much of getting me out a week before his 40th birthday.

And that was that. The senior players rocked up and I was back to my proper spot in the pecking order. At the time I was disappointed, but now I realise what a great opportunity it was to get a dry run at being an IPL player before I really was one.

My place was made yet more clear when we had away games and they didn't bother to take me as there was no way I was getting in the team. Doug Bracewell was in the same boat, so we struck up a friendship, hanging out while everyone else was on the road. What we didn't know, remembering these are the days before WhatsApp groups, was that there were special training sessions arranged for us while we were having a great time hanging around the hotel pool and golf courses. Whoops.

Doug and I went our separate ways when we were released, in my case to England for my first stint as a county pro. Our paths from there have taken us in different directions and it's improbable that we'll play together again, but it's a moment we shared in a time that had a big influence on me wanting to get back to the tournament in 2013.

Did I ever. I mentioned how quickly stocks can rise in T20 land, especially early in your career, and my timing was everything before the next auction. Despite having been peripheral in 2012, Delhi offered to retain me for the next season and quadrupled the price tag. But a year on in cricket's meat market, I'd had the chance to play for Australia in both white-ball formats. The advice at the time was to play the game, risk the money, and see what happens. So we did.

Two days before the auction, we were playing a one-dayer against West Indies at Perth. My international career was still in its infancy. I was scarcely required to do much with the bat in one-day cricket, and after a few brisk contributions against Pakistan in Sharjah I had done very little that summer at home. I probably wasn't far off losing my place and having to prove myself again. On a number of fronts, it was useful timing for a day out. I didn't look likely to get a hit after we rolled them for 70, but Michael Clarke asked if I would be keen to open to get the runs quickly. Would I? My 51 not out in 35 balls was flashy and couldn't have gone much better, even if it was beating up on an attack who had no runs to play with, but I'd taken my chance.

Swept up in everything that is part of being an international cricketer, I didn't even remember when the IPL auction was held – it was two days later, while we were playing another ODI. In a classic chocolates-to-boiled-lollies effort, I chopped on Darren Sammy for a first-ball duck off the toe of the bat, went back to the rooms and had a tantrum. My parents were over to watch me and I'd stuffed it up, back when I didn't handle failure well.

After I settled down, Pup and Mickey Arthur came in and grabbed me – they wanted to talk in the next room. Privately. There I was thinking that I was in strife for blowing up. What a day. But no. They had word from the IPL auction. Did I want to know what had happened? Having not given it a thought, and still thinking about my wicket, I guessed it was bad news, so I told them to go ahead. 'Okay,' I remember Mickey saying. 'We'll tell you. But only if you promise not to let it change the rest of your game?' Righto, lads, lay it on me . . .

'You've been sold to Mumbai Indians for one million dollars.'

My reply: 'Fuck off.'

How was this possible? Was this a prank? A million bucks. These were the days before IPL auctions were global TV events. You needed to have your wits about you to find it online. But I was assured it was true, and it's amazing how fast some news spreads. Back in the viewing room, the rest of the boys were giggling away, calling me Maximillion and all the rest. I had told Mickey it wouldn't distract me but there's no way to keep a promise like that.

In the short term, maybe that was a good thing – after seven attempts at the bowling crease in ODIs, I finally snared my first wicket, then turned that into four of them by the time the game was won. We don't need to dwell on Sunil Narine tonking me for four sixes before I got him. It summed up the wild day it had been. Then getting to soak it all in with Mum and Dad was the best way cap it off.

Naturally, my mind went to how on Earth this had happened, and later I found out that it's a great little story. Given their proximity and stature, plus the clout of the Ambani Empire, Mumbai are the biggest club going and there were always stories flying around about just how well they treated their players. Mukesh Ambani is one of the richest men in the world, and his son Akash had seen a bit of me playing, and had watched that quick half-century two days before. They had salary cap space, and they tend to get what they want.

Tom Moody, then coach of Sunrisers Hyderabad, picked up on just how enthusiastic Mumbai were, and knew they had form when it came to bidding wars. So he encouraged his team to play along and keep putting their paddle up – and on and on it went. From Moods' perspective, every dollar Mumbai spent on me was money they wouldn't have later in the auction. It was shrewd work on Hyderabad's part. The big fella has said to me in the past that I owe him a beer for his part in that final price and he's not wrong.

Hyderabad had another present for me in the months that followed. Not the team, but the city, because that's where I made my Test debut. Both there and at Delhi I was offering more with the ball than the bat, but it meant by the time the IPL rolled around, I had already been in the country for nearly two months and was eager to get to the Wankhede and get to work justifying the price tag that was now attached to every word that was said about me. I was secure enough not to see this as a burden – I was probably acting my age and being more interested in how many social media followers it would get me – but it was time to act like a top-dollar overseas import.

The other factor that set Mumbai apart in that era was that it was Sachin Tendulkar's team. This was his final year as an international cricketer and the celebration of his career was non-stop. Even more than usual, he was feted everywhere he went, especially by fellow Indians, and that included our teammates. So I figured the best way to develop a relationship as a newcomer would be to take the opposite approach, and to talk to him like a person instead of a deity.

Rather than tiptoeing around Sachin when entering a room, I'd go out of my way to put my cricket bag next to his. I'd speak to him casually, ask how his day was, rib him about how rubbish his bats looked for someone who had made so many runs. He seemed to warm to me, so I kept on taking the piss and he gradually came out of his shell to me. It was a different story when he was batting – I took in everything he said and did. There's a shot I treasure standing behind him in the nets, shadow batting to every stroke that he was playing. Even now, every time I run into him at a match or a hotel, he meets me with a big smile and recalls those weeks together.

In terms of my on-field opportunities, it was like the season at Delhi where there were so many international players to pick from. I wasn't in the first choice XI too often – my selection, to an extent, was one with future seasons in mind. In fact, the only game where I started to get on top of the opposition attack was against Rajasthan Royals in a match we later found out was spot fixed by some of their players. That was a bit of a blow to the confidence in retrospect.

One of those overseas stars who kept my season to three appearances was Ricky Ponting – my childhood hero – in his last IPL campaign. I take from that vivid memories of him addressing that group of players, having spent so long at the top as Australian skipper. I was in total awe of him and hung off every word, even though I was sitting on the bench. I had a hunger for knowledge, and sitting next to Sachin while listening to Ricky was a buffet.

We had played a little bit against each other in domestic cricket by this stage, but the real thrill of being on the same team as Punter was fielding practice. Growing up, he was one of the players I watched and tried to emulate, along with Andrew Symonds and Michael Clarke. But in our coaching group that year was Jonty Rhodes, almost a mythical figure in the field. On one occasion, it was Jonty running a high-intensity drill: Punter versus me, head-to-head, aiming to ping the stumps down as often as we could. For a fielding nuffie, this really was heaven and an experience that will live with me forever.

Off the field as well, Ricky was taking an interest in who I was and what I wanted to achieve, so we started spending time together playing golf. His support and backing, often at low times in my career, has helped me walk tallest. When he's coached me, he's understood me. So often the difference at the very top level with coaches is being able to tailor your message from player to player, and there's nobody better at that than Punter. I'm not at all surprised to see the rise of Jake Fraser-McGurk under him as Delhi coach as I write this.

By the business end of the tournament, we were on a roll and won the IPL. I was out of the XI, but to be part of a group that had achieved that success was yet another stepping stone. The same when coming back to India later in the year for the Champions League, where we won again to complete the double. Playing an important role in the final there, hitting 37 in 14 balls to get us over 200 against the Royals, was a great full stop on my million-dollar Mumbai year, and meant that from their perspective it was money well spent.

Between times, it was Ricky that I went to England with for my second stint over there, this time with Surrey. I was getting into the groove: autumns in India, winters in England, summers in Australia. Learning as I went, it meant by the time the next IPL was rolling around for season 2014 I had learned a thing or two about the process and didn't feel much anxiety about going back into the hat for the triennial mega-auction.

When the music stopped this time, I was off to the north of the country with Kings XI Punjab. I arrived in great spirits, knowing Bails was the captain, who by that point was playing a lot of international cricket with me. That included the T20 World Cup in Bangladesh immediately before the IPL, where I peeled off 74 from 33 balls against Pakistan, 45 from 22 against West Indies and 23 from 12 against India. We didn't win often, but it was enough to get me named in the team of the tournament – my best run yet in green and gold.

The other quirk to begin the 2014 season was that the first five games were played in Dubai due to security concerns around India's general election. To say that everything clicked in the UAE is an understatement. Firstly, the team was flying – we won all those games. I went on a run of 95 from 43, 89 from 45, and 95 from 43 again for three Player of the Match gongs on the trot. It has been a feature of my career that when I hit a hot streak, it can make me difficult to suppress, and the World T20 into this was the best run I'd had in the big time. I was loving life.

Upon returning to Chandigarh and Mohali, the team and personal success made everything feel a lot different to when I was in and out at Delhi and Mumbai. There were fan signs all over the ground with my name or giant pictures of my face. It's wise to keep a check on your ego, but any athlete who says they aren't chuffed when there's so much love coming their way is almost certainly telling a fib. The Bash Brothers thing I had going on with David Miller, who was also seeing them beautifully, made everything that much easier. It was also a great time to be sharing a dressing room with Mitch Johnson out of the back of an Ashes series that he had dominated like few others. A chilled-out operator like Sanjay Bangar was the perfect coach, and Bails the ideal leader.

Only dropping three games, we finished top by a healthy margin and earned the double chance, which we ended up needing on losing to Kolkata. We won through to the final in a high-scoring qualifier. Sehwag had also joined Punjab and he smashed 122 from 58. I've never been shy about an unconventional shot first ball, and that's what I went for in the final, but the reverse sweep didn't clear Morne Morkel – a touch unlucky to the tallest bloke in the game. Setting KKR 200 for victory should have been enough but we went down in the final over. As close to the perfect season as you get in the IPL, but no trophy.

I was player of the tournament with 552 runs – I'd ridden the wave, hit more sixes than anyone, and was told clearly that the franchise was going to be built around me to go one step better. But just as I'm prone to runs of great form, it usually runs the other way as well – when I'm in a rut it takes some breaking.

Having topped the table in 2014, we collected the wooden spoon two years running. My own numbers, sure enough, went off a cliff. The IPL is such a difficult place to be at times like this, and for me the key for me has been learning how to avoid inflating cricketing failure into a catastrophe. As a younger player this was more difficult. I doubted myself, felt the negativity, saw the social media posts. I'm proud of never trying to defend my way out of a funk, which is the most selfish thing you can do as a T20 batter, but willing myself to be a matchwinner doesn't always make it so.

These experiences combined to make 2017 a huge test for me. By now, I was earning plenty of money each season but that had little to do with my motivation – it was time to demonstrate to the world that 2014 wasn't a fluke, that I could boss the IPL again. The big boost I had on the way back into the Kings XI orbit was that Test century in Ranchi a few weeks before. I felt primed to go big.

This time there was a twist. I was going to be captain, which Sehwag told me when we met during the Test series. We had played together, but now he had retired into what was described at the time as a 'mentor' role. We discussed how the team would operate and I thought we were all on the same page.

How I wrong I was. Our coach, J Arunkumar, was coming in for his first season, and it became clear to him that he was coach in name only with Sehwag pulling the strings. Winning papers over cracks, and as we got up in the first two games, the confusion behind the scenes was ignored. Privately, though, I had coaches and players coming to me asking what on earth was going on, and I found it difficult to give them a straight answer.

When it came to selection, I thought it might be a good idea to bring the coaches into a WhatsApp group to make our decisions. Everyone agreed to this and shared their teams, with the exception of Sehwag. At the end of the process, he made it clear that he would pick the starting XI, end of story. We were losing on and off the field by now, with Sehwag on more than one occasion making decisions that didn't necessarily make sense.

Take poor old Ishant Sharma. At one point he was told not to bother coming to our game that day in Mumbai, having not been picked in a while. We had several other local bowlers, plus the Kiwi quick Matt Henry had just come into the side. Doing the right thing, Ishant did a gym session and came along anyway, bowling at full pace in the warm-up. Then Eoin Morgan was told that he would be a new inclusion that day, taking the last overseas player spot from Matt. Morgs protested that it wasn't fair to drop Matt after only playing one game, so they rejigged again, left out Morgs, and both Henry and Ishant played.

It was hard to figure out how the organisation was allowed to be run so erratically.

The season came down to our final group game against Pune away from home and we had a shocker batting first on a wet wicket, rolled for 73. It was all over. In the context of what was going on, I'm still quite proud of how we were able to broadly keep the show on the road until that stage. I was also happy with how I performed, doing the right thing as leader by giving myself the chance to influence games at the right time with bat and ball. Of course, we were all flat not to make the post-season, but it could have been so much worse.

I volunteered to do press that night, but Sehwag said he would instead. Upon getting onto the team bus, I found I'd been deleted from the main WhatsApp group. What was going on here? By the time we reached the hotel my phone was blowing up, with

Sehwag having unloaded on me as a 'big disappointment', blaming me for not taking responsibility as captain and all the rest. It was unpleasant, especially when I thought we had parted on good terms.

I texted him to say how much it hurt to read those comments and added that he had lost a fan in me for the way he had conducted himself. Sehwag's response was simple: 'Don't need fan like you.' We never spoke again. I knew my time was at an end and told the owners as much: if Sehwag was going to stick around, they were making a mistake and not to bother with me. He only lasted one more season.

Entering my thirties, I'd experienced the best and worst of what the IPL had to offer. A fallow season in 2018 back at Delhi was frustrating as I wanted to make it work for Punter, who by now was my coach. There was so much else going on that year, which I'll detail in a later chapter, that maybe I was destined to miss out.

As for the pandemic season that was postponed until late 2020, I found myself back at Kings XI in the post-Sehwag era. But I couldn't take a trick. Not for lack of trying, I didn't clear the rope in the whole tournament, something that became an internet joke building game by game. Returning home for a one-dayer against India straight after the tournament, nine balls into my knock, there was that sweet feeling of a switch-hit coming out of the middle for six. I added two more in a minute. When I turned around, I remembered that my Kings captain KL Rahul was behind the stumps for India. The look on his face could best be described as 'What the fuck?' All I could do was shrug and say sorry. At some point you need to surrender to the reality of what you are. This is me.

But I still felt there had to be a twist in this story, and there was. Who to thank? Virat Kohli. On that same tour of Australia, he wanted to whisper an idea to me: him, me and AB de Villiers to be the middle order at Royal Challengers Bangalore in 2021. I was in love with this before he finished his sentence. Having started with Sachin and Ricky, the chance to bat with the equivalent of them in my own generation, in those gold pads no less, was irresistible.

Before then, auctions had come and gone. This time though, I was obsessed. When the paddle came down for me from RCB, I was the happiest cricketer in the world. It was in Bangalore where I would begin my second act as a player. And it is what I learned in Bangalore colours that would allow me to play the most important cricket of my life.

5

The King and I

By the time my third season at RCB rolled around – the crucial months of 2023 as far as my leg was concerned – the place felt like a home away from home. It had become a bit like that after a few seasons at Kings XI, but this was still different. It was a relief playing somewhere with a really clear solid system in place, with owners who hired cricket professionals to handle the cricket while they took care of the business side. Those sides rarely clashed, while the owners were extremely supportive after every match – win, lose, or draw.

My first memories from 2021 are along these lines. It was set to be another frustrating Covid season – the most hectic of the lot, with the initial games bouncing between Chennai and Mumbai before the whole thing was postponed for a few months. But the presence of Simon Katich as coach and Mike Hesson as director of cricket was immediately comforting.

Virat had given me the short version of the plan when we were playing against each other in Australia. To be honest, it wasn't much more sophisticated when the big bosses briefed me on joining. My selection was all about overs 6–14, and to their mind there was nobody better at managing that period against spin than me. I'd never had role clarity like it. I was their missing piece.

I had a great feeling about playing under Kato for many reasons. It won't surprise anyone that he's a diamond of a bloke, one of the best people in cricket, so that was a great start. He had been a big supporter of mine in his media roles, and I had always thought that had to do with him having spent a season with me in my early days as an overseas player, at Hampshire in 2012.

We had been at opposite ends of our journeys at this stage, Kato a couple of years after his excellent Australian career, me a few months before I was first called up. I could sense that he wanted to try to leave a positive mark to help me on my way – the definition of a classy senior pro. Our working relationship underpinned my productive run for Hants, an influence that helped propel me into Aussie squads.

My favourite moment with Kato as a mentor came when we were playing Essex in a T20 match. Batting together after I had missed a reverse sweep early on, he came down the pitch to let me have it. 'Cut that fucking shit out,' he growled. 'I want you to plant every ball over deep midwicket. No more reversing. Fucking pump this bloke.' I reckon I hit the next four balls for six. At the end of the over he came up with a huge smile on his face: 'Now you can reverse! Now you can reverse!' I went back, reverse sweep, four. And he was fired up even more: 'That's fucking batting! That's fucking batting!' Happy memories.

We were coming back together at a great time after a couple of tricky IPL seasons. With mutual respect and familiarity, it was much easier coming into a new environment. People think that T20 players don't care, but a lot of us feel anxiety going into a new franchise. You want to make it work, you want to earn respect, and if it doesn't it can be brutal. With RCB's extraordinary supporter numbers, it would be a lousy time (especially online) if I didn't perform. And this is where Kato was so good for me, where I could provide honest feedback on how I was tracking and he could squash negative thoughts. There will always be a debate about the role of a coach in cricket, less defined than in other professional sports, but a non-negotiable is getting players to believe in themselves. I had that going into 2021.

No surprise how I started that season, then. On debut, a strong contribution in a winning chase against Mumbai. Next up, 59 in a hurry against Hyderabad, then 78 playing Kolkata, two more victories. In the latter it was so hot at Chennai that I had to take refuge under the shade of a light tower after I was out. At ground level it was a good view of AB teeing off at the end after I'd done my job in the middle, just as it was set out to me by Virat, Kato and Hess.

Occasionally IPL owners can get quite hands-on riding the rollercoaster, which I can understand given the level of investment and scrutiny. But we were flying with six wins from seven starts, and they were content to leave us be. It added to the positive energy; we were clearly on a good thing.

Then there was the skipper. This would be Virat's final season in charge at RCB, having been in the job for a decade, which is an eternity in a competition this intense. Across his time there had been plenty of heartbreak, a couple of lost finals, and several playoff campaigns that should have ended better. Winning one of these tournaments had become an obsession for him as a leader alongside everything he had achieved as India's number one. You never said it out loud, but this felt like the time where we were going to come together and put that right for him and the fans.

He will always be known for his next-level intensity, especially in the field when his emotions spilled over more than occasionally, but there was a calm to Virat through that winning start to 2021. That extended to the off-field life, where we were all happy in each other's company watching games together in lockdown on a big screen. We were united.

Predictably, we'd had a run-in or two across our years playing against each other. There was a little bit going on during that Ranchi Test in 2017 where I'd posted my ton. Virat had a bad start to the week, injuring his shoulder on day one when diving to stop a boundary. When he was batting, I put in a similar dive at the same part of the ground. On impulse, I mocked him by grabbing my shoulder the way he had a couple of days earlier.

This was all in the context of a wild series for Virat's relationship with us, essentially calling Smudge a cheat in the previous

Test at Bangalore for looking up at the dressing room when considering a DRS challenge. That was against the rules from our captain, who called it a 'brain fade'. Virat's presence through that series was as intense as anything I'd experienced in the game. After my little pantomime act, he was on strike. Next ball? Caught Smith, bowled Cummins. Big Patty, in his first Test for six years, had got King Kohli in single digits and we went nuts with excitement.

Even though it had been Virat who had sounded me out to play with RCB, in the back of my mind I still remembered all that carry-on. So as we were developing this lovely relationship at my new club, I thought I should follow him on Instagram. But I couldn't find him anywhere in the search bar despite having tens of millions of followers. Had he . . . blocked me? He sure had. Four years prior, when I'd pissed him off so badly that he couldn't stand to see me online. By that point we were able to have a laugh about it, and these days, our families hang out and I'm sure we'll remain mates for the rest of our days. Yes, he has unblocked me.

We came into each other's lives at RCB when he had just become a dad. I could tell that had changed him, as it would me in turn, helping us both find it easier to understand when things didn't go our way. He still had his moments, but most of his intensity was well directed, certainly when compared with the adversary of our younger days.

Another example was his willingness to essentially share some of the captaincy duties with me in the field. Specifically with the bowlers, he gave me space to talk with them and keep them focused on the plans for each batter. As captain he was instrumental in all we did before a game, but it reflected how he had grown as a leader, sensing that I was the right person to deliver those messages, giving him space to focus on the tactical back and forth.

That we were humming along as a group made the suspension of that tournament even more frustrating. Not that our camp questioned the correctness of the decision once Covid started ripping through India at a ferocity not seen before. The daily death toll was horrendous, as were the pictures on television each night. It was the right thing to do to shut the IPL down and come back later in the year. But purely from a cricket perspective, it interrupted us when we were tracking perfectly.

Departure from India was as chaotic as you might imagine. Thankfully I had Vini with me, but the first step was to lock everyone in hotel rooms for a few days as decisions were made about how to transport us home. Australian Government policy at the time had the border to India shut, so it was never going to be easy. I pondered whether Adam Zampa and Kane Richardson, who had left earlier to avoid this problem, might have gotten it right. Word got through to us that we would need to spend the next couple of weeks in a third country, and that would be the Maldives. Okay, maybe not so bad.

But it didn't play out how we thought when the 20-odd Australian and New Zealanders from the IPL bubble reached our designated accommodation. We arrived after some of the broadcast crew, who were in the same boat as us. At a stressful time, it was no surprise that everyone congregated at the bar, and we joined as soon as we could. But as I've learned over the years, sometimes the hard way, if someone has had a decent head start in a situation like that, they rarely get hauled in. This night, nobody was catching the lead pack.

Michael Slater was out front, with the peloton including one Davey Warner. Often happy to needle someone for his amusement, Bull started prodding Slats and never stopped. It didn't go down well, the tension rising to the point where Slats made it clear he would whack Davey if it kept going. Davey of course carried on, prompting what nearly turned into a physical encounter. I was in the middle of it and took Slats back to his room, very agitated. It had been a long day and night.

Enough of this exchange made it back to Australia to prompt media reports about a punch on. It may have had that potential, but it was cut off at the pass by those in the vicinity. It wasn't long before the two of them shook hands and made up, just like my best mate Rob and I would after a scrap as kids. More than anything, it was a function of the strange times we had all been through. Nobody was at their best.

Most of all I felt for Neroli Meadows, a good friend who had also been in the broadcast contingent. As the only journalist on the island, so to speak, people assumed she had briefed the story back to her colleagues, which wasn't the case. Vini and I spent a lot of time with her and made sure when speaking to others that we didn't let the idea stand.

Day two went little better than day one. Far from using downtime to recharge, we had a monsoon sweeping through the island and waves nearly lapping at our door. It didn't stop for a week. First the altercation and now this – it was taking a toll. We were spent emotionally, and most people took refuge in their rooms, calling room service. The worst bit was knowing that as soon as this was over, another fortnight was to follow in Australian quarantine. We agreed with what needed doing, but it didn't make it easier after so much of it for more than a year. I was cooked.

The Zoom chats with teammates in quarantine in Australia revolved around the white-ball tours to the West Indies and Bangladesh and how we simply had to get out of them. We weren't popular with Cricket Australia advancing these views – the response, as is often the case, was that we had chosen to be at the IPL rather than taking that time to rest as contracted players. That is true. But the counter is that we learn so much to use while playing for Australia. I'd declined the IPL before – in 2019, for instance, when I was giving myself a chance of playing Tests again with a World Cup in England right before the Ashes – but in 2021 it was about making sure we were at the peak of our powers for the T20 World Cup. It made sense to go.

Calmer heads prevailed, and a different squad was sent on those winter tours, giving some respite for those of us in the never-ending bubble. Between times, it was decided that the second half of the IPL would be staged back in the UAE, where we had been the previous October – familiar terrain for all battle-hardened white-ballers.

Where our RCB team had been so dynamic in our first seven games, the opposite was true in Dubai and Abu Dhabi. We started with a thrashing from KKR. I was player of the match against Mumbai, a game we needed to win, with a satisfying innings in tough conditions where I had to get creative and it worked. I made a second fifty in another triumph over Rajasthan, and a third on the trot against my old club Kings XI. That hat-trick of wins took us to the playoffs, and I was in the form of my IPL life – even better than that magical 2014.

But a close loss to the Sunrisers, where I was run out by Kane Williamson just when it looked like I was going to get us home, meant we coughed up a double chance. Even so, I felt calm going into the eliminator, having finished the group stage with 51 not out as we beat Delhi. I had over 500 runs at a fast pace with six half centuries – I wanted the big stage.

Some people find it difficult to tell one T20 match from the other in long tournaments, and having played over 400 of them, I understand this perspective. But I won't forget that night as the best chance I've ever had to play in a championship team faded away. I wasn't set when trying to play a slice cut that looks a million bucks when it comes off but sloppy when it doesn't. I was beaten in the air, caught at short third off Sunil Narine for 15. With only 138 to defend, Virat's last night as leader ended in a tight loss. It hurt.

The nature of the sport is that we need to dust ourselves off quickly. The T20 World Cup, also in the Emirates, was starting within days of the IPL final. There'll be different views on whether that's a good or bad thing, and I certainly could have done with another breather, but everyone was in the same boat.

To understand the evolution and success of the Australian white-ball team over the last few years, it's worth going back a bit – specifically, to England for the lockdown series we played there in September 2020. And when I say lockdown series, I really mean it – this was the first time we had played under these conditions, all coming together at a time months before there was even a Covid vaccine.

Once it was agreed that we would visit England for these six matches, the only way we could leave the country was on a chartered flight that operated like a school bus – from Essendon Airport, we picked up teammates in Adelaide and Perth before the trip to London. Upon landing, we were whisked away not through the airport but a different process altogether. It felt like we were evading the law as we were ushered onto a bus to Derbyshire's county ground, where we were isolated under the strictest controls.

When we eventually made it to Southampton for the T20s, specifically the Hilton Hotel built into the stadium at the Rose Bowl, it was quite a different story with the on-site golf course available to us at any time and a lot of effort going into making us comfortable. At Manchester, where we went next for three ODIs, it was better still, with the giant corporate facility opened to us and turned into something of an arcade – a golf simulator, table tennis tables, even a basketball hoop. As for the field of play, this was our recreation area to hang out and treat like a public park. It didn't take long for us to start enjoying it.

The level of camaraderie is something that has set us apart since we fell short at the 2019 World Cup. It turned into a different group to any I've played in for Australia, or any professional set-up. *The Test* documentaries have given a feel for this via Zampa and Stoinis, but it goes beyond them. Personalities like Agar, Nic Maddinson, Kane Richardson, aren't people focused on every last detail of playing. They avoid getting consumed by it by having other interests.

On that England tour, we were far happier soaking up the sun in our budgie smugglers sitting on our balconies, listening to music and drinking coffees made by Marnus, Smudge or Zamps. We didn't need extra hours in the nets or talking tactics. People talk about work–life balance, and we found it. It broke the mould in terms of what people expect of Aussie cricketers but we're all healthier for the influence of teammates who don't let that drive them.

The trip ended on a high for the team and for me personally. Set 303 to win the third and deciding ODI, we were in strife at 5 for 73 when I walked in to join Alex Carey – another polite, kind human being who just happens to be an excellent player. Given so much cricket had been played on the Manchester square as one of only two venues the England men played at in 2020, by mid-September it was tired, slow and tough to score at all, let alone at better than a run a ball. Nobody gave us a chance from there.

Kez got lucky early on, caught off a no-ball when Jofra Archer overstepped. But that seemed to do him the world of good as he started to bat with freedom. Then it got fun as I got into that zone where I feel like I'm able to hit most balls for six, doing so seven times. A few were large, thudding into the building that was our big-kids indoor playground. Because there was no crowd, it was left to teammates who weren't playing up on their hotel balconies to make as much noise as they could.

For Kez, it was his first ton for Australia after a few years in the team. For me, it was the first time I'd reached three figures in an ODI since the World Cup of 2015. With a little bit of help from Starcy in the final over, we got the job done. Yet another bilateral series, some might say it doesn't look like much. But to that group, right then, in a series behind closed doors where we were living at the ground, it was a win that brought us even tighter. The beers that night as we sat around in a circle were special. It was then that we found the belief in ourselves that as a group, we could go on and win some World Cups.

The reality is – and I genuinely think in hindsight he would agree with this analysis – the direction the team was heading by this stage was at odds with the way that our coach Justin Langer ran his operation. As our playing group matured and grew together, we wanted autonomy.

This would come up all the time behind closed doors when talking to each other, but it was another thing working out how that would be raised with a guy we have so much respect for. This was the coach who showed up after Sandpaper with the reputation of Australian cricket in tatters, and took on the task of repairing it. Adjustment to life under him was jarring at times and didn't always work for me personally. But looking at where we were in 2018 compared to a couple of years later, we outgrew such a hands-on method.

I have so much admiration for the way the leadership group within the Australian teams went about advancing the position of the dressing room by 2021. It was down to Tim Paine, Finchy and Patty to provide the feedback to JL, and a lot of that happened in the middle of that year on the Gold Coast in a team camp that was well reported on. By this stage, everything tended to leak.

It was awkward when JL backed over what was being told to him privately – that those leaders wanted him to back right off and let the players work with him more on their terms, and work more with the specialist coaches on specifics. He asked if the room felt that way and everyone nodded along. The message did cut through, and JL said as much publicly.

The first test of this, with the full senior squad back, was the T20 World Cup in 2021. And again, to JL's credit, he got on board and played the role he was being asked to, which gave space to Ronnie, Michael Di Venuto, Jeff Vaughan, and Sridharan Sriram to play more of an active hand as skills coaches.

The pressure was right on us early in the tournament, scraping by against South Africa – holding our nerve in a low-scoring chase – before England obliterated us. We had hit the point early in this competition where we had to run the table from that point; any loss would put us on a plane. In an earlier iteration of JL's tenure, that would have led to him reading the riot act and demanding more training. This time, we were allowed to do the opposite.

The day following that loss, a lot of us were scheduled to play golf and the rest of the squad joined us for a long meal and a big night together outside. Despite what had happened not even 24 hours beforehand, there was this buzz around the table. All the tension and pressure vanished. On the way home on the bus, the speakers were blaring as we sang at the top of our lungs in the dark.

This was the way our group wanted to respond to adversity and it had the desired result – to a person, upon waking up a little dusty the next morning, the attitude was 'Okay, now we're ready. Let's go and win this fucken thing.' We never looked back. Some big wins to finish the group stage, an exhilarating semi-final chase with Wadey and Stoin, and on to the final.

There was so much trust in each other. It meant that as soon as the coin fell Finchy's way in the decider against New Zealand, looking around the dressing room before going out to field there was a powerful sense that we couldn't lose. That sounds arrogant, but it captures the faith that had been developed from years of work and evolution as cricketers and people.

In the heart of it all was Mitch Marsh. During the middle of that year when we were all trying to get some time away, it was Bison taking every opportunity presented to him in New

Zealand, the Caribbean and Bangladesh. By the time the World Cup rolled around he had earned the number three position. In a practice game against the Black Caps before the tournament on the secondary ground at Abu Dhabi, he pulled his first ball over forward square leg for what must have been a 100-metre six off Tim Southee. All of the senior players felt that we had rarely seen anyone strike the ball so cleanly, and that he would be the man to win us this Cup.

Sure enough, against Southee and company again in the final, he struck 77 of the sweetest runs one could ever see to break the back of a chase of 173. When I came out to join him with 63 to go, it was already party time. It's all been said about Mitch since his triumphant return to all the Aussie teams, but there's nobody we want to win more than him. He is loved. As it turned out, it was me who hit the winning runs with an ugly reverse pull that trickled to the rope. The ball was still at least 10 metres from the boundary by the time Zamps and Stoin made it to Mitch to leap all over him.

The plan had worked. We wanted to do things our way, the case was argued respectfully and accepted. I have no doubt it was the extra confidence from that freedom that made the difference when the going got tough and it was a key driver behind us winning that cup.

When JL eventually left the job a few months later, following a home Ashes win, the fallout was ugly and we weren't immune to it. But the way I saw the situation then, and still do now, is that the foundation was laid in that 2018–19 period, which provided us with the chance to build from there. That is to his credit and the legacy he leaves our generation.

———

Following that T20 World Cup win with a good Big Bash season and my wedding, I was happy as could be with the IPL as my next assignment in the March of 2022. Having the confidence of the RCB top brass, who made sure they held on to me in a revamped line-up where Faf was taking over as captain from Virat, had me fired up again. Unfinished business and all that. The downside was that we still wouldn't have the excitement of playing at the Chinnaswamy Stadium in the heart of Bangalore. That would have to wait, with Covid still demanding some level of quarantine.

I had a few nerves, too, having missed a few games for the wedding while the rest of my Australian teammates were touring Pakistan. RCB had been winning but I hadn't yet been part of it, and I know all about the second-year-blues at IPL teams. Where anything felt possible in 2021, the following season we just wanted to make the playoffs. From there, we had belief in our matchwinners. I was consistent, my strike rate up towards 170, but I wasn't winning games myself as I had twelve months prior. Getting rolled on a seaming pitch on reaching the elimination stage summed up where we were at. For another year, we had to move on.

And so, our lap around my IPL experiences takes us back to where we started: leading into the 2023 season, with no certainty that my reconstructed ankle would be up to the task. For all the work I'd been doing to be as ready as I could for the opening game, I knew in my heart this had the potential to go wrong; that it could be my toughest competition yet.

I wrote earlier about Virat's growth as a leader. In my case, I was proud of the way I presented my situation and positioned expectations about how much work I could do. For the first time in my career I felt like I was going to need to be managed rather than playing every game. It was humbling to make such a concession, but I couldn't risk another setback, lest the chat move to whether I was finished. I didn't think so, but I had sensed that sort of drumbeat starting after my ill-fated Aussie return.

In past seasons, wherever I've played, I've been a good sport when doing every piece of filming asked by my franchises and sponsors. I'm a people-pleaser, for better or worse. But these are seriously long days, especially at the start of the tournament, when commercial partners are getting their deserved pound of flesh. Overseas players like me have a reputation of leaning into these requests, and the sillier they are, the better my theatrical performance, or so I tell anyone who listens.

But to pad up for every commercial this time was going to compromise my rigorous agenda: pool, gym, training, physio, massage, more pool . . . Before this stage in my career, I never would have had the courage to put myself first like this, but it felt good. And sure enough, I received no negative feedback in making this call. This might sound like a small thing, but it meant the world to me that once again we were all on the same page. They had my back.

With my body getting stronger by the session, my confidence growing as I stuck religiously to my routine, I was fresh and filled with the same hope from that first season two years prior. And just like 2021, we were off to a flyer – the team and me.

I wasn't much needed, but I remember so clearly the two sixes I hit upon reaching the middle to finish off the first win against Mumbai. It had been a long time since I'd done that in a game, and hitting the ball well is why I get to do what I do. My leg might have been weary but my eyes, hands and coordination hadn't changed. A half-century striking at better than 200 against a Lucknow attack including Mark Wood, who on his day is one of the bowlers who has given me difficulty with his extreme pace, told the world I was back in business. That was underlined by eight sixes against Chennai; I made 76 from 36 balls, then 77 against Rajasthan.

It was like I had gone in a time machine to the very start of my Victorian career – that night at Hobart against Tasmania a dozen years earlier. The freedom to trust and swing and know that when I'm having one of those innings, I'm a nightmare to bowl to. The hot streak abated – it always will, with the way I play. But a couple of further brisk fifties made it five for the season with 400 runs to my name at a strike rate of 183, having hit 31 sixes in the process.

In the end, though, for the team, it was another unsatisfying effort. This time we didn't even make the playoffs. My favourite moments of the season were the batting partnerships I shared with Faf. Doing so much work together at training, and having so much admiration for his career, it was special to spend time in the middle together. In that Chennai chase, he had been down the other end for most of it, smashing the ball everywhere. It was the cleanest and most consistently that I'd hit the ball in a long time, and it was the sign that I was ready to play the best cricket of my life.

6

Mirage City

It may not look like it, but a lot of planning goes into determining where players on the T20 circuit will end up at different times of the year. When my manager Ben and I were having these discussions early in 2023, with my foot still a mess, I was concerned about the prospect of not having much on between the end of the IPL and the ramp-up to the World Cup. If my RCB stint got cut short with the injury, I needed a back-up plan. And where better than England?

As it turned out, given my time in India exceeded expectations for my recovery, the trip to Warwickshire and their T20 side the Birmingham Bears ended up scratching a different itch.

In Melbourne's lockdown days, the most precious hours of my day were getting out to the Junction Oval to train. Wanting to extend that permitted window as far as possible, I appointed myself something of an assistant coach for the Victorian women's team. I'd have a net set up for anyone who wanted to come in for an individual session, a system that worked well. I had done a lot of coaching for kids when I was in my later teens and early twenties, but doing it at this higher level gave me the bug in a big way.

It's probably clear by this stage that my personality is to go all-in on any new interest, and so it was for this. I was fully invested in what was going on with the women I'd worked with for the Stars in the Big Bash: Tess Flintoff, Nicole Faltum, Annabel Sutherland and Kim Garth. I rode the emotion of how their games were progressing as I did my own, like seeing Annabel and Kim go from strength to strength with the Aussie women's team. It helped my cricket too, reminding myself in the process of teaching about what is and isn't important.

The suggestion of playing in this edition of the Blast came up at the end of the previous English season. Alex Davies, an old teammate from a stint at Lancashire in 2019, had since moved to Warks and suggested it might be a fit. I'm so glad that I went through with it. It was trickier to keep up with my rehabilitation at the same levels as the IPL, not helped by the relentless schedule that feels like you're living on motorways, but I got so much out of the chance to be a playing coach.

This wasn't formalised and it didn't need to be. With captain Moeen Ali having an unexpected Ashes recall, Alex was in charge, and Mark Robinson as head coach was more than happy to let me work on range hitting and fielding and other finer T20 points that can be lost in the helter-skelter of an English season. Someone like Sam Hain, who has one of the best 50-over records in the world, was especially rewarding to work with as he tried to tweak his approach to be as dominant across 20 overs. We were inseparable, nerding out all day on technique. When he went on to make his ODI debut a few months later, I was bursting with pride.

I'm sure it will be the same when some of the younger lads make their next step. I kept trying to reinforce to them that the job wasn't only the number of runs, but whether the way they scored kept improving the team's position. That's something that gets missed early on. Jacob Bethell and Chris Benjamin were both living in town near where I was being put up. We complemented endless nets with plenty of dinners and a few beers to bed in what we had talked about during work hours. I was so invested in Bethell's progress that I tried to get the Stars to draft him when I got home. And just before this book was finished in 2024, there he was in an England shirt playing against me.

The off-field highlight of my time at Edgbaston was heading along to watch my mates from the Australian team on day two of the extraordinary Ashes Test. Vini had joined me by this stage and the Aussie team left us a couple of tickets. But when we rocked up to find our seats, not far from the viewing room, we realised it was right alongside one of the formal tour groups. With respect to the fans who had travelled around the world to be there, I realised our location would make the type of day I was envisaging quite difficult to pull off.

The alternative was to find the aforementioned Bears crew, plus Olly Hannon-Dalby and a few others. Their spot was perfect: alongside the sight screen opposite the pavilion end, as far as possible from the media centre, right up the back with a wall behind us. It was anonymous enough to let our hair down with a day of Pimms and cheering every run like I was a kid back at the MCG. And what a day for it, with Stuart Broad on a hat-trick after nicking off Marnus Labuschagne first ball, then Uzzy Khawaja fighting back to register his first ton in England. You might expect that I was jealous of the guys in the middle, but in my little sanctuary that afternoon I couldn't have been happier.

My original schedule for 2023 had me moving from Birmingham to London to take part in The Hundred for a second season with the Spirit, based at Lord's. In the end, CA decided that after the rigours of the Blast, I would be better served in full-time rehab at home. Given how close we were to Vini giving birth, getting back home was the right call for everyone.

However, the cricket part of my brain was sad not to get back to The Hundred after a brief stint in 2022 that didn't shoot the lights out. Again, what I enjoyed most was getting involved on the coaching side, like an old-fashioned senior professional. At the Spirit, my coaching project was Jamie Smith. He was well on his way to taking the next step, and as I write he has done so with a flying start as a Test player, but it's rewarding getting a look under the hood before someone goes big. After I'm done playing, I'd like this to be part of my future.

Of course, I had ended up on the Spirit's radar in the first place because Warney was their inaugural coach. I mentioned earlier playing against him in my second game of first-team cricket for Richmond in 2006. I didn't witness his century, as that happened in week one of the match before I was substituted in for our departing Shield players. But as a lad who was still in high school, walking out to face Warney was something else.

As a disciple of his growing up – weren't we all? – I had watched the coaching tape so often that I genuinely believe I picked every ball in that first over he sent down to me. There they all were: the aggressive toppie, the wrong'un, the flipper, the zooter, the slow leggie – or at least that's how I like to remember it. Of course I had no chance to score, but the very idea of being in a battle with Shane Warne was barely believable. It was like a computer game. He had so much control, letting the ball drop as he wished, always at the last moment, drifting and ripping and making me look foolish. I'm smiling thinking about it. On Monday, the principal announced to the school that I had played a game of cricket against the best spinner of all time and hit him for a boundary, presenting me a prize. A total dream.

The next time we were in each other's orbit was in the lead-up to the 2012–13 Australian season, when he was instrumental in getting me to join him at the Stars. I had been down the road at the Melbourne Renegades in the first season of the Big Bash, but Warney liked my style. He wasn't just the captain of the club in those early years, he *was* the club. I have vivid memories of a practice match with him talking me through every delivery I was bowling, getting my field and angles just right. I see now that the way he was with me when I was learning the game is how I try to be with young players now.

His investment in me continued. It's fair to say he always had my back on commentary, feeling like he was part of my journey from those days when we crossed paths in the MCG rooms. It was from there that I entered what can best be described as Warney World.

It was a brief but brilliant period when he took me into his inner sanctum, just before the pandemic. Once he realised we had similar interests, including playing cards, I started getting a regular invite to the poker games he would run at his house in Brighton. When he decided to put that mansion onto the market, he tried to sell it to me first. He got me around early one night to give me the full tour – what a pad. It wasn't quite what Vini and I were looking for, but it was fun being taken around by a guy who was so proud of what he had helped create there over the years for him and his family.

As for the nights down in the theatre, in many ways it felt like being back at a kid's birthday party. A bunch of Warney's mates would gather, with plenty of regulars at almost every game, but even when there were high-profile names at the table, it was still mostly a bunch of blokes eating M&Ms and jelly snakes, drinking Coke Zero, and hanging shit on each other. No glamour, just fun.

Warney's sell to get me to London was that we could enjoy taking on a new tournament in The Hundred and also play plenty of golf together. It's so sad that this wasn't possible in 2021 with the pandemic, and by the time the comp rolled around again the next year he was gone. I'm eternally grateful that he made me, a kid who adored him, one of his people, and the baton has been passed, with the poker games now arranged by his son Jackson.

Something that has been watched more often than any shot I played with the Spirit was a batting masterclass I did in the middle of The Oval with some young players on Sky Cricket – always amusing segments to be involved in. It wasn't the first time I'd been on that network, though. We have to go back to a much earlier stint in England in 2012.

I was playing for South Wilts in Hampshire and we had been called up to attend a taping of a playful Saturday morning show called Cricket AM. My teammates decided to make the most of it the previous night on the town, not factoring in that we would have to speak on telly first thing. That's what I've always blamed for mishearing a question when asked in the quiz segment what the currency of Japan was. My answer: Tokyo. I swear the host said capital! A note to Sky producers reading this: you don't need to revisit that archive.

The South Wilts diversion is one of the weirder tales of my career. Remembering that I'd played my first IPL season in 2012, the plan was for me to make the most of my UK passport in England and turn out in all formats for Hampshire. The deal had been nutted out between David Hussey and Dimi Mascarenhas – I didn't know much about it, but I was thrilled.

After a few training sessions with the senior squad, finding my feet and getting ready for the long campaign, it was explained to me that in order to take the field as a local, I would need to front a judge to declare that I had no intention of playing for Australia within the next year. This didn't feel risky – I'd only played a dozen games of state cricket and I felt miles away from the national team. Giles White, the cricket boss at Hants, had a different view – he didn't want to scupper any chance I might have of playing for Australia in the short term, which was the risk of playing this hand. I'm grateful for his judgement, as in a lovely turn of events, I ended up making my Australian ODI debut four months later, in August 2012.

So instead of being a local for Hampshire, I would play if they had vacancies for an international, and spend the rest of my time playing club cricket and county second XI fixtures. Not what I was expecting, but not the end of the world, especially given I'd still train with the main professional group at the Rose Bowl. On Saturdays, I would run around in the top division Southern Premier League with South Wilts as their overseas.

It was all ticking over as planned, making the most of my season in the 50-over fare for the seconds, and enjoying my Saturdays even more with ball than the bat, including a 7-for. Ahead of the Blast season, the county second teams play T20s to fine-tune as required, which saw me taking the field in May against MCC's Young Cricketers. Well, 44 balls later I'd hit 115 against an attack led by Jamie Porter, who would soon be one of the best bowlers in England. With doubts around Shahid Afridi's availability as the second overseas player in the Blast, Hampshire handed me a contract as soon as that innings was complete. My first professional stint in England was secured.

I explained earlier how important Simon Katich was as a teammate in that Blast season, opening my eyes to what it was like for the players who really made it count in Australian teams. A match-winning effort at Chelmsford, where I made a quick, unbeaten 60, was the innings where it started to click at that level, giving me the belief I needed to take the next step. It made other people pay attention too, and my Australia days soon arrived.

Four years earlier, a similar pattern had played out when I was a club player aspiring to make it for Victoria, also coming off some vital months in England. As a 19-year-old in 2008 my first season at Fitzroy-Doncaster had ended awfully: I don't think my batting average in first XI cricket got far into double figures. It was a big setback, having moved from Richmond for more opportunities but blowing almost all of them.

A conversation with a teammate towards the end of that season included a reference to his brother-in-law looking for an Australian to play for them that winter. This sort of opportunity hadn't been on my radar before, so I jumped at the chance to follow the sun. Once my brother, Daniel, learned of this plan, he became part of it: we were off to Norfolk. Specifically to Saham Toney CC about 50 kilometres west of Norwich, a village of 1500 people.

For a lad who had never lived away from my parents, the setting was ideal. We were put up with the vice-captain's family, his mum cooking a feast every night. It took her until about the third week to double up something she had made for dinner; we were totally spoilt and loving it. They talk about the Heathrow Injection for Australians spending time in the UK. I put on stacks of weight, with a pair of chunky sideburns to match.

Like most players who go to England, we were taken in by the club and made to feel at home. To say we were in the East Anglia Premier League is broadly true, but our first XI was in the fourth division of the competition. It was a fair way down the pyramid from the Victorian and occasionally Australian players I had been facing in Melbourne club cricket over three seasons. So to lay a marker, the first ball I faced for the season I sent straight back over the sight screen for six.

From there, it was cocky of me to ask what the league record was for runs, but it was right to set a goal and give it a red-hot go. I got there by rattling off five centuries on the trot to finish the season, including 217 against a club called Mundford. More importantly, we won the league and earned promotion. It's something I'm still proud of, and knowing they still have my photo in the club house means a lot too.

That isn't the full story of my 2008 in England, though. Despite my success in the middle, this was the first time I had a really bad run with what I now understand to be depression. The fact that it peaked immediately after making a century should have been a sign that it had very little to do with cricket, and much more to do with a chemical imbalance. I sobbed to my brother – it all came out.

I'm lucky he was there with me. With nine years between us, Daniel and I had played senior cricket together when I was 15 and 16 at South Belgrave, but when I moved to premier cricket our paths diverged. While I was playing, he was doing his computer engineering masters. As the dux of our school, he's always been sharp.

In that moment, I just wanted to stop. My life had been on a certain path since I was a little boy, through the underage ranks to where I was now. But I'd found the adjustment difficult and the dream of going on to make it as a professional felt so far away. There are photos of us at Lord's on the tour that summer up in the media centre and on the side of the field – I didn't for the life of me believe I'd ever end up playing there. My greatest hope was getting to the Victorian team, and, irrational as it was, I felt like I'd already blown that in 2007–08.

He nailed his job as a big brother in that moment by taking all the pressure off. No, don't go home. Stay here; enjoy the experience. Let's stop fixating on cricket and let it just be something you do rather than defining every part of your life. It struck a chord. Instead of packing off back to the airport and burning my bridges, I did stick around, I enjoyed it a lot more and that distinction between cricket and who I am has been a slow work in progress ever since. It all started with that brotherly conversation. My sister Lisa is 11 years older and has the life experience of extensive travel, so she has been a strong support too.

In hindsight, that should have been when I put in place the type of processes that I have now. Things to help when my brain gets the better of me, often for no reason at all. But this wasn't talked about in the game then, not in the way it is these days. It would be years later before I had to figure that out.

In the same way that 2012 helped propel me into the national team, this stint in rural England laid the foundation for getting me into the Victorian squad. On getting home to Melbourne, I had by far my most dominant first-grade season, which prompted a rookie contract for 2009–10. I'd bounced out of my mini-crisis ready for my new life.

In the same way that going to India each autumn would become an annual ritual, so would spending the time that followed in England. In 2013 it was Surrey, in 2014 back to Hampshire. These were times to be enjoyed and I found myself in a Brat Pack of sorts with James Vince, Liam Dawson and Chris Wood – all part of the wider cultural experience.

Then in 2015, months after becoming a one-day World Cup winner on my home ground with the Australian team, I was off to join another juggernaut: Yorkshire. Finchy and I had been signed as the overseas pair, me essentially as his understudy, and we would play in the Blast together where there was provision for both of us. Despite being such a red-ball machine at the time under Jason Gillespie's coaching, the T20 side didn't click.

Of course, I made the best of the situation by making friends with a number of new teammates including Liam Plunkett, Jonny Bairstow, Jack Brooks and Steve Patterson – these bonds were one of the best things about floating around the county circuit. They strengthened for me at Yorkshire when Finchy had to finish up through injury, so I was given the chance to turn out in the four-day competition as well – something I'd been craving since 2012.

It was in this window where I put in one of my best career performances. The Scarborough Festival is an iconic part of the English calendar, played on the best out-ground in the country, with loads of history – it's always packed, a true carnival atmosphere. We were up against Durham and ball was dominating bat for the first half of the game, but I'd made it to 36 the first time around before gloving one off Graham Onions down the leg side.

Onions was leading a quality attack made up of my Vics teammate John Hastings and Durham's record wicket-taker Chris Rushworth but in the second innings I felt within me that I was on the cusp of a special performance. At 5 for 79, it was the type of day that needed it. Adil Rashid, who at that stage was much more of an all-rounder, walked out to join me. Without doing anything unconventional, the two of us put on 248 at a run a ball, and I made 140 from 144. I've rarely felt in such control or played with such confidence.

This game was being played on the same date when the Test boys were rolled for 60 at Nottingham after Stuart Broad's 8 for 15 – two days later they had conceded the Ashes. It was obvious that there was going to be a generation change, with Pup and Bucky announcing their retirements ahead of the following game at The Oval and other senior players like Watto and Brad Haddin unlikely to play again.

It might have been naïve, but I did think upon getting home for the summer of 2015–16 that my time to get a proper go in the Test side was coming. Sure, my two previous stints were in Asia and the last was twelve months earlier. But I had always been clear in my own mind and in my messaging that I was happiest playing red-ball cricket on pitches like those in Australia and England, where seamers rather than spinners set the agenda. My career as a resourceful middle-order batter who bowled spin had been born of necessity as the only way I could bang down the door to get into the strong Vic team.

But I missed selection for the reset to start that summer. Then again when Uzzy did a hamstring in Perth but it was Shaun Marsh who got the nod. He caressed a ton against the West Indies in Hobart, sharing a monster partnership with Adam Voges. I knew that SOS was good enough to deserve another crack, but it's hard not to ponder what might have happened had it gone the other way.

A second fork in the road came a couple of years on, when I actually was a Test incumbent. My century in Ranchi came in my first game back, then 45 in Dharamsala, where we should have won had we not botched our second innings. I made 23 and 14 in Mirpur, where we lost by a whisker, then corrected that in Chittagong with 25 not out in a winning chase, having made 38 in the first dig while helping add 96 in some of the hottest, most sapping conditions imaginable. I know all too well that my numbers weren't earth-shattering, but they were a meaningful contribution, so it struck me as total bullshit to throw it all up in the air ahead of the home Ashes of 2017–18. Apparently, all spots were now vacant.

Naturally, Victoria were aware how much my Test spot meant to me, and gave me a chance to bat at three early in the season. Andrew McDonald was the coach ahead of moving to the national team, and his decision was reflective of how much the relationship had improved between me and the state since I was one foot out the door to New South Wales a year earlier.

Yet when the call was there to be made, it went the other way and SOS got the nod ahead of me again. Of course he went on to make an important fifty in Brisbane, a match-defining hundred at Adelaide, and finished the series with another in Sydney. He made the very most of his recall. But as it had been in 2015, it was impossible not to imagine me as a Test batter in my home conditions, perhaps walking out on Boxing Day with my family watching on.

For about five minutes at the start of the series I was back in the frame, called up urgently to Brisbane before the first Test when SOS twinged his neck. He came good the next morning and I was just as quickly released to play a Shield game at North Sydney. It led to one of one my stranger pieces of success, still my highest first-class score. Against five bowlers who had played for Australia, I walked in at first drop and left with 278 to my name from 318 balls. It wasn't fuelled by anger or emotion, it was just a time when I felt so comfortable against the red ball and was so confident playing in a way to meet the challenge.

My most demoralising moment with selectors, though, came shortly afterwards, when I'd backed up the 278 with 96 against Western Australia before copping a bad leg before decision. This all happening while I was out of the side led to a conversation with Trevor Hohns, where I asked why I was surplus to requirements when going through such a purple patch with a Test hundred close behind me. The answer was blunt: not enough tons. It's the only time I've come close to losing it in a situation like that. So, had the umpire credited four runs instead of leg byes from an inside edge against WA, my innings would be seen as a success, but having recorded four short of 100 meant it wasn't? That was the difference?

All of these close calls came years after the first, one that almost nobody knows about. That was Boxing Day 2012, a few months after my first limited-overs internationals. At 7:30 in the morning after celebrating Christmas, I woke up to a urgent call from Mickey Arthur, the national coach at the time. 'We need you to get to the MCG right now,' he said. 'Bring your kit and I'll explain when you get here.' I was still living at Mum and Dad's, so I got straight in the car for the 50-minute drive from South Belgrave.

What was this all about? I hadn't been with the team in the lead-up, and certainly wasn't in the squad. When I arrived, Mickey told me that Watto had a calf problem. 'He's about to have a fitness test and if he doesn't pass it, you're playing.' Stunned but obviously excited, I nipped down to the nets right away for a bowl and a hit – it was Big Bash time, and I hadn't played with a red ball for weeks.

International cricket's anti-corruption measures mean that as soon as I reached the dressing room, I had to hand my phone over. A change to the team wouldn't be announced until the toss. So there was also a chance that I would be making a Test debut at my home ground and my family and friends wouldn't be there.

It wasn't to be – Watto got the green light, I got released, and had to rush back home to get my luggage before setting off for our next BBL trip. When we touched down in Perth we saw that Watto had sent down three overs in the first session before blowing out that calf.

Who knows what might have happened had that fitness test been more robust. Watto batted well despite the injury in a big win, but was ruled out for Sydney. That absence got me officially into the squad. And this time, as the only all-rounder, it was made clear that I was going to get my baggy green. Predictably I told people, and a cohort from my family and South Belgrave Cricket Club made plans to be at the SCG on day one.

Only for another twist. Mitch Johnson not only beat up the Sri Lankans in Melbourne with his pace, he carved them up with the bat, nearly making his second Test ton. So in Sydney the selectors decided to push him up to seven and have Wadey as wicketkeeper at six, with Mitch Starc coming back in. It was the first Australian XI to play four fast bowlers in Sydney since 1954. I would debut in India a month later, but never at home.

With that opportunity just about gone, although I'll never stop hoping, these are reflections more in sorrow than in anger. I know my career has been an enviable one in so many ways, and I needn't fixate on the piece that hasn't been satisfying. I try to see it that way. But those tales still exist, and are still part of my story.

Returning to where we started in Birmingham in 2023, there was a red-ball twist after we had been eliminated from the T20 tournament. They asked if I would like to play in a four-day game against Kent before going home. I was mindful of how taxing it might be on my leg, but I was pumped about getting to do this in England again. It did require a phone call to Kookaburra to ask for some white pads. I remember the response of the contact there who took the call: 'Glenn Maxwell and white pads? Is this a prank call?' Fair question!

The plan was for me to bat at seven and bowl some spin – yes please. By the time I got the chance to bat at Canterbury, having rolled the hosts for 171 on the opening day, we were well ahead in the match. But playing my way to 81 from 67 balls was a thrill – a reminder to myself that I could still more than match it in the longer version of the game.

There was never any prospect of Bails picking up the phone after that to tell me to stick around for the Old Trafford Test, but given the boys had been beaten at Leeds the week before, there was media speculation that it might not be the worst shout. Remember, this was against an England team playing with the type of freedom that would have suited my game down to the ground.

My final commitment in England was a great day on BBC radio commentary for Blast Finals Day, something that was very different to my other jobs. So ended a stint of six weeks where I packed so much in and felt nourished, and I can't wait to get back over there when the planets align. But after the better part of five months on the road, it really was time to get home: rehab, regroup, and go again.

7

Such Great Heights

I know I won't get to do this forever, so when it comes to time on the road, I try to resist the temptation to complain. It's always a privilege, even when it isn't going well. When I say that I love few things more than a winter break in Melbourne, it's said with self-awareness. But getting on that plane home for the first time since February, even for a month or so, got me very excited. See mates, go to the footy, put my cricket gear away, get a scarf out – outstanding.

The reason CA were keen for me to skip The Hundred was to put in some more of that intense rehabilitation work on my foot before the big World Cup run coming up, only three months away. This isn't exciting work, but it was how I spent most of my days, in a throwback to the previous summer when I was basically living at the Junction Oval gym and pool. Returning, I took a moment to appreciate just how far I'd come from the point when I wouldn't have been able to walk through those doors.

When I wasn't at the office, so to speak, we were nesting at home. With Vini's due date a couple of months off, we were going way over the top as all expectant parents do, buying and borrowing anything we were told might be vaguely useful. I had a couple of weeks in the UK on my own towards the end of my stint at Birmingham and had made the most of the long summer nights, but it was always in the back of my mind that life was about to change radically. I can't remember ever being more excited.

As we prepared for what was to come, we did reflect on how different life was when we initially and belatedly moved in together. This had been our most recent stint of getting any decent length of time together in the winter, during the 2020 Covid season.

In so many ways, a domestic arrangement had been a long time coming. Vini was raised in a Hindu tradition that frowns upon couples shacking up before marriage, but it became pretty obvious that lockdown was going to make it impossible to be darting back and forth between our places. Marriage wasn't far off – we had got engaged right before the whole world stopped. In fact, our party, with about 200 people flocking in, was our last night of anything being vaguely normal before it suddenly became clear that nothing was anymore.

Having never lived together it was quite an experience to suddenly be in each other's pockets, not just under the same roof for four straight months but forbidden by law from leaving the house. If it was an early test for marriage and kids, we came through it with flying colours. But this test came a long way into our story, one that goes all the way back to 2012 in a chance meeting at the Melbourne Stars family day.

Casey Fields is a long way from the city, but similar in distance and feel to where I grew up in South Belgrave. I always like being out there. And having moved to the Stars from the Renegades during the winter thanks to Warney, as well as being a new member of two national teams, they immediately put me front and centre of all the marketing. That meant a long trip out to Cranbourne on a Sunday morning in December, having of course been out late the night before.

When we were taking photos with fans, I noticed one of the people holding a camera. 'Oh my god, she's beautiful,' was my immediate thought. As it turned out, Vini was only there having been dragged along by a friend who was the one posing for the photo. Vini jumped in for one as well, and I had just enough time to ask her name. Unable to stop thinking about her, I got home and wondered how we might ever run into each other again. Then came the idea. What if she'd posted the photo? What if she'd tagged me? Boom! She had, on Twitter of all places. Of course, I followed her account and soon we were messaging.

I was stoked at these quick developments, and we went on a date, but my conversation included the fact I was about to go overseas for six to nine months, and she fairly assumed I wasn't interested. That's how things continued, with me so often away.

We danced around it for years, had different partners in between times, were in contact now and then, but our timing never lined up. Her career as a pharmacist was building. She wasn't preoccupied with my life and I couldn't blame her.

Still, there were moments along the way when I felt that there was clearly something between us, and perhaps it had to have its moment eventually. That came in late 2017, in the form of another date and an ultimatum. Either I would get my act together and we could give it a real go, or she would make the decision for us and get on with her life.

Thankfully, after a long time getting there, I had my act together enough to see the good thing staring me in the face. My previous relationships could never adapt to the unpredictability of life on the road. I wasn't at peace with myself and made immature mistakes. Yet none of this repeated once Vini and I were together. She understood all of it, and was the first person I had been with who did. We fitted into each other's lives seamlessly.

Her parents Viji and Venkat emigrated from India in the 1990s before she was born, but they were so busy making a suburban life for themselves in their new country that when we met, my day job wasn't too important. That's different now, they're hugely supportive as any family would be, but cricket wasn't a religion to them. It was quite refreshing to get questions from people who didn't have much of an idea about the game, counter to the cliché about those from India.

Thinking about my volatile days, a lot was down to how badly I handled being in the public eye. It's a big adjustment for anyone, and in my case it happened quickly. From relative anonymity to the Australian team in the space of a year. Batting the way I do added another layer of curiosity. I hadn't been on the professional pathway, enrolling in TAFE and teacher's college. When I was going out on the town as a younger guy, people noticed the football players who were drafted as they ended high school. Rory Sloane was one example. A year below me at school, I coached him at cricket and footy. He was flying from the moment he went to the Adelaide Crows.

Then suddenly there was a feeling of knowing that sometimes people were whispering to each other when I came into a room. I wasn't me, I was Glenn Maxwell the Australian cricketer, and they had seen me on TV. It was a big adjustment, it made me self-conscious, and it was happening right at the time Vini first came onto my radar.

Part of the difficulty was the strong opinions people formed about me, often based on little more than watching me bat in a way that was different to the norm. I understood how it happened, but it still didn't seem fair that I was being painted as an arrogant, aloof prick purely because I didn't mind reversing my hands or taking on the first ball I faced. In part, I was lapping up the fun that comes from the attention, but in another way I was resisting the judgement of strangers. I've eventually found peace with not being able to control what people decide about who I am; it just took me longer to get there than some.

A lot of my growing up was helped by my manager, Tony Connelly. He was with me through the time when life shifted up several gears through those early IPL experiences and into the Australian team. I couldn't have asked for a more professional or calm operator in charge as my responsibilities grew on and off the field. I trusted him implicitly. He'd often say how easy I was to handle, how low-maintenance. 'You don't need a lot do you?' he once joked. 'As long as you have a few bats you're good to go.' I imagine this observation had a bit to do with my contrast to another of his clients, Davey Warner, who commercially has a lot more fingers in a lot more pies.

Tony understood how precious time with family was to me when I did get windows at home, and didn't urge me to take on extra commitments. That might sound counterintuitive as an agent with a business model that revolves around me being busy, but it spoke to the wider duty he felt to me and others he was looking after. It's why my family loved him as much as I did. He took care of me because he cared about me.

His bowel cancer diagnosis in 2019 shook everyone who knew him. He tried his best to give the impression of business as usual, but it was increasingly clear that this was serious. He wouldn't be getting better. The decline was quick, devastating to follow, and made all the worse by Covid. Instead of being able to fly up to see him in Sydney, the best I could do was communicate on the phone for support, which didn't feel enough, given everything he had done for me. He was dying, at age 46, with two little boys.

When we took off for that bizarre closed-door series in England in September 2020, the end wasn't far away. Tony was about to marry Monique, his partner, as a special final moment with their family. I'm so pleased he was able to do that. None of this was far from the surface for those on the trip who were closest to him: Adam Zampa, Alex Carey, batting coach Trent Woodhill, and Davey, who had changed management but remained close to Tony as a mate and a sounding board.

Kez and I never said it to each other in the middle when stitching together that 212-run partnership at Old Trafford to win the ODI series, but as we both reached three figures that night we were only thinking of Tony. In the dressing room after the game, getting into the swing of celebrations, we got together to send him a photo. We later found out that he was still awake, watching the end of that match. It meant so much that he got to see us do that for Australia, together, and for him. He passed away a week later.

———

It wasn't the first time that grief had been part of my life in the game. Nearly a decade from the intense tragedy of November 2014 – an amount of time that in itself is impossible to believe – I'm always grateful that I had the privilege of taking the field with Phillip Hughes.

Bloody hell, Hughesy. What a remarkable fella, and a staggering talent. We first played against each other in Under 15s state cricket, Victoria versus New South Wales, always the biggest clash of the carnival. So striking, even as a pocket rocket, was how hard he hit his cover drive. I'd never experienced anything like it. Fielding there at the start of the game, balls were pinging past me before I had a chance to dive, not that I wanted any part of my hand to get in the way of those bullets. Anyone who saw him at that age was of the same view: this guy was destined to be a great.

We had been on a couple of early Australian tours together and I was in the team when he made a perfect ODI century on debut at the MCG. He was our generation's most talented player, bar none. I've no doubt that he would have ended up with 30 Test tons and 20 in white-ball cricket for Australia, it just felt inevitable.

We were fielding for Victoria when he was hit in Sydney, day one of a Shield game against Western Australia. Half an hour before tea, I'll never forget hearing the words yelled out by someone in the sparse crowd, echoing around an empty MCG: 'Phil Hughes is dead.' What was this all about? It was such a jarring thing to hear, but surely not literal. It made us all a bit angry in the middle – why would someone yell that sort of thing? It was a weird passage of play before tea, nobody fully concentrating after hearing that comment.

As we rushed off the field for tea, we were met by ashen-faced coaching staff. We checked our phones, and everyone caught up with the horrific vision of Phil collapsing, and the online reporting from the ground about resuscitation. There was immediate panic and disbelief, then silence. I still can't believe the decision to send us back out there after the 20-minute break, but we did as directed. We bowled, they batted, nobody uttered a single word for two hours. Everyone was numb, jumping to the worst conclusions.

Two days later those were realised. Our world became a different place.

I was living with Finchy at the time, one of Hughesy's closest mates, along with Wadey from our Vics team. They joined the bedside vigil and said their goodbyes. The days that followed were horrific. Watching New Zealand take the field a day later, sobbing through their minute of silence, sharpened up what a collective heartbreak this was for everyone who played. There was a much wider sense of tragedy too. When we returned from the funeral a week later, with Finchy one of the pallbearers who carried our mate from the service, we could barely speak a sentence to each other.

Even though the show went on, with cricket restarting a fortnight later, the events of those days followed us long after it stopped being the news of the day. We didn't want to forget either. It was there every time I picked up a bat, immediately transported back to what happened. We all had to be rebuilt with time and with the support of therapy. The best way to sum up that 2014–15 home summer is that we played because we were made to, not through any desire.

To be honest, I find it hard to give an accurate representation of the next couple of months. I suppose I've blocked a lot of it out. What I do know is, having been in the one-day team for two years, my spot was far from certain until the weeks before the World Cup. My results weren't there in any game I was playing. I hadn't quarantined the grief as well as others, and it was showing in all sorts of ways.

The low point was a Big Bash game at the Gabba. A few days after Christmas, in the era when the BBL was must-see-TV, we were chasing 165 and I was coming in at three inside the first over to face Ryan Duffield. No offence to the left-armer, he was a good cricketer, but his career was a modest one, so there was nothing about him that should have caused me panic. Regardless, I totally froze. His first ball came down, I backed away, then inexplicably left it alone. It bowled me middle stump. What was going on?

Those who loudly speculated that I was cooked were just about right. The clip went round the world and I couldn't get away from it. Realising that my World Cup dream was about to slide away, I sent a message to Ricky Ponting. We met before a Big Bash game for a chat in the stands of the MCG before anyone else arrived.

I was as vulnerable with Punter as I had been with anyone, letting him into how little motivation I had. He replied that this wasn't something that had ever happened to him, but suggested a remedy: for me to pick a fight with the opposition right away. In my next outing with the Stars I did just that. Ben Hilfenhaus is a lovely bloke with whom I had no beef, but I ran at him and hit a furious boundary. It'll sound like I'm putting an awful lot of weight on one delivery, but in that moment I did feel liberated and finally turned the corner.

A couple of games later I enjoyed a partnership with Kevin Pietersen when we got stuck into the Renegades at the MCG, hitting the ball as cleanly as I had in the middle of the previous year when smashing it for Hampshire and winning games for Australia. Against England in the tri-series final before the World Cup, I was player of the match for scoring 95 followed by taking 4 for 46. I'd got my act together in the nick of time.

That home World Cup to end the summer was one that there's every chance Hughesy would've been part of – I'm sure the form he was in would have been enough. We had to go on and win it for him, something that Michael Clarke didn't say directly but we all understood. Pup, of course, was struggling himself, having done a lot of damage to his back and hamstring during the staggering century he made at Adelaide in tribute to Phil. He'd just made it back in time.

Ahead of the tournament, we had a warm-up against India at Adelaide. I had one of those days, 122 not out in 57 balls with sixes pinging everywhere. They retired me with five overs to go. It wasn't an official match, so I still didn't have a ton for Australia, having been out three times in the 90s. But it was a sign of things to come when the real stuff started against England on Valentine's Day. I got hold of them at the end of a hot Melbourne afternoon for 66 from 40 – an easy win. Two games on, I made the most of a developing Afghanistan attack with 88 from 39 balls as we hit top gear. Our next assignment was Sri Lanka at Sydney.

In contrast to those beautiful flat pitches with generous fielding conditions, in the blessed days of four fielders outside the circle in the final overs, I found myself in the middle of a break-up. With great timing, everything had blown up the day after we beat England in the tournament opener. Realising when we reached

Perth that I needed support, I knocked on Shane Watson's door. Something about Watto made me feel he was the right person to trust, and I was right. Putting his giant arms around me, he said that he would look after me, and he did.

Every day he would check in on me, see how I was going. He knew me well enough to see the risk that I would spiral with too many late nights to distract myself, and he never allowed me to hit that self-destruct button. At Sydney, we were in the middle together. Having dropped a crazy match to New Zealand in Auckland, this was a big game in the context of our group and was built up accordingly in the media.

My attitude was different to a couple of months prior. I wanted this so badly now and it showed. At my most ruthless, there wasn't a lot the Sri Lankans could do. I motored to a 52-ball ton – finally my first for Australia, and every cricketer's dream come true.

With Watto there, with Phil's 408 cap number written on the back of my bat, with all that had played out over the previous few months, I jumped into the big guy's arms and sobbed. Not a conventional way to celebrate but it was this full-circle moment for me as a player and a human being. There would still be moments where I'd grieve, and even now I find myself drifting there from time to time. But the heartbreak felt by all of us was turned into the energy we needed for the business end of the tournament.

Pup led that final push, even if his hamstring was on the edge and risked becoming a sideshow. He had the inner strength to push through alongside a group of experienced players. Later he wrote that he was never the same after what happened to Hughesy, and about how much it took him to get to the finish line. I'm proud that I was part of that dressing room.

The day of the final was another belter. My home ground was as packed as it is for any Grand Final – more stuff I'd dreamed about my whole life, be it running down the wing for the Saints or playing for my country. As it turned out, I wasn't needed with the bat as we chased down New Zealand's target easily, but I did send down seven overs and hit Marty Guptill's off stump before nailing a direct hit run-out of Tim Southee. We were world champions.

———

Eight years later and 20 kilometres down the road from the G, having a much quieter day on the couch in Black Rock, Vini and I were happy that we had done everything we could over the previous month at home together to be ready for becoming parents. There was only one thing left for me to do before that: nip over to South Africa for a quick white-ball series.

Bails and the leadership team understood that I couldn't take any chances about being home for the birth, so our solution was that I would play in the three T20s and come home before the one-dayers, well ahead of the due date. It wasn't the same format as the World Cup, but we had all been through so much, they trusted me to get the big calls right.

8

Your Song

It would have been different once, but in my dozen years playing for Australia, the organisation has been good at making family a priority. I've noticed it more as I've got older, and there was no better example than how much effort from CA went into my planning to be with Vini when it mattered most. I never had to ask. They knew I had to be there for our baby's birth and sorted it without question.

The schedule has evolved too. These days we're conditioned to shorter series but more of them, especially when playing both white-ball formats. Decision-makers can give more debuts to younger players, which over time should lead to greater depth and the good selection problems you want in Australian cricket, with healthy pressure on all.

For me and Ashton Agar, who was also attempting an injury return and had a baby due, the fix was to be picked for the T20s in South Africa that finished on September 3rd, but to go home straight afterwards. This would let us be with the white-ball group for the first time in five months, even if we weren't able to take the field in the ODIs. The baby's due date was September 20th, but given how rubbery those predictions can be, Vini and I didn't want to take any chances.

Even though I wouldn't be playing 50-over cricket, the idea of getting back on the park for the Australian team in any capacity filled me with happiness. I'd been in India in March for all of one fielding innings before my body gave way. Before that, it went back to the T20 World Cup in Adelaide nearly 12 months prior. By now that felt like an eternity.

That preceding month of fitness training at home in July and August had been as intense as any I've undertaken through my professional career. The jargon they use now is 'overtraining' – where, out of competition, you are flogged. It feels old-school, how I'd imagine an AFL pre-season to be, but the method is that the core fitness you build can make you more resilient when in competition.

Truth told, I needed to be battled-hardened and everyone knew it. I'd made it through the IPL and my T20s in England, but there is a huge difference between 20 overs and the rigours of a one-day international. I hadn't proven to anyone else, let alone myself, that my leg was going to be up to everything that would be asked of it.

Until now this had never been an issue. I've been lucky that my standard base of fitness is high and my body is wiry, so I've never needed a huge amount of extra work to meet the standards wanted from me in the field. From the moment I walked into the Australian team, I've gravitated to the places the ball goes most: backward point early in an innings, sweeping on the leg side late. I love being in the game, so I've never wanted it any other way. But now, it was fielding where I risked becoming a liability until proven otherwise. Back in February and March, on the comeback trail, fielding was what made me feel most at risk of further injury.

I've known Ronnie for so long, as a teammate then coach, that we could be honest about this with each other. Along with André Borovec, our assistant coach in the Aussie camp, who focuses primarily on fielding, they ran a specific session for me, which is unusual. At the Junction Oval for the better part of an hour they gave it to me with constant sprints and fielding. This was mixed up with periods to cool down, only to sprint again – with a niggle, this can be where it hurts most. The idea was to replicate the toughest hour I could anticipate in the field on a hot Indian day. I got through it and was proud of myself. I could tell they were relieved.

The rigour of my routine was maintained by one of Cricket Victoria's strength and conditioning team, Chris Williams, who went after me like a personal trainer ahead of a wedding. Extra sprints, extra reps, sessions in the field that only got longer each day. I had an idea of what I was coming back to after that lovely English summer, but reality exceeded expectation. It was brutal, but I was ready.

An added complication before South Africa was that I had to return to England only a couple of weeks after the Blast for a sponsor. Nearly a year earlier I'd signed as an ambassador with the travel website Booking.com for the World Cup, which included a commercial shoot with Jos Buttler and Rohit Sharma. This was designed to be as convenient as possible: shot in Manchester, when my team was playing Jos's team during The Hundred at Old Trafford. Except I got pulled out of the tournament to go home. But I had a contract to meet. I had to do both.

I don't want to pretend that flying up the front of the plane is a burden – we're bloody lucky to be looked after so well as athletes. Even in the best circumstances, though, flying that distance takes a toll on your body. To mitigate, we decided I would stay for five days and continue training in Manchester before flying back, rather than smashing myself with two flights in three days. It worked as well as it could, with Lancashire kindly letting me use their gym as a former player. I love that club.

It's always nice to spend time with Jos, someone wired in a similar way to me as a cricketer. I've felt for him over the last couple of years, with the timing of his Test career not lining up with the Bazball era, when he would have been perfectly suited to that freedom. I've occasionally thought about how I would have fared as an England player when Brendon McCullum and Ben Stokes decided to revolutionise their approach. I'm not saying that I wish I'd used my British passport to turn out for England – let's not say things we can't take back – but you can understand the workings of the imagination.

As for Rohit, I'm in awe of how he's made the very most of opportunities later in his career to become an all-format superstar, having found himself stuck in a similar way to me at different points. I knew we'd be seeing plenty more of each other, not only at the World Cup but in our ODI warm-ups straight before the tournament.

I was back in Melbourne with 10 days to go before taking off for South Africa, but in hindsight, I've wondered about the extent to which this set me back. Everyone was trying to do the right thing, everything did the right thing, but there was drama to come in Durban just as we started to get into the swing of things.

Drama in this part of the world? That was something I had experience in.

———

Let's take this chance to go back to my previous visit to South Africa – in March 2018, for some of the most dramatic days of my life, setting in train the most dispiriting time of my career.

For me, Australia's sandpaper debacle begins at the Harp of Erin, a well known pub in Kew. It was nearing the end of a long summer which had already been an emotional rollercoaster. Dropped from the Test team before the Ashes, that double ton in the Shield, my second T20 century for Australia when I got hold of England in Hobart, a full BBL season, and missing out on the Test squad for the South Africa trip. I was drained. Quality time with old mates on a Saturday night would be time well spent.

It turned into an end-of-season occasion with friends I'd played with, played against, gone to TAFE with – guys who didn't treat me any differently because of where I play now. I'm at my best in that environment. On this infamous night, the Test in Cape Town was on the telly and we were half watching. Around the table, I remember distinctly, were Aaron Daniel, Brendon and Nathan Walsh, and Anthony Davies. I can even remember where we were all sitting when realising something was up.

'Boys,' I declared. 'I guarantee I'll be going to South Africa tomorrow.' A bold statement, but my instincts were on the money. I couldn't believe what we were seeing, and even before it was confirmed that it was a square of sandpaper being brandished in the field, I just knew this was going to blow up like nothing we had ever seen before.

I wasn't entirely correct – I thought they would bring the entire team home – but sure enough three players got suspended and the call came through first thing Sunday morning to get on the next flight. So much for a few gentle weeks at home recharging for the IPL. But of course, my mindset shifted quickly to the very real prospect of putting on my baggy green again at Johannesburg.

Fresh off their successful Shield final for Queensland, Joe Burns and Matt Renshaw were also making their way from Brisbane, the three of us replacing Smudge, Davey and Cam Bancroft. We talked about what we might be walking into, but still had no idea how devastated the touring party was. Exhausted and heartbroken, it felt like nobody could so much

I started batting in nappies (*left*) and learned to switch hands early (*right*).

Tagged as a white ball player from day dot when I was given yellow pads.

Supplied

Supplied

Supplied

Supplied

Seven years old, playing an unofficial game at Kings Park. I was on the sidelines watching and asked if I could join in and they said yes.

Supplied

Eleven years old playing Mitchell Shield for Ferntree Gully District Cricket Association (top level for U12s in the region).

I won the player of the tournament for the RM Hatch Shield. This was the premier comp for U14s in Metro Victoria.

Playing cricket with my brother, Daniel. I was 17 and Daniel was 27. This was my last game for South Belgrave CC playing De Coite Shield in the 2nd division.

Presentation night for Victorian Premier Cricket with Daniel. I was named in the team of the season.

With my sister, Lisa, after a Stars game at the MCG.

My parents, Joy and Neil, at the MCG.

Modern technology assisting with family photos while travelling. This was a family reunion in Cairns for the McPhersons (Mum's maiden name). I was away at the time, but able to join via videocall.

Wearing the Australian shirt for the first time. 28 was my first number before I changed to 32.

Post-game at the MCG for the 2015 ICC Cricket World Cup, after Finchy's amazing hundred.

Finchy and I with the trophy after beating New Zealand at the 2015 ICC Cricket World Cup final.

The first Australian Cricket Awards with Vini, February 2019.

Dubai, 2019.

as make eye contact with each other, let alone with the blokes who had just rocked up.

There were a lot of tears; it was difficult to observe. Teammates who I'd enjoyed so much success with looked destroyed. Enough time had passed for them to realise how intense the reaction had been at home and around the world. The disgraceful behaviour directed at Davey's wife, which was not an excuse but was relevant as a catalyst, had barely registered. We were the disgrace, as far as the public was concerned, and we would stay that way for a long time.

I took an immediate decision not to ask what had happened in the dressing room that day. It's not as if anyone wanted to talk anyway, but I was wary of prying. Instead, I tried to help as best I could by keeping the conversation elsewhere and trying to be a distraction. Remember the intruders they would throw into the Big Brother house to change the direction of the show? The three of us felt like that.

There was only so much we could do when preparations for the final Test began. On reaching training that day, Darren Lehmann walked into the press conference and promptly resigned as coach, in yet more tears. Two days earlier, when the punishments were handed down, Boof said he would be the right man to lead Australian cricket in a new direction, but he had soon realised that wasn't going to fly. There wouldn't be total collective responsibility, but a full leadership change was the only step.

I've been asked over the years whether I'd ever seen ball tampering in the Australian team or had an inkling of what was going on in South Africa. My answer is that every team I've seen around the world has its own way of trying to affect the ball, from club cricket to county to state to international, and that every team gives it a shot. The Cape Town version was extreme but the preconditions had clearly been emerging for a while. The cultural review that CA undertook got this pretty much spot on, about an obsessive attitude to winning having taken hold.

Recently we've seen what is possible when players from my generation are allowed and encouraged to be who they are. That was missing in this earlier period. It was rammed home to us what Australian cricket *should* be like, and according to some former greats, that was the not-so-secret part of their success. It came loud and clear after the Hobart Test thrashing in 2016, as the team got cleared out: this generation was too weak and too soft to win.

The following season, by the time the South Africa tour rolled around after a home Ashes with all its added hype and pressure, it was ingrained that hunting in a vicious pack could help get a series win in extremely hostile surrounds. But for the most part, it was an act, and little wonder in hindsight that it fell apart. Needless to say it's a healthier dressing room these days.

Boof had been able to relate to me personally, even if at times I'd not ended up where I wanted. We had our moments – he never held back when giving forceful feedback, shall we say. I knew he had my back, though, and I knew he and I wanted me to get to the same place. Our bond from my early days, including that first World Cup win, will always be there. His heartache in

Johannesburg was palpable, but we all knew he was right to pull the pin.

Another selection call went against me, with Burnsy and Renners replacing the banned openers and Petey Handscomb as the spare batter on tour taking Smudge's spot. They were the logical choices, but by this point I was so raring to go that it still felt like a body blow. Returning at such a fraught time would probably have put me on a hiding to nothing, but honestly the degree of difficulty made me want a piece of the action even more. The Test itself was the longest five days imaginable, Faf's side squeezing us into submission. From the dugout, it was tough to watch. The guys were giving all they had but also clearly wanted to be out of there.

Once the first layer of dust had settled, it really did look like I could now make a go of being a Test player. I didn't want anybody to be serving bans, with so many spots open in the top six, there was a logic to what could play out. Our next series six months later was against Pakistan in the UAE, where I'd been picked four years earlier, so it was a fair expectation that I would be getting another chance. From there, if I made the most of it, a precious home season against India was in my grasp.

To make sure I had the best run-up for an opportunity like this, I jumped at an offer to return to Surrey for some first-class action. Having played T20 for the club in 2013, it was a great fit and would be better still due to the Aussie team having a limited-overs series scheduled in England for the middle of the year.

But the directive from Cricket Australia, specifically from selection chair Trevor Hohns and high-performance boss

Pat Howard, was to take downtime instead. I was disappointed at the call, but it suggested goodwill, and that was reinforced when I got my next contract. National deals come with a ranking number. It's not exact but it bluntly reflects the pecking order, and mine in this round was the highest it has ever been. The message was clear in meetings too: right now, I was an all-format Australian player and was going to be part of the Test team again.

Then the whole thing went weirdly off the rails. There was an Australia A trip to India ahead of the Tests, and the stated plan from those same administrators was that I would use it to get some red-ball cricket under my belt before the important stuff. Good as gold, I thought – no Surrey, but this will do. However, the squad was announced and my name wasn't there. I called Cracker Hohns right away, who was pretty casual, along the lines of, 'Don't worry about this – we know what you can do. This is about having a look at a few new blokes. Everything is still on track.'

Alright – a bit odd again, but in a way, reassuring. I trusted the people in charge. Even if it meant one of those unusual blocks at home in Melbourne in August and September with absolutely no cricket leading into two of the most important matches of my life.

Or so I thought. I was so fresh and so excited that I had already packed my kit at home with all the bits and pieces I would need for Test cricket, including, of course, my baggy green. A bit keen, but confident about what was coming. And then it didn't. The Test squad came out, the email landed, I scrolled down my phone, and my name was nowhere.

It was such a cruel blow and underpinned with such dishonesty. Of course selectors have the prerogative to go different ways – things change. In this case, though, I'd been denied the chance to bolster my case in England, denied the A tour because I was deemed too senior, and after all that got the kick in the teeth. It was handled abysmally by all involved. The year that promised so much instead left me empty.

There was a postscript in January 2019, the next time selectors were looking to replenish Test ranks at home against Sri Lanka after getting whipped by India. In one of my regular spots with Gerard Whateley on SEN radio, I'd given a diplomatic but detailed enough answer when the UAE squad was released, and this all came to the surface when I got overlooked again for the Sri Lanka games.

At a press conference, asked why I'd been blocked from playing more first-class cricket and making my case in 2018, Cracker tried to talk his way out of what happened in our exchanges. The alternative history was disappointing to say the least. When Justin Langer copped a few similar questions the following day, he blew up at the journalist, describing the whole story as a series of 'careless whispers'. They were nothing of the sort.

———

Five and a half years on from that previous trip to South Africa, at a vastly different point in my career, I was relishing the chance to do the most basic thing for a cricketer: go to training with my teammates and hit some balls.

That first full session began like any other: a very gentle lap, having a laugh as we handballed the footy around, ahead of some stretching. The type of process I've gone through hundreds of times since I was a kid. But this time was different. When I got up to complete the lap, I felt my foot. Yes, *that* foot. It was a sharp pain; I couldn't take off properly, let alone run. The most innocuous lap was flooring me? What on earth was this?

Hobbling off the ground, panic set in. All this work behind the scenes was designed to demonstrate that I could get through a rigorous World Cup, and I'd broken down within a couple of hundred metres of my Australian return. I got to the physio room and blew up, furious and confused. I could tell there and then I would be sent home without playing.

In those two days between the injury and my inevitable flight, my year was crashing down around me. I couldn't help but flash forward to what Ronnie and Bails might think of this setback. Could my body be trusted anymore? Might they replace me? Could that be it for me as an Aussie cricketer? There were some leaps of logic, my anxiety making it worse, but the questions were rational. I was in a dark place and spiralling.

The lads on the trip were a comfort, especially Mitch Marsh, but my impression is that most people were of the view that this was good timing for an injury as I could get home well ahead of Vini having our baby. That was true, and the thought of an early labour had certainly gone through my mind plenty of times before leaving, but nobody seemed to clock that this injury might be much more damaging than something short-term.

I remember the flight. Stuck inside these negative thoughts, on my own. All roads in my head went towards the World Cup in India. Not just any tournament, but probably my final opportunity to win the trophy that matters most in cricket. Instead, was the end coming in a hurry?

When I got home, Vini was the best possible distraction. By this stage she was big, nearly ready to drop, and that alone was such a source of comfort. We were still two weeks out from the due date, so I was able to switch back into gear as a dad-to-be at home.

I needed to use this time wisely. The scan diagnosis was that I'd strained a different part of my foot, the inside bottom right. Because that is some distance from the outside left, where the metalwork was put in, I was told to take this as good news. It wasn't unrelated to the break but at least it wasn't going to require rehab on that former section.

Instead, it was back to the good old Game Ready ice machine for every moment I could get into it, and, yes, back to that Junction Oval gym for the same low-impact work that had dominated the early part of my year. It was January all over again, my very own Groundhog Month. Getting to India now hinged on getting this latest rehab spot on. On September the 5th, the squad was announced, and this time, my name was on the press release.

———

On September the 10th, with all the bags packed, I drove us to Cabrini Hospital. Vini was induced into labour. I was expecting the television-style instant result more than the reality of the long day and night that took us into the 11th. Where I was flying blind, Vini was all over it, and in the fullness of time, in the birthing suite as we planned, our baby boy emerged.

I hadn't given much thought beforehand to cutting the cord, but caught up in the emotion and spirit of the occasion, I was given the scissors and didn't say no. We took turns at holding him close and sobbed, uncontrollably in my case. He was out and crying and safe. We were parents.

We were so well looked after by the midwives over the next few days, getting supervised practice in the practical components of cradling a newborn, changing nappies, putting clothes on. It was a magical time in the baby bubble, welcoming our closest family members to meet this beautiful boy of ours.

In a quiet moment, we also took time to reflect on the emotion of it all. Ultimately we had been lucky. There was the anguish of our miscarriage followed by months of apprehension and medication. But knowing we were getting that profound happiness, that sense of achievement, and the pride I had in Vini, was strong. There are so many people out there who have done it tough on this front, including friends in our lives. We feel for them, and know that it's a lottery. We'll always be grateful for Logan.

Logan Maverick, actually. Quite a name, isn't it? I know when we announced the birth to the world, via an Instagram post of his little hand holding ours, it prompted a lot of speculation and interest. Were we massive *Succession* fans? The boring answer is no, we've never seen it. Instead, it was landed through a combination of what I'd describe as baby-name Tinder and me catching Vini at a weak moment.

There's an app that throws names up at you and you can swipe yes or no. Your partner does the same and you're left with a shortlist. I remembered that this is not how some people use Tinder, instead swiping yes to every person and thinking about the next step later, so to get on the same page as Vini as quickly as possible, I followed that technique. Logan jumped out immediately. It was a lock.

The only other name I'd thrown into the mix was Maverick. I'm not sure where I spotted it, but I thought it would be different, fun and give him plenty of cool nicknames when he was older. Initially Vini dismissed it out of hand. But I kept it in the back of my mind, and after landing Logan, I popped up Maverick again, this time for the middle name. Exhausted after all that she had gone through, Vini gave it the green light – you beauty! Our little Logie Bear had a full name.

The time came to leave the safety net of hospital and get my family home. I'd heard stories of how scary that first drive is for a new parent, and I felt every bit of this. What should have been a half hour drive was nearly twice that long as I stayed way below the speed limit, totally shitting myself. But we got home, and this was real.

My teammates were brilliant, the dads quickly welcoming me to their club. It reflects how we have evolved and matured over time that so many of my generation are now parents – so different to the 2015 World Cup, for instance. From big nights and lapping up all that comes with being an Aussie cricketer to looking for a quick dinner and maybe a quiet whiskey before making the most of an early bedtime.

It also means we relate to each other in different ways. You can be immune to depth as younger players, when your whole life is defined by what happens on the field – it can make friendships superficial. These days we bond as friends on a different level, working through the wider challenges of life together. It's not the entire reason behind our success but I think it's a bigger part than meets the eye.

As Vini and I tried to find a rhythm at home, I had no choice but to literally get back on the bike at the Junction Oval for this latest insufferable stretch of rehab. I had a fortnight left before flying to India, which became my new deadline. It was going well, my progress was swift, but this really was my last chance. One further setback, however modest, and I knew it would be too difficult to carry me, given they were already doing that with Travis Head, who had broken his hand in South Africa. If a gentle lap had botched my foot, what would a rigorous fielding session bring? The risk sat with me every day.

I started getting up before the crack of dawn to smash out as much of this work as I could before anyone arrived. It also meant that I would be back home by breakfast, ready to roll up my sleeves and put in a shift through the morning so that Vini could bank some rest, having been up and down all night breastfeeding. It made jumping out of bed at this unfriendly hour easy as I knew the payoff was quality time bonding with my boy.

At the same time, it dawned on me that I was soon going to be taking myself out of our precious baby bubble. Yes, they would join me in India, but it weighed heavily on me that soon, I would be a continent away from my crew. I'd never felt more attached, and separation was coming fast. I broke down when getting into that taxi to the airport; part of me couldn't believe I was leaving. But everything I had done for my cricket hinged on this moment of truth in India. Could I do this? Would I be able to get through, and perform? Whatever happened, would it be worth it?

9

Spinning Around

It didn't take long once back into the Australian camp to see that I was badly underdone. Rocking up in South Africa a month earlier, I had felt like I was flying but now? The fresh injury had done for that. And between times, I'd become a father. At home with nappies and feeding and worrying about any small thing, it was bursts of intense activity while also feeling like nothing was moving at all. But now, that period of staying still was over.

Once again, I was so grateful to George Bailey for understanding what I needed. The selectors could have had me fly to India for the first of the three ODIs before the World Cup, but that would have been just a few days after Vini gave birth. Instead, they had me drop into camp a few days before the third match, which gave me 10 days of being a dad. It doesn't sound like much, but that balanced approach made a big difference.

At the same time, it ratcheted up the importance of me getting through that one game in Rajkot. In India the previous time in March I'd barely made it through 20 overs, and my previous ODI before that had been in September 2022, up in Cairns against New Zealand, months before breaking my ankle.

There were two official warm-up games in the calendar to follow, but they are never the same intensity as a full international. So I knew I had one chance, and there was an expectation of me being able to do things like I had through my career, things like sprint to a ball in the 45th over having not touched it for half an hour, making a play for a run-out with a one-handed pick up and throw. You can replicate that in training all you want, but it's another thing in the heat of battle.

I was realistic enough to know that if I looked like an old man out there, a drumbeat would start about my suitability for selection before we'd even reached the tournament. It was pressure that I put on myself as well, really locking in that day and focusing on making my mark.

As it turned out we batted first and batted well, so I wasn't walking in until the 37th over. I would have to get moving. Looking at the scorecard, it says I was bowled by Bumrah for five from seven balls. But walking off, I honestly felt really good. Not because he'd snuck a yorker past me while I tried to steer it away – that's a normal risk at that stage of an innings – but because in two overs throwing myself back and forward at the crease, I hadn't thought about my leg at all. It felt just how it's meant to.

So at the innings break, I was up on confidence and ready to push myself in the field. I knew from IPL matches earlier in the year that sometimes when we batted first my ankle would stiffen before fielding, but I made it clear to Patty as captain that I didn't want to be looked after. I needed to get back into those hot spots.

The other thing I had to do was bowl. We had 352 to defend, which on a good day might mean starting my spell after early wickets, turning the screws without pressure as they chased the game. On this night, however, Rohit was on, getting stuck into all our quicks the way he does so well, pulling them miles whenever he had the chance. He hit five sixes in his half-century and was motoring to another ton against us.

Patty threw me the ball for over number 11 – the moment the fielders could drop back. From the first delivery, much as it had been with the bat, I was able to launch into my action and twist on that front foot without feeling a twinge. It was that twisting part of my action that had me worried – there's a lot of energy going through that ankle, and to not pivot is to end up bowling doorknobs instead of spin. But it worked; another bar was cleared.

It helped that from my fifth ball, thrown up outside off stump, Washington Sundar took me on inside-out with just enough room for Marnus to motor around from long off to take a ripper of a catch. As any bowler will tell you, getting in the book early does your confidence the world of good. I didn't mind that I was straight back out of the attack with Patty going to a different match-up for two right-handers: the cool-down and warm-up process would be good for me with the bigger picture in mind.

I was back in the 21st over, with Rohit still there and Virat helping keep the required rate at just past seven an over – well on track. Rohit, seeing them like beach balls, welcomed me back with a step down the track before the ball even left my hand and pumped me over long on to go to 81. Uh oh. We've all seen how it can play out when somebody is going like this – it takes one to know one, I suppose. How to respond?

It ended up being the moment that reinforced to me, and anyone carrying doubts, that I was going to make this World Cup. Two balls after the big one, Rohit tried to do the same thing, but it was quicker and angled at leg stump. Instead of him getting it over mid on, he had me squarely in the firing line in my follow through.

Now, I've taken some decent snaffles across the journey. There was one at Leeds in 2015, jumping back and forth over the rope, that got attention at the time, as did a one-hander in the Big Bash against the Heat, running back with the flight like my old mate Nick Reiwoldt for the Saints. But for whatever reason, I've always been a liability off my own bowling, much to my enormous frustration.

So for those who know my game well, the probability of dragging a Rohit rocket out of the sky with one hand was not high. On the replays, my face tells the story: I cannot believe it. It was harder still because the ball was coming out of the sight screen behind the batter's end, where the advertising display was predominantly white. So it was all reflex.

Supplied

Flying to the UK for the first series during Covid, September 2020.

Centuries to me and Alex Carey helped chase down a record total in Manchester and seal the ODI series in September 2020.

Stu Forster/Getty Images

Gareth Copley/Getty Images

Alex Carey and I celebrating our centuries after a thrilling ODI series-clinching victory at Old Trafford, 17 September 2020.

The photo we sent to Tony Connelly, who was in hospital, after the game.

Supplied

Philip Brown/Popperfoto/Getty Images

Sharing a laugh with Hardik Pandya and Virat Kohli as we wait for the presentations after Australia won game three of the T20 International series against India at the SCG on 8 December 2020.

Gareth Copley/ICC/Getty Images

Celebrating following the ICC Men's T20 World Cup final match between New Zealand and Australia at Dubai International Stadium on 14 November 2021 in Dubai, United Arab Emirates.

The swelling in my foot post-op, November 2022. You can see why I came close to losing it!

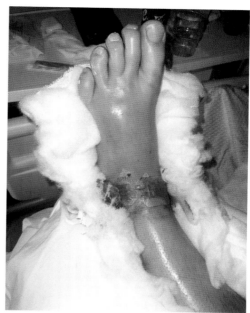

The Australian team celebrate our World Cup triumph in India, November 2023. I had so many doubts I'd ever get to this tournament over the preceding 12 months so this moment was extra special.

Our wedding day,
18 March 2022.

Rob was my best man.

Vini and I with my parents, Neil and Joy, and long-time mates, Anthony Davies, Brendon Walsh, Nathan Walsh, and Aaron Daniels, in Bangalore during the IPL in 2023.

Dad life in Dharamshala during the World Cup in 2023.

Morning of the AUS V AFG T20 match when I made 201. The pre-game routine was a dip in the pool with Logan.

Inset: 201 not out against Afghanistan in Mumbai during the ICC Men's Cricket World Cup, November 2023.

IT TAKES ONE DAY

MAXWELL
32

#CWC23

Making my way back to the changing rooms after scoring 201 not out.

Tour life is different now . . .
Hyderabad IPL 2024.

A BBL match between
the Melbourne Stars
and the Melbourne
Renegades at the MCG,
2 January 2024.

Playing a shot for
six runs during the
ICC Men's T20 Cricket
World Cup Super
8 match between
Australia and India
at Daren Sammy
National Cricket
Stadium in Gros Islet,
Saint Lucia, 24 June
2024.

The sharp move across didn't put pressure on my leg specifically, but having the agility to get into the right position got me on a roll. I got Virat on 56 when he made a mistake against my quicker ball, then Shreyas on 48 with one I was very happy with that was good enough to beat the outside edge and smash into his off stump. That was the game.

So, 4 for 40 from my 10 overs, and player of the match in what turned out to be a 66-run win after a couple of losses. I celebrated each wicket with more enthusiasm. Plus I didn't put a foot wrong haring around on the ropes, took a second catch at deep midwicket, and only once had to come off to get my strapping redone. I'd done put in a proper performance in a proper game – everything I wanted.

I felt such relief, slumping back into my trusty ice machine for the recovery, proud of myself in an Australian shirt for the first time since the T20 World Cup more than 10 months before. In a way, it was even better that I'd made it count with ball rather than bat, in what will always be seen as my second discipline.

————

How did I end up as an off-spinner? We have to go back to my time in the Victorian Under-19s in 2007. I was our medium pacer, something I'd been developing at Richmond, and through the Vics set-up I had the chance to work with David Saker and was gaining pace. Of course, like everyone in Australia of a certain age, I had been a kid trying to bowl leggies like Warney.

And like most of us, I lost confidence after too many half trackers. But I'd never bowled offies.

I had good energy to the crease, and when playing twos for Richmond would even get the new ball. At that level I was quick enough to land a skiddy bouncer and it was good fun. But at the grade above, where my batting had taken me, low-120s medium pace was never going to fly, along with the risk that I could hurt my back if I went too hard. I still bowled fast in England in 2008 because it was so much fun to do there, but I knew it had a limited shelf life.

As I've explained, those teenage years didn't have me at the front of Victoria's thinking. I played the Under-19s carnival but was some way from cracking the code at grade level, and miles away from state. Most of what I did was open the batting and take shine off the ball conventionally. But I was close enough to pick up some feedback that the state coach, Greg Shipperd, and the selectors were thinking about my bowling.

For years, Brad Hodge and David Hussey had bowled very useful finger spin from the top order, and thinking to the future, management wondered whether I could do something similar. Once I got a sniff of this, I went all in. If there was any sort of opening, I wanted to show that I would try whatever might give me a chance to get through it to the next level.

Part of this was putting up my hand any time an email asked for net bowlers when there was international cricket at the MCG, which occasionally had me in the nets with the Aussies. It was a huge thrill, even when Andrew Symonds took a particular liking to my offerings. It made great memories and was part of learning how to bowl under pressure.

The best of my net-bowler days was with the Vics. Early in the morning, the first day of a Shield match, a call came in asking whether I could come down to bowl to Rob Quiney. I reckon I made it into the car in no more than two minutes, onto the freeway for the long drive. They were playing South Australia, where Dan Cullen was in residence, and Bobby wanted to tighten up his game against finger spin.

After his net he had to dash off to get ready for the match and threw me his car keys, telling me to look in the back seat. He had left a gift for me, a bottle of Jim Beam. It was such a thoughtful touch from a guy who I would go on to respect as a teammate when I finally got into that dressing room, and it was something I've never forgotten when it comes to the way we treat others in and around the teams who try to help us be at our best.

I was nearing 20 at this point and at the level below the Victorian team, in an emerging players squad made up of district youngsters with a dream of taking the next step. On getting home from England in 2008, this gave me a season with a lot more time in the nets bowling to state players. My best season of Premier cricket followed with the bat and I was making inroads with the ball. Having taken strides towards becoming an all-rounder, I was rookie listed by the state for 2009–10.

The next major step on the development path was being sent to the National Cricket Academy in Brisbane in 2010. By this stage I'd been given a go in the Victorian 2nd XI, or the Under-23s as it was known then, and now had this opportunity in the finishing school of Australian cricket. It was a buzz getting the invitation, given how far away I had been a couple of winters before.

This was the place for players who would go on to get a baggy green, I thought. Many from that intake did make it for Australia across formats: Mitch Starc, Josh Hazlewood, Adam Zampa, Nic Maddinson, James Pattinson, James Faulkner, Moises Henriques, Sean Abbott. There were so many other excellent players, and more senior ones like Ryan Harris would sometimes show up and bowl to us.

We were all convinced it would be Luke Pomersbach and Ben Dunk who would make it as the next superstars of Australian cricket – they were the two complete players, so accomplished against anything they faced. I'd have these conversations every night on the apartment balcony with Jimmy Faulkner, who became a kindred spirit as we debriefed over a beer from our long and structured days at Allan Border Field.

Playing for any side with 'Australia' at the front of the name was a massive thrill, like when I got to the Hong Kong Sixes tournament in 2010. It wasn't proper international cricket, but it wasn't nothing. One other game stands out in the same respect from the two seasons I was eligible for the Australian Institute of Sport.

In the middle of 2011, we were up against the South African Emerging Players at the ground where the University club play in Brisbane grade cricket. We were led by Ryan Carters, my roommate at the Academy, who went on to have a good domestic career before retiring at 26 to become a scholar at Harvard, as you do. We had Alex Keath, who also finished young to become a successful AFL player, as well as Sam Whiteman, Marcus Harris, Jon Holland, Sean Abbott, and a leggie named Nathan Brain who we all thought was going to make it.

It's easier to remember what happened next because thankfully it got posted on YouTube. I had a day out and lamped 110 not out in 52 balls, taking down Kyle Abbott. Their batting was stronger still, with Richard Levi, Reeza Hendricks, Stiaan van Zyl and Temba Bavuma their top four. I raise this story because it ended badly for me, when all-rounder Obus Pienaar took me for 20 runs in five balls to chase the target in the final over.

And guess who I should run into while writing this book, at the same time as preparing to play for the Washington Freedom in Major League Cricket? Obus never made it for South Africa, but moved to the USA and has played for more teams than he's had hot dogs. From a left-arm quick who gave it a whack, he's now a middle order T20 gun, and we are premiership team-mates after we beat Pat Cummins and his San Francisco team in the final. Needless to say, Obus remembers his match-winning 20 runs off me too.

Despite that chastening experience, I made leaps with my bowling in Brisbane, working day-to-day with John Davison. To this point I had done what felt natural, trying to copy what I'd seen on TV, but from a seam-up background I was limited to darts at leg stump. Davo got into my action with video analysis so I could understand how I was bowling rather than focusing on what was coming out. It didn't take long before I was shortening my bowling stride to generate drift and drop, along with shape and more turn. All of a sudden I was an actual spinner, and having started to understand the craft I was excited to let rip.

On getting back into the Victorian set-up, with this role that had been carved out, I was able to start having an impact with the ball. I got my career going with eight games through the 2011–12 Shield season, and 16 wickets at 29 was a good return. I'd dismissed players like Ed Cowan, Nic Maddinson, Joe Burns, Adam Voges and Shaun Marsh. I wasn't a world-beater, but it showed the decision-makers that over a couple of years I had turned myself into what they wanted. Before long, it was what Australia wanted too, and helped get me my big break in 2012.

———

After the Rajkot win, our next assignments were the two warm-ups the ICC put on. These are always unusual, trying to fine-tune for serious cricket in match conditions on TV, but with literally nothing riding on it. Even the stats don't count on your List A record because teams use more than 11 players. It's like a Sunday friendly but with both teams stacked with stars, all doing their own thing.

We had drawn the Dutch for the first of these games in Thiruvananthapuram on the south-west coast. It's a lovely little spot, except for the fact that on match day it was hosing down rain. Given we'd played two days prior, this suited most of us down to the ground – Rajkot was the 11th international Australia had played in less than a month between South Africa and India.

Most of the squad did as you do when you have an unexpected day off – a haircut, a massage, an afternoon nap. Some of the crew were still in bed at 5pm, three hours after the scheduled start, when a message went around the WhatsApp group saying we needed to be on the bus in 15 minutes for a 6:15pm start. Chaos ensued as management herded cats, but we got there in time for a 23-over slog.

I thought a reduced-overs match wasn't a bad thing, as there's always a chance that could happen in a World Cup. And I still needed to get as much cricket into my body as possible, even if this was going to be the low-intensity variety. They were poor conditions, my innings was brief, but we slogged away to something credible with Smudge and Kez getting a decent hit in the top three.

As soon as we went out to field, Starcy had the ball hooping in the air and decking off the lively surface. Once he'd claimed a hat-trick, it was decided he had better come out of the attack so there would be time for the rest of us to bowl. The rain set in not long afterwards, so it was all a bit silly, but another tiny step for me.

Three days on, we were up against Pakistan in Hyderabad in happier conditions – a proper road. We took this a bit more seriously and lined up as we expected we would in our opening game, with Davey and Mitch opening, Smudge and Marnus following in the engine room, then Kez and me to finish it off. We got off to a flyer, with everyone spending time in the middle as planned.

I walked in during the 25th over, which gave me a chance to work into a longer innings before trying to tee off. I put some manufactured pressure on myself when walking out, which was helped by the fact that Pakistan were giving all of their bowlers a run: four front-line quicks and three spinners, so it was going to be a proper workout. So it proved across an hour in the middle, facing 71 balls for 77, clearing the ropes half a dozen times with various shots. This put enough pressure on my foot to test me, but as in Rajkot, there was no pain. At last, I felt like I was good to play freely in the real stuff.

More than my batting, it's our comical defence of 351 that sticks with me. Because we were so close to the World Cup, we were only playing three quicks, and strict instructions said that Starcy, Patty and Sean Abbott were each to be given no more than six overs. Sure enough, once the batters learned of this directive, they were excited about their chance to have a trundle.

It won't surprise you to learn that Davey was front of the queue, talking up his leggies, which once upon a time were pretty bloody good. Not so much on this occasion, as he had 41 taken off two overs. He was unlucky that a waist-high full toss he bowled to start with got dropped at long on by Josh Inglis – and didn't Dave let him know about it. It was little better for Smudge, with 0 for 40 from four overs, while Marnus bowled twice as many and ended up an expensive matchwinner with 3 for 78. When Babar Azam got to 90 from 59 balls, a few of us went up and suggested he was wasting his time. He looked up, agreed with us, and walked off retired out.

It's a ridiculous scorecard, reading that we won by 13 runs. Amongst it, though, I had a tidy eight overs with 1 for 34, Fakhar Zaman caught in the deep after I beat him in flight. Alongside runs earlier in the day, it was the last confidence boost I needed with India waiting for us at Chennai for our World Cup opener five days later.

I felt like India was a great match-up for me to begin the round-robin stage, knowing their players as well as I do from international cricket and more than a decade of IPL. Playing at any venue in that country, I feel as much at home as I do on Australian grounds. I compare it to how Smudge must feel when walking out in an Ashes Test – the familiarity shorts out any added aura.

This history goes back to my first one-day series in India, exactly a decade before the 2023 World Cup. A seven-game stretch with scores from both teams like the format had never seen – a sign of things to come with T20 starting to influence ODIs. Mitch Johnson was bowling rockets and Rohit hit a double ton. I clocked innings of 53 from 32 in Jaipur, 92 from 77 at Ranchi, where I'd later get my Test ton, and 60 from 22 on what would later become my RCB home deck.

From that point, I always had belief that I could take down Indian attacks no matter the location, and did that in the World Cup semi in 2015 when setting them a chase that proved too big. Early 2016 included another important moment in my

Aussie career, my first big night at home at the MCG. I'd hit a rapid 66 there against England the previous season, but we were already well ahead. This other time, on a Sunday night in the middle of summer, we were behind the game, chasing 296.

A big crowd, lots of eyes, a competitive series between the two best teams in the world – this was perfect. It was like I was back in a time machine to my childhood, watching every ball of, say, Michael Bevan batting with Andy Bichel or Paul Reiffel in support. The nights that helped develop my love for it all.

Watching the highlights back, it was even better that Bill Lawry was up there commentating that night. He was building this sense of 'Can the Victorian do it?' as Jimmy Faulkner, my old Academy mate, started mowing down the target with me in the final 10 overs. We had to play it smart, too. This wasn't a road, it was slow, so my tricks to manipulate the field were more important than power. With scores level as I reached 96, I tried to muscle a ball over mid off to get the perfect finish and was caught, but by then we had the game in hand. It didn't take much gloss off for me, with the buzz of getting to do that on the G.

So by the 2023 World Cup, there had been many important nights for me against India or in India, including at Chennai in the IPL. With my leg back to full strength at the perfect time, with a couple of strong performances under my belt during my brief stint in the country, this was where I wanted to be. I know how damaging I could be, getting on a roll at the start of a tournament, and that was my plan. Get out of the blocks fast, leave them for dead.

Then we botched it. Batting first was understandable: get in before the pitch becomes a mess. But from the moment the coin came down in our favour on a surface that was cracked and challenging, we didn't get much right. India picked three spinners, the ideal call. An early wicket, a sluggish Powerplay, a slow passage in the middle overs, a scorching hot and sweaty humid night, and through it all the noise and intensity of the Chepauk beat down.

In theory, this is where I'm meant to shake it up. I walked in for the 28th over at number five, with our score only 110. I wanted to accelerate. But I was caught in the net as well. Those contrasting finger spinners in Ashwin and Jadeja had the left-arm wrist spin of Kuldeep Yadav to join them, and between them gave me very little. It was Kuldeep who got me a treat. I've played him for years and can pick his slider, so I went back to it knowing that it almost always skids across me outside off stump. This time, though, the ball followed me, spinning back in sharply from one of those cracks, and I was no chance of catching up with it. He chopped me in half and knocked down my leg stump.

Walking off with 15 off 25 balls after 44 unconvincing minutes was not what I had in mind, but I tried to console myself with the fact that it was very tough going and that maybe our 199 would prove competitive after dark. For about 20 minutes it was, when 'Hoff' Hazlewood blew Rohit's pad off and had Shreyas caught at cover after Starc had Ishan Kishan caught behind. Three guns, three ducks, with two runs on the board.

And how close it was to being 4 for 21, when Hoff should have had his third. Virat skied his bumper. I was at backward point and saw big Mitch Marsh running in while Alex Carey went from his keeping position towards square leg. Either might have taken it without someone coming the other way. I don't think anyone was calling, not that it would have mattered with the crowd somewhere between a gasp and a shriek as the ball hung in the air. Sure enough, down went the catch and the game – we took one further wicket all night. India cruised to the extent that they ended up trying to nurse KL Rahul towards a ton, which was odd and didn't work out for him anyway.

I had a good first couple of spells while the game was live, 20 runs from my first seven overs. Operating at the end, as KL chased three figures, he got 13 off what became my last over. But the ball was a bar of soap by that stage, and I knew that at least my bowling was in good shape.

Knowing what we know now, I wouldn't change a thing about how that result played out. If we had made the most of our opportunity that first night, it could have been a different journey for both teams through the group stage, but I wonder whether India getting into a such a strong position early on in the competition served us better at the end.

As for our crew, there were some frustrated players, especially those who had already spent a longer lead-up bouncing from city to city. They knew there were seven more weeks of World Cup pressure to come, and South Africa waiting for us in Lucknow. Kez paid for getting into a rut at the wrong time at the end of a marathon year across formats: our keeper lost his spot after that one game, Josh Inglis given the chance.

INDIA V AUSTRALIA

Venue: MA Chidambaram Stadium, Chepauk, Chennai
Toss: Australia, elected to bat first
Points: India 2, Australia 0
TV Umpire: Chris Brown (New Zealand)
Referee: Richie Richardson (West Indies)

Date: October 08 2023
Result: India won by 6 wickets (with 52 balls remaining)
Umpires: Chris Gaffaney (New Zealand), Richard Kettleborough (England)
Reserve Umpire: Adrian Holdstock (South Africa)
Player of the Match: KL Rahul, (India) 97* (115)

AUSTRALIA		R	B
David Warner	c & b Kuldeep Yadav	41	52
Mitchell Marsh	c Kohli b Bumrah	0	6
Steven Smith	b Jadeja	46	71
Marnus Labuschagne	c †Rahul b Jadeja	27	41
Glenn Maxwell	b Kuldeep Yadav	15	25
Alex Carey †	lbw b Jadeja	0	2
Cameron Green	c Pandya b Ashwin	8	20
Pat Cummins (c)	c Iyer b Bumrah	15	24
Mitchell Starc	c Iyer b Mohammed Siraj	28	35
Adam Zampa	c Kohli b Pandya	6	20
Josh Hazlewood	not out	1	1
Extras	(lb 6, w 6)	12	
Total	(10 wickets, 49.3 overs)	199	

Fall of wickets: 1-5 (Mitchell Marsh, 2.2 ov), 2-74 (David Warner, 16.3 ov), 3-110 (Steven Smith, 27.1 ov), 4-119 (Marnus Labuschagne, 29.2 ov), 5-119 (Alex Carey, 29.4 ov), 6-140 (Glenn Maxwell, 35.5 ov), 7-140 (Cameron Green, 36.2 ov), 8-165 (Pat Cummins, 42.2 ov), 9-189 (Adam Zampa, 48.2 ov), 10-199 (Mitchell Starc, 49.3 ov)

INDIA	O	M	R	W	Wd	Nb
Jasprit Bumrah	10	0	35	2	4	0
Mohammed Siraj	6.3	1	26	1	2	0
Hardik Pandya	3	0	28	1	0	0
Ravichandran Ashwin	10	1	34	1	0	0
Kuldeep Yadav	10	0	42	2	0	0
Ravindra Jadeja	10	2	28	3	0	0

INDIA		R	B
Rohit Sharma (c)	lbw b Hazlewood	0	6
Ishan Kishan	c Green b Starc	0	1
Virat Kohli	c Labuschagne b Hazlewood	85	116
Shreyas Iyer	c Warner b Hazlewood	0	3
KL Rahul †	not out	97	115
Hardik Pandya	not out	11	8
Ravindra Jadeja			
Ravichandran Ashwin			
Kuldeep Yadav			
Jasprit Bumrah			
Mohammed Siraj			
Extras	(b 1, lb 1, nb 1, w 5)	8	
Total	(4 wickets, 41.2 overs)	201	

Fall of wickets: 1-2 (Ishan Kishan, 0.4 ov), 2-2 (Rohit Sharma, 1.3 ov), 3-2 (Shreyas Iyer, 1.6 ov), 4-167 (Virat Kohli, 37.4 ov)

AUSTRALIA	O	M	R	W	Wd	Nb
Mitchell Starc	8	0	31	1	3	0
Josh Hazlewood	9	1	38	3	1	0
Pat Cummins	6.2	0	33	0	1	1
Glenn Maxwell	8	0	33	0	0	0
Cameron Green	2	0	11	0	0	0
Adam Zampa	8	0	52	0	0	0

Having at least had a sniff after trailing against India, it was a different story altogether against South Africa. We were nowhere. There was a window early with the ball seaming around but we didn't get it right. Quinton de Kock got himself in, his ton looking certain from the time he reached 30. Closing out with Aiden Markram, David Miller, Heinrich Klaasen and Marco Jansen, only a couple of them needed to get away to make sure we'd end up chasing plenty, and 312 was the target.

My happy time at the bowling crease continued, jagging 2 for 34 from my full allotment, with a great catch from Davey at deep midwicket getting rid of Bavuma, while I eventually bowled de Kock when he tried a reverse pull on 109. More worryingly, it was also the first time since getting to India that I had started to feel pressure in my leg, so I jumped straight into my ice machine at the break to try sorting that out, knowing I'd be needed if we were to win.

Well, we didn't, and it turned into one of the worst performances with the bat I've been involved in for Australia. To say they were all over us would be an understatement. We couldn't find the boundary, let alone clear it. We had no partnerships. When I walked in at 4 for 56 in the 12th over, the game had all but slipped away. I didn't help the situation, unable to get any rhythm, stinking the joint up to the tune of 3 from 17 balls. The damage was done by the time I offered a limp leading edge back to Keshav Maharaj. I still don't understand how I ended up in such a mess, but it made two failures in a row.

The only mitigation was that this pitch turned into a nightmare after dark. In the many 20-over games I've seen at Lucknow, it has been slow to the point that 120 is enough to get well into a match. Then they relaid the square, and it became the very opposite. The South Africans had the ball talking early and it never stopped. We were all out 177, and even that flattered us with the fast bowlers getting some boundaries away before the end.

Under Patty's leadership, we are quite good at not bringing external noise into our inner sanctum, but we all knew what would be coming from former players in the media after the loss. That's fine for the most part – everyone has a job to do, we had been dismal, and were perhaps one loss away from being bounced out of contention altogether, given the hiding our net run rate had already taken. But the tenor of criticism had changed since Justin Langer had finished as coach, with some people still blaming us for that, on top of sad bullshit from dickheads outside cricket aimed at our captain because he wants something to be done about climate change.

From my vantage point, I also found our predicament exciting. As we've discussed, I'm a cricket nut. I love the game. Not everyone who plays at the highest level is like that – they think about their own game but not the history. For me, my immediate reference point when the rockets started firing was to talk about the 1999 World Cup, played when I was 10. I knew all about what Steve Waugh's team did there, cooked after some early losses but then winning seven on the trot to take it home.

Sure, we had let it slip against India and never got ourselves a chance against South Africa. A lot of the guys were feeling the pinch more than they should have so early in a tournament. But what if we could get on a roll? I was all-in on the fairytale, even if in hindsight it was premature – some teams would end up making the semis with more than two losses. But had other teams gone better, one more loss could have been the end of us. So I tried to use that story to break us out of a spiral, to stop catastrophising and get us into a different mindset. In short, time to fire up, lads. Now or never. Convince ourselves that this was just the way we like it.

SOUTH AFRICA V AUSTRALIA

Venue: Bharat Ratna Shri Atal Bihari Vajpayee Ekana Cricket Stadium, Lucknow

Toss: Australia, elected to field first

Points: South Africa 2, Australia 0

TV Umpire: Richard Kettleborough (England)

Referee: Javagal Srinath (India)

Date: October 12 2023

Result: South Africa won by 134 runs

Umpires: Joel Wilson (West Indies), Richard Illingworth (England)

Reserve Umpire: Chris Brown (New Zealand)

Player of the Match: Quinton de Kock, (South Africa) 109 (106) & 2 catches

SOUTH AFRICA		R	B
Quinton de Kock †	b Maxwell	109	106
Temba Bavuma (c)	c Warner b Maxwell	35	55
Rassie van der Dussen	c sub (SA Abbott) b Zampa	26	30
Aiden Markram	c Hazlewood b Cummins	56	44
Heinrich Klaasen	c †Inglis b Hazlewood	29	27
David Miller	b Starc	17	13
Marco Jansen	c Warner b Starc	26	22
Kagiso Rabada	not out	0	1
Keshav Maharaj	not out	0	2
Lungi Ngidi			
Tabraiz Shamsi			
Extras	(b 4, lb 2, w 7)	13	
Total	(7 wickets, 50 overs)	311	

AUSTRALIA	O	M	R	W	Wd	Nb
Mitchell Starc	9	1	53	2	1	0
Josh Hazlewood	9	0	60	1	3	0
Glenn Maxwell	10	1	34	2	2	0
Pat Cummins	9	0	71	1	0	0
Adam Zampa	10	0	70	1	1	0
Mitchell Marsh	1	0	6	0	0	0
Marcus Stoinis	2	0	11	0	0	0

Fall of wickets: 1-108 (Temba Bavuma, 19.4 ov), 2-158 (Rassie van der Dussen, 28.3 ov), 3-197 (Quinton de Kock, 34.5 ov), 4-263 (Aiden Markram, 43.1 ov), 5-267 (Heinrich Klaasen, 44.1 ov), 6-310 (Marco Jansen, 49.1 ov), 7-311 (David Miller, 49.4 ov)

AUSTRALIA		R	B
Mitchell Marsh	c Bavuma b Jansen	7	14
David Warner	c van der Dussen b Ngidi	13	27
Steven Smith	lbw b Rabada	19	16
Marnus Labuschagne	c Bavuma b Maharaj	46	74
Josh Inglis †	b Rabada	5	4
Glenn Maxwell	c & b Maharaj	3	17
Marcus Stoinis	c †de Kock b Rabada	5	4
Mitchell Starc	c †de Kock b Jansen	27	51
Pat Cummins (c)	c Miller b Shamsi	22	21
Adam Zampa	not out	11	16
Josh Hazlewood	c Rabada b Shamsi	2	2
Extras	(lb 4, nb 2, w 11)	17	
Total	(10 wickets, 40.5 overs)	177	

SOUTH AFRICA	O	M	R	W	Wd	Nb
Lungi Ngidi	8	2	18	1	1	0
Marco Jansen	7	0	54	2	3	1
Kagiso Rabada	8	1	33	3	1	1
Keshav Maharaj	10	0	30	2	2	0
Tabraiz Shamsi	7.5	0	38	2	0	0

Fall of wickets: 1-27 (Mitchell Marsh, 5.5 ov), 2-27 (David Warner, 6.6 ov), 3-50 (Steven Smith, 9.5 ov), 4-56 (Josh Inglis, 11.1 ov), 5-65 (Glenn Maxwell, 16.1 ov), 6-70 (Marcus Stoinis, 17.2 ov), 7-139 (Mitchell Starc, 33.3 ov), 8-143 (Marnus Labuschagne, 34.4 ov), 9-175 (Pat Cummins, 40.3 ov), 10-177 (Josh Hazlewood, 40.5 ov)

10

Time to Pretend

You might recall me saying that when we turned around the T20 World Cup in 2021, it was a heroically long lunch that did the trick. This time around was a bit different because most of the lads were just so relieved that we could stay in the same beds for more than a few nights in a row. The way this tournament was structured, most teams only got once chance to play back-to-back games at the same venue – a couple of teams got two chances, while India and England were on the road non-stop.

Our double-up came at the right time, following South Africa in Lucknow with Sri Lanka four days later. There was a bit of socialising but mostly we took the chance to rehab and regroup, taking our time and doing it our way. I can't tell you how important this proved in helping get over such a bad loss.

In my case, I know all too well how tough it can be to arrest a negative spiral during a major tournament with the added scrutiny. It had happened to me at the previous ODI World Cup in England. In 2019 it was all the more galling, because instead of coming into the competition underdone after injury, I had been purring. In our lead-up series against Pakistan in the UAE, I'd rattled off three very different innings in different situations: 71 from 55 balls, 98 from 82, then 70 from 33 in a man-of-the-match effort that saw us wrap up it up five-nil.

I had opted out of that year's IPL and gone straight into the county system with Lancashire to get as much cricket in England as possible before the rest of the world arrived. Given how well I was playing, I thought I would be into the swing of things right away, get on a roll, win the big trophy, and be in such great shape that they would have to add me to the Ashes squad for the summer of my life.

I was even more confident after my Aussie teammates arrived for a couple of intra-squad practice matches at Whitgift School in Surrey. It's never easy facing our quicks at training – I remember seeing that attack compared to the class of a Ferrari, and I couldn't agree more. But in those lead-up days, I was getting hold of all of them. Media talk was comparing me to Kohli, and I really believed this was my moment.

You've probably worked out what happened in the real stuff. At Bristol against Afghanistan, there were only four runs to get when I walked in. Against West Indies at Trent Bridge, we were in some strife at 3 for 36 in the seventh over. From the rooms, I saw Sheldon Cottrell doing his thing with the new ball and reckoned he wouldn't be quick enough to worry me, and that with the field still up I should take on anything he banged in short. It's also true that I had never faced him before, so my pre-emptive call wasn't my finest. As it turns out, his bumper is far livelier than his stock ball, I got a top edge that went nowhere, and walked off for a second-ball duck with the team in even deeper strife. Bugger.

Nathan Coulter-Nile bailed us out of that game with the bat, so I didn't cost the team, and I found some rhythm in the games that followed against India, Pakistan and Sri Lanka. I was reaching the 20s in a hurry but not going on. In that third game I was 46 not out from 25 balls, which looks handy, but I was still frustrated because I knew the way I had been hitting it recently, I could have piled on more.

Against Bangladesh, it looked like it would finally be my day to explode, galloping to 32 in nine balls with four overs to come. It felt like the innings I needed to turbocharge everything. Until it ended in a mix-up, with me left not best pleased when Uzzy Khawaja stopped running after I went for a single. It's just one of those cricket things, we've all made the same mistake, but the last thing I needed was a decisive moment of bad luck.

And so without having any understanding of what was coming, I began what proved to be the worst time of my cricket career, and would deepen into the worst time of my life.

At Lord's against England with a packed house and our semi-final spot within reach, I felt again like this could be the day for me to get on a roll. It started with serious pace, Mark Wood at one end and Jofra Archer at the other. Mark got one up me immediately, which I managed to keep down safely. Jofra

I played on my terms, picking him up over long on for a six that went nearly a hundred metres. Next ball he went short, and I crunched him over midwicket for four. Giddy up.

Wood came again, and I did what my instincts tell me when I'm in the zone, trying to uppercut and use his pace against him. Instead of clearing the cordon, I misjudged the line enough to get a tiny nick to Jos behind the stumps.

To those paying attention, it was the end of a brief eventful innings where I looked to break it open after Finchy laid a base with a ton. But with 12 runs to your name, people naturally focus on the dismissal. Having been out second ball trying to pull Cottrell into Nottingham Forrest football ground, then out to a short delivery here, along came ridiculous snap judgments.

I've been around the game long enough to know how these stories get a life of their own, and I'm pretty good at ignoring them, but this one got to me. A problem with short bowling? Me? Are you fucking joking? I've made a career out of smashing the quickest bowlers in the world all over the park when they have a crack at me, and I relish this part of the contest. In all my time, nobody had even hinted that this might be a flaw in my game, and now, on the evidence of two dismissals going after the bowling, it was coming up everywhere I looked. I couldn't believe it.

After doing the job easily against England, we stuck around at Lord's to play New Zealand. If my run out against Bangladesh was rough, I could also have done without Jimmy Neesham dragging in one of the best return catches I've seen. Jimmy might be 30 kilometres an hour slower than Woody, but again it was a short ball. I was through the shot early, somehow squeezed it off the toe of the bat, and he dived left at full stretch an inch from the turf. Unforgiving as cricket is, the fact is I was out again for one run.

We won comfortably and were locked in for semi-finals. I was frustrated with my lack of contribution but there was a group game yet to go, up the motorway to Manchester. South Africa after a poor run were at the other end of the table. And it would be at Old Trafford, a ground where I had loved playing for Lancashire as recently as a month earlier, where everything went right off the rails.

It started in the nets. Training sessions the day before the game are typically where you top up on a few exact things you need. There is a time and place for major technical work, and in my time in the Australian team, it has never been here. This doesn't mean avoiding the quicks, but it means training sensibly because the last thing you want at this stage is to risk an injury. It's common sense.

This day was different. In my net, I got a proper full-tilt short ball from Starcy and ducked it. Okay, a touch unusual, but play on. Next, something even more potent from Patty from back of a length that reared up and hit me in the middle of the forearm. I threw the bat and walked out of the net, fuming, my immediate thought being that I'd broken my arm. Meaning the end of my World Cup. Off to the rooms.

What I didn't realise, but what got back to me later, was that our quicks were following a directive from JL. The written press get up close when watching our net sessions, and our coach had said in their direction something to the effect of 'If you think he has a problem with the short ball, watch this!' Then told our guys to bump the shit out of me.

Stepping back with five years of space, I can see what he was trying to do. Media chat was doing the rounds, so he could have seen this as my chance to prove it wrong and steer the conversation another way. But at what risk, and potential cost? Added to that was JL's own quote to the media that same day, saying I needed to 'work really hard' against short bowling. It probably wasn't meant to, but it suggested this involved me remedying a problem rather than doing the work that any player does. That made it a very poor read of the room and on how I was travelling.

In the professional game there are times when you are managed well and times when you aren't, and all you can do is try not to get too flat during the latter. Me and JL, with all of our shared history, knew each other well. Well enough that after our blow-up earlier that year with the 'careless whispers' press conference and my efforts to get back to Test cricket, we dusted ourselves off and got on with it. We were both focused on winning.

This time though, JL knew me well enough to understand that I didn't need horseshit about not being able to play short bowling coming back to me in a feedback loop that now included my coach. His job was to get in between me and that stuff, to repudiate the suggestion. Or if he genuinely thought I did need to address something, to have that conversation with me directly, whether formally or over a coffee. There had been ample opportunity to do that, but instead I was sitting in the dressing room with a confused mind and a throbbing arm.

Not even five minutes later, poor old Shaun Marsh came down the steps as well. Well, first of all came his batting helmet, which bounced over and knocked me off the bench where I was being treated by the doc. 'Oh, fuck, so sorry, Maxi,' he grumbled, sincerely. Here was another arm that looked like it might be broken. The poor bastard was right on the edge, right at the end, with his last chance as an Australian player hanging in the balance. From the sick bay to the hospital, off we went together.

It was in that car that I came to the realisation that I wanted my arm to be broken. If I wasn't delivering, and the perception was that I was a drag on the team, then fuck it – I may as well be out of there. At least it would be over. I couldn't put it into words, and certainly couldn't voice this thought to a single soul, but it was my true feeling. Within a few months I would be able to figure out that something deceptive was happening inside my head, but right then I believed it. I was lost and I was desperate.

The scan came back with a green light for me – bruise, not break. I was lucky, the doctor said, little knowing that it was the opposite of what I wanted to hear. So all I could feel was guilt that SOS was getting the opposite news. His arm was broken, his World Cup was done, and as it turned out he never played for Australia again. I consoled the big guy. He was devastated. I was cooked.

Nevertheless, upon waking up in the morning, for all that had played out across that horrible Friday afternoon, I had a job to do. That is, as long as I could pass a fitness test. There are lots of ways to go about this, but I didn't anticipate it would involve going back to those same dusty, used nets for JL and Punter to wang bouncers at me. Part of my mind was angry, thinking this was fucking ridiculous. And part of it thought this was good, because there was some chance they would ping me on the arm again and finish the job, letting me escape responsibility. Talk about an unhealthy place.

Declared fit, my anxiety was overtaken by anger. It was obvious I was going to be bombed by South Africa's fast bowlers, and I was determined to go down swinging. Chasing 326, I was in before the halfway mark with loads of work to do. My second ball from pace was short, and I got inside the line to punish it past mid on. The next bouncer coming my way was from Kagiso Rabada and there was no way I was going to duck it. In position to hook, too enthusiastically, I got a top edge and de Kock took a blinding one-hander. There is never any happiness in being dismissed for Australia, but I had to smile to myself: 'Of course, that'd be right'.

Losing that game stuffed our chance of staying in Manchester to play New Zealand, instead heading to Birmingham against England, who by this stage had got their shit together. Uzzy did a hammy too, so along with SOS there was another player done. Petey Handscomb was next in line, and Matthew Wade got called up as cover from the Australia A tour. And boy, he was flying – he looked like I had six weeks earlier. Reversing, lapping, pumping it everywhere, nobody could bowl to him in the nets. Without a doubt in my mind, he was the in-form Australian player of the moment and should have been rushed into the starting XI for a knockout game.

The problem was, it was my spot he should have taken. Those thoughts started dominating my mind again: 'You are keeping this bloke out of the side.' Instead of priming myself for one of the most important games of my life, I was embarrassed to be in the team ahead of Wadey. I was nowhere close to the right state to play, but didn't feel there was anything I could do other than front up and hope. My confidence was shot, positivity had vanished. I felt like the worst player in the team and drew the conclusion that everyone else must be thinking the same thing.

In a training session on the Edgbaston pitch before the game, JL famously told us to take off our shoes and socks for a wander on the grass. Earthing, as it's called, might have worked at a different time for a different dressing room, but I don't think anyone was feeling it. We went around the circle, everyone being asked to tell the group what we would do to make us win. I think that was the question. I was a million miles away.

Game day. As with South Africa, with the routine of playing, the machine kicked into gear, and I talked myself into believing I could do something special. I got reshuffled to number seven, we had a shocking start, and I was needed by the 29th over. My old Yorkshire teammate Adil Rashid was all over me but I felt good against Jofra, pulling him right out the middle of the bat. Next ball I faced from Adil I crunched straight over his head for six. Maybe muscle memory would be enough here?

But on 22, I was done. A catch to cover with no power at all. Look at that replay, and my face on the way off is complete confusion – how was it possible the pitch had misbehaved to such an extent? It took 10 minutes back in the dressing room to be told that the pitch had nothing to do with it – it was Jofra's knuckle ball, one of his standard variations. My head was so swamped that I had stopped watching for my normal cues when reading the ball out of the hand, in favour of preparing to smash bouncers for six. I had lost the plot.

England chased down the runs without breaking a sweat, destroying us by eight wickets with 18 overs in hand. I hadn't even been called on to bowl – fair enough, given I'd failed to take a wicket in the World Cup. With each run they scored, I felt pain and relief in equal measure. It was almost over now, at last.

My parents were there for this debacle, and were straight down into the rooms with me. Most of the chat around the tournament itself was that Australia, in the context of only having got Smudge and Davey back from their year's suspension on the eve of it, had done alright in the circumstances. I took zero solace from this. When I saw Mum, who was just as emotional as me, everything came rushing out. Dad had to console us both.

At the time, I was surprised how shattered she looked. In time I understood that it wasn't about my performances – she could tell that her boy was hurting far more than that. Her sixth sense had kicked in when seeing how little of my on-field persona was there, and how fake it was when I tried. I'm normally the centre of energy on a team, and even when I'm not scoring runs,

I'm only ever a shot or two away from getting it back. Now I was anything but.

I had no clue what to do. It's obvious now, and will be to you, that I needed to be as far away from a cricket ground as possible. But what did I do? Ran straight back to Manchester the next morning and was playing for Lancs two days later. In my mind, if I could get away from the national team and get some runs, everything would reset. I could forget the previous six weeks. Instead, the problem compounded. I barely remember taking the field in that Blast season. I masked it by doing alright, and we made the finals, but the whole thing is still a blur.

We have hit the point now where the end of the English season runs straight into the Australian domestic season, and so it was in 2019 – there was barely two weeks between me boarding the plane home to padding up for the Vics. Normally I'm resilient enough to bounce around when the schedule requires, but this just meant more of the same. My memory says I played a couple of 50-over games upon getting home, where the records say it was five and a couple of Shield games. I'm good at recalling detail on just about any game I've been a part of, but from these, almost nothing has stuck. They happened, I was there, and I was numb.

Afterwards, it was straight into the Australian camp for six T20 matches against Sri Lanka and Pakistan. Adelaide was first. I tried my best to rationalise what was ahead on a flight over from Perth, where my Vics game had been. Yes, by now it had been three months of feeling worse and worse. But surely seeing my mates would snap me out of it this time, and I'd be good again?

On the contrary, it was breaking point.

We were greeted with a team meeting. At the Playford Hotel where we were staying, team psychologist Michael Lloyd addressed the group. The message was clear: we were to treat these six games with professionalism and win them all. But the way this was depicted hit me. To do this, everyone would need to give '100 per cent commitment, 100 per cent focus, 100 per cent energy.' There was nothing wrong with the sentiment. But I was hearing this and thinking, 'Bloody hell, I might have 60 per cent tops.'

It was more than that, too. I was petrified by the idea of someone wanting 100 per cent from me. Something about the finality of that number made me realise this had reached a point of no return. I was shocked by how I was responding; it felt like a panic attack. As soon as the meeting ended, I went to Lloydy and completely broke down. We had a great relationship going back to the Academy days and I knew he would respect honesty. It all came out: how sick I felt, how scared, what my mind was doing to me.

Of course, he got it. We moved into an action plan to get me out of the pressure cooker. From Adelaide, we were off to Brisbane then home to Melbourne – how about jumping off at that point? Yes! The moment he said those words, a weight started to lift. I felt like I had been copping a battering in the boxing ring but couldn't fall to the mat. Now, the top rope had been taken away and I could tip backwards over it. The next conversation was with JL, and despite being surprised, he understood this wasn't flippant. Him being supportive was such a relief.

There was still the small matter of two matches to play for Australia. I felt sorrow looking at my cricket kit, and the anguish hadn't dissipated, but knowing it was a couple of hits then home did clear my mind. So much so that I've never worried less during a game of cricket than when I walked in at Adelaide. We were already in a good spot with Davey smashing it, so I told myself I was going to follow my first instinct every ball. Reverse, slog, I wouldn't be judging myself.

Liberated to a ludicrous extent, I never missed the middle of the bat across 28 balls, creaming 62 to get us up to 233. When it was our turn to field, Fox wanted to mic me up, and as usual I'll do what I'm told. It included a passage where I was able to basically commentate a run out from the boundary as I was executing it – that's good telly. There were lines in reports to the effect that 'Maxi is back!' Little did they know. All I had done that afternoon was pop my mask on, be it batting or commentating. I would learn a lot about this in the weeks to come – how for so long I had been doing a version of this, trying to do what I thought everybody wanted.

One more stop, Brisbane, before I could hide from the world. It was such an easy win that I didn't need to bat. It was over. After the game, I told the team the short version of what had been going on, explaining that I was taking an indefinite break from all cricket. I remember saying that it might appear strange but I wasn't okay, it had taken me a long time to accept this, and I had to get myself right. I left it by saying I hoped to see them at some stage during the summer, but at that moment I didn't have any inner belief that I would be playing again so soon.

I think they were stunned, even the captain Finchy, who knew me so well beyond the dressing room. Their confusion was mirrored by the public – didn't I just smash a quick fifty and sound happy on TV? A version of this assumption drove so much of what was wrong. When I was making runs, I was a good boy. Low scores meant the opposite. Who I was as a person had given way to how well I batted, to the extent that I didn't know who I was. But using this façade to appear okay had turned into me being a cardboard cut-out of the guy who was there before. I knew it was a risk walking away from the team, but it would only get worse if I stayed.

Home. Windows closed. Relief. My house in Aberfeldie, a place I'd lived for five years, was to become my cocoon. By now Cricket Australia had put out a statement that referred directly to 'difficulties with regard to mental health', so there was no confusion. I had to stay away from my phone because there were going to be hundreds of messages, and while they would have been supportive, I needed to be out of communication. The exception was Vini, who had been there in Adelaide. She kept my family in the loop, and that was it.

I'd returned to that house exhausted before, home from tour, but this was different. There was no next game to turn my attention to or next training session to consider. I was left completely to my own devices to work it out on my own terms. I didn't leave the house. Even the idea of a hit of golf was joyless for me by this point.

At the end of that first weekend, I picked up the phone to Moises Henriques. I didn't want to engage with anyone in cricket, but there were parallels between what had been happening to me and what I knew he'd been through. We had played a lot with and against each other from the start, and I have a lot of respect for him as a human being. It wasn't a marathon call and didn't need to be, but it was an important first step.

Slowly, my mind turned to what cricket represented to me. The CA statement didn't say the word 'indefinite' but that was how I felt. It was more than a passing thought in that first fortnight that maybe this was it for me as a player. I went through the exercise of thinking what else I might do, trying to put a line through cricket in favour of anything else that could bring me happiness. The spilling over of stress and anxiety was not something I wanted to happen again.

Of course, I didn't have the answers, and after some quiet days I was ready to turn to psychological support. This was when Dr Ranjit Menon was introduced to my life. A psychiatrist specialising in sportspeople who have suffered breakdowns, he got into it with me right away. I don't imagine it was a difficult diagnosis of depression and anxiety, with antidepressants prescribed to help us unpack my state of mind.

He was able to go back with me to understand that this was not only about what happened in England recently, it had been building for years. The way I was handled during the World Cup, the things that made me so angry, weren't the reason I had this breakdown. It wasn't JL's fault or anyone else's. It was on the way to happening anyway, and could have spilled over at any time. When I told Dr Menon about nearly quitting the game as a teenager at Saham Toney CC, it all tallied. I'd been wearing this mask for as long as I'd been in the public eye, and when it had slipped everything fell apart. It was so reassuring to know that this is not unusual, and that we could find a balance.

As these conversations continued, I started to feel lifted from my funk. Dr Menon had me doing very small things, small wins. Going for a run around the block. Catching up with old friends, the ones who knew Glenn Maxwell before the persona became Maxi the international cricketer. I needed people who had no need for my mask. Going back to my life of 15 years earlier helped sharpen up a sense of who I am at the core.

Alongside this, after more than a month of not going anywhere near my cricket kit, I made my first tentative steps back. There was no pressure on me to turn out for the Stars in that BBL season, but I wanted to test the waters. Some solo sessions, mostly working on fitness, turned into a couple of bowling-machine nets. Nothing competitive.

But I was going to have to play somewhere before returning to a professional game. With my club Fitzroy-Doncaster in the middle of a two-day game in Geelong, this was perfect. They were able to sub me in for the second weekend at the very last minute, far enough from Melbourne that I could do it without media glare. Sitting in the dressing room putting my pads on, I broke down again, but this was different. It was a strong, positive feeling, going into my kit to begin the ritual of preparing to face up in a match. A step in the right direction. It didn't matter that I only needed to face a few balls before we declared, the process was the thing.

On getting to the middle, a Geelong player came by and said, 'It's good to see you back, Maxi.' It was the sincerest comment ever directed at me by an opponent during a game, and I could feel that goodwill from everyone. It was time to get back to it.

My most complete Big Bash season to date followed. First game back I made 83 from 39, one of three player-of-the-match performances. Nearly 400 runs with an average right on 40, scored quickly, and 10 wickets too. We finished top of the table, the key metric as captain. More important than the successful run was the fact that I wanted to be there. The pressure valve had been released, I'd given myself permission to just be me, and it was working. What an extraordinary difference the time away had made. I'm forever grateful to Lloydy for making it happen and Dr Menon for helping me help myself at that point of crisis.

I know that this can happen again. There have already been moments in the years since when anxiety and stress begin to build and I get too deep within my own head. I know this is true of most people, and I know that I have a risk of spiralling as quickly as I did in 2019. I know there's plenty I can do every day to help, and I know that practising a form of mindfulness is one of those things, even though I'm not perfect at it.

That BBL season ended in frustrating circumstances. It had rained all day in Sydney, just for a change when the cricket's on. Then somehow we got a 12-over match against the Sixers, our fault giving away home advantage to them in our earlier playoff match at the MCG. We fell short in that shortened final, something we've made a habit of.

Just as frustrating was picking up an elbow injury at the pointy end of that tournament. The best way I can describe is it that the joint would click when playing some shots, and felt like there was something out of place. By the post-season matches, it stopped me playing my reverses and I couldn't go inside-out over cover. There was no way I could quit the tournament but it didn't help that I was playing one-handed at the end, getting out sweeping Steve O'Keefe in the final when I would normally reverse.

By this point I had been picked for an upcoming tour of South Africa through February and March, my Aussie comeback. I was relieved, but there was a clash with my closest friend's wedding. I wrote about Rob Cockerell and our shared childhood earlier in the book, and now my best mate had asked me to be his best man. I floated with management the chance of missing the final game to get home in time. That got knocked back. It was a bloody difficult phone call to make to Rob. As with so many things, playing for Australia came first.

That was, until I had my elbow scan, when I was surprised by how insistent the doctor was that I needed surgery right away and that I wasn't to hit another ball until it happened. There was loose bone and cartilage floating in there and I was going to make it much worse. My whole South African tour was off.

Injuries happen, that's life. But there was more to play out. Two nights after the BBL final we gathered for Allan Border Medal night in Melbourne, by which time I already knew the bad news from the scan. It had gone up the chain. When JL saw me, he was not pleased. He brought up the wedding, putting it to me directly that I had engineered missing the tour, and adding that my first games back for Australia should have been the priority.

I blew up. 'Are you saying I've faked an injury?' I said, probably with several expletives in there for decoration. He replied that I had been fine for the BBL final, I was going to be fine in time for the IPL, yet was suddenly unfit for this tour.

I reminded him, forcefully again, that it was CA's medical staff who had recommended this immediate operation, and that I couldn't bat properly at the end of the Big Bash because of the problem that hadn't then been diagnosed. He seemed to think I could tough it out and be fine to play, despite the scan and the doctor's advice. It was only a couple of months since JL had been brilliant when realising that I was in strife, and had given the support I needed. But this latest episode was another example of where, for whatever reason, there was some sort of block for him when it came to me. I never could explain it.

I went under the knife as planned, and recovered quickly enough that I was fit for the one-day series against New Zealand through the middle of March. Eventually the call was made not to rush me back, but it ended up mattering little. Along came the pandemic, stopping the series after one match and the world along with it. At least before that happened I did get to Rob's wedding and gave his best man speech, one of the happiest nights of my life.

———

Back to the 2023 World Cup, nearly four years later, the healthy, grown-up team environment that by then we enjoyed was the biggest asset we had. Seeing it from my trajectory, within that team I felt at ease to be who I am in a way that hopefully means I'll never get back to the low place I was in 2019. Across the board, we're able to retain perspective when things don't go as planned. Those two losses to start the tournament meant they very much hadn't.

For our third game, as refreshed as we could be after a precious couple of days to ourselves, the planning against Sri Lanka was all about trying to make the running. We know that when we're ahead, we're difficult to catch. But that didn't play out at all – we were the ones with the big gap to make up, gasping for breath. It felt like the start of the South Africa game, getting into a dangerous rhythm as Pathum Nissanka and Kusal Perera got off to a flyer. As they crossed 20 overs at a run a ball with no wicket down, a few of us were starting to fret.

Enter Patty. I had bowled four tidy overs but no wicket. He got himself straight into the act. Four balls into the 22nd over, banging one in at Nissanka, he was pulled out to deep midwicket where Davey sprinted around to take a diving catch to his left. It's been a long time since the Bull had a strong arm from the deep, but he takes himself out to those spots anyway, and his pace across the ground makes him an asset on the ropes. The way he celebrated that wicket reminded me of Warney in the 1999 semi, bowling Herschelle Gibbs before screaming at his teammates that they had to lift. There was also some Warne theatre about the way Patty knocked over Perera for 78 with the most superb off-cutter.

It might have taken us two hours too long, but the switch was flicked. Davey took a second screamer in the deep, this time to his right, huge for Zamps after having copped a lot of stick for the earlier losses. He had back spasms causing him endless grief but he found a way. He finished with four wickets and we had run through them for 209. I'd done my bit, taking the final wicket, going at under four an over, and only giving up a couple of boundaries. My bowling felt great and also meant we could plug me in while Zamps went off to get his back treated, a pattern we would follow for the rest of the tournament.

Davey hit a huge six to get us going in the chase, and even though he was soon out, it set the tone for how we were going to do this. Mitch Marsh played a series of booming drives that reinforced our approach, and we were on the way to victory after he got to 50. Josh Inglis and Marnus built another stand, and we were 57 away when I walked in at number six.

After my shocker against South Africa I saw this as a chance to make a statement myself, and went for it. My first four scoring shots were boundaries. I clobbered Maheesh Theekshana for two big ones to go from 16 to 28. Marcus Stoinis came and joined me for the last bit and played in the same way. Neither of us wanted to bat as we had against the Proteas ever again.

There at the end together, we had held our nerve and smashed them with nearly 15 overs to spare. Now it was time to get busy through the middle of the tournament, and make our presence felt. Our next stop was my IPL home – Bangalore.

SRI LANKA V AUSTRALIA

Venue: Bharat Ratna Shri Atal Bihari Vajpayee Ekana Cricket Stadium, Lucknow
Toss: Sri Lanka, elected to bat first
Points: Australia 2, Sri Lanka 0
TV Umpire: Chris Brown (New Zealand)
Referee: Richie Richardson (West Indies)

Date: October 16 2023
Result: Australia won by 5 wickets (with 88 balls remaining)
Umpires: Chris Gaffaney (New Zealand), Joel Wilson (West Indies)
Reserve Umpire: No umpire recognised
Player of the Match: Adam Zampa, (Australia) 4/47

SRI LANKA		R	B
Pathum Nissanka	c Warner b Cummins	61	67
Kusal Perera	b Cummins	78	82
Kusal Mendis (c)†	c Warner b Zampa	9	13
Sadeera Samarawickrama	lbw b Zampa	8	8
Charith Asalanka	c Labuschagne b Maxwell	25	39
Dhananjaya de Silva	b Starc	7	13
Dunith Wellalage	run out (Cummins)	2	9
Chamika Karunaratne	lbw b Zampa	20	11
Maheesh Theekshana	lbw b Zampa	0	5
Lahiru Kumara	b Starc	4	8
Dilshan Madushanka	not out	0	6
Extras	(b 2, lb 2, w 9)	13	
Total	(10 wickets, 43.3 overs)	209	

AUSTRALIA		R	B
Mitchell Marsh	run out (Karunaratne/†Mendis)	52	51
David Warner	lbw b Madushanka	11	6
Steven Smith	lbw b Madushanka	0	5
Marnus Labuschagne	c Karunaratne b Madushanka	40	60
Josh Inglis †	c Theekshana b Wellalage	58	59
Glenn Maxwell	not out	31	21
Marcus Stoinis	not out	20	10
Mitchell Starc			
Pat Cummins (c)			
Adam Zampa			
Josh Hazlewood			
Extras	(w 3)	3	
Total	(5 wickets, 35.2 overs)	215	

Fall of wickets: 1-125 (Pathum Nissanka, 21.4 ov), 2-157 (Kusal Perera, 26.2 ov), 3-165 (Dhananjaya de Silva, 32.3 ov), 4-166 (Sadeera Samarawickrama, 29.1 ov), 5-178 (Dhananjaya de Silva, 32.3 ov), 6-184 (Dunith Wellalage, 34.5 ov), 7-196 (Chamika Karunaratne, 37.6 ov), 8-199 (Maheesh Theekshana, 39.2 ov), 9-204 (Lahiru Kumara, 40.5 ov), 10-209 (Charith Asalanka, 43.3 ov)

AUSTRALIA	O	M	R	W	Wd	Nb
Mitchell Starc	10	0	43	2	4	0
Josh Hazlewood	7	1	36	0	1	0
Pat Cummins	7	0	32	2	1	0
Glenn Maxwell	9.3	0	36	1	1	0
Adam Zampa	8	1	47	4	2	0
Marcus Stoinis	2	0	11	0	0	0

SRI LANKA	O	M	R	W	Wd	Nb
Lahiru Kumara	4	0	47	0	0	0
Dilshan Madushanka	9	2	38	3	1	0
Maheesh Theekshana	7	0	49	0	0	0
Dunith Wellalage	9.2	0	53	1	0	0
Chamika Karunaratne	3	0	15	0	2	0
Dhananjaya de Silva	3	0	13	0	0	0

Fall of wickets: 1-24 (David Warner, 3.1 ov), 2-24 (Steven Smith, 3.6 ov), 3-81 (Mitchell Marsh, 14.3 ov), 4-158 (Marnus Labuschagne, 28.5 ov), 5-192 (Josh Inglis, 33.1 ov)

11

U-Turn

I'm lucky to have many grounds that feel like home, and the Chinnaswamy Stadium is one of them. The passion of IPL season is like nothing else I've experienced, and the Virat factor in Bangalore takes it to another level again. Rocking up here in the World Cup was ideal for me, doubly so with our opponent being Pakistan. Despite us being one of India's tournament rivals, Pakistan are India's ultimate rival, so we were always going to get crowd support. My RCB allegiance topped it up. I felt it from the moment I walked out to warm up, with Maxi signs and chants in the stands.

Neither could my arrival in the middle have been designed any better. Gifted the chance to bat first on a belter, Davey and Bison went to town. The partnership grew and grew, so once they had each made centuries, Patty asked me to pop the pads on and come in next. First drop with 259 on the board in the 34th over? This was perfect. The crowd went nuts as they clocked the change in batting order, seeing me come down the stairs to push us beyond 400.

Except I botched it. After having Bison caught at short fine leg, Shaheen Afridi had one ball left in the over. He brought up mid on and mid off. So I thought if it pitched anywhere full, I could clear either fielder to get going with a four. The second I swung the bat, I thought to myself: 'Glenn, you're an idiot.' Miscued to Babar Azam at mid on, I bagged myself a first-ball duck. The moment had got the better of me while I had got ahead of myself, a bad combination. After that good outing against Sri Lanka, I was back in the hole and furious.

More important than runs, I'd given Pakistan two wickets in two balls and a route back into the game. They did a decent job of taking it. We lost nine wickets, and our 50 overs ended up worth 367, far fewer than what was on the cards. I felt responsible and hadn't moved since ditching my pads. When Hoff made a duck in the final over, promoted from his usual number eleven spot with Zamps having back trouble, he said wryly, 'That's what happens when you bat out of position!' All I could reply was, 'Tell me about it.'

At first Pakistan were in the chase, taking their opening stand to 134 by the 22nd over. Finally, Stoin nailed his bouncer with his first ball and Abdullah Shafique's top edge landed with me. His partner Imam-ul-Haq went in similar fashion and we were into them. Stoin had turned the game our way and we were pumped for him. That let Zamps do what he does best through

AUSTRALIA V PAKISTAN

Venue: M Chinnaswamy Stadium, Bengaluru
Toss: Pakistan, elected to field first
Points: Australia 2, Pakistan 0
TV Umpire: Michael Gough (England)
Referee: Richie Richardson (West Indies)

Date: October 20 2023
Result: Australia won by 62 runs
Umpires: Chris Brown (New Zealand), Richard Illingworth (England)
Reserve Umpire: Jayaraman Madanagopal (India)
Player of the Match: David Warner, (Australia) 163 (124)

AUSTRALIA		R	B
David Warner	c sub (Shadab Khan) b Haris Rauf	163	124
Mitchell Marsh	c Usama Mir b Shaheen Shah Afridi	121	108
Glenn Maxwell	c Babar Azam b Shaheen Shah Afridi	0	1
Steven Smith	c & b Usama Mir	7	9
Marcus Stoinis	lbw b Shaheen Shah Afridi	21	24
Josh Inglis †	c †Mohammad Rizwan b Haris Rauf	13	9
Marnus Labuschagne	c sub (Shadab Khan) b Haris Rauf	8	12
Pat Cummins (c)	not out	6	8
Mitchell Starc	c Saud Shakeel b Shaheen Shah Afridi	2	3
Josh Hazlewood	c †Mohammad Rizwan b S S Afridi	0	1
Adam Zampa	not out	1	1
Extras	(b 1, lb 10, w 14)	25	
Total	(9 wickets, 50 overs)	367	

PAKISTAN		R	B
Abdullah Shafique	c Maxwell b Stoinis	64	61
Imam-ul-Haq	c Starc b Stoinis	70	71
Babar Azam (c)	c Cummins b Zampa	18	14
Mohammad Rizwan †	lbw b Zampa	46	40
Saud Shakeel	c Stoinis b Cummins	30	31
Iftikhar Ahmed	lbw b Zampa	26	20
Mohammad Nawaz	st †Inglis b Zampa	14	16
Usama Mir	c Starc b Hazlewood	0	3
Shaheen Shah Afridi	c Labuschagne b Cummins	10	8
Hasan Ali	c †Inglis b Starc	8	8
Haris Rauf	not out	0	1
Extras	(b 1, lb 7, w 11)	19	
Total	(10 wickets, 45.3 overs)	305	

Fall of wickets: 1-259 (Mitchell Marsh, 33.5 ov), 2-259 (Glenn Maxwell, 33.6 ov), 3-284 (Steven Smith, 38.1 ov), 4-325 (David Warner, 42.2 ov), 5-339 (Josh Inglis, 44.2 ov), 6-354 (Marcus Stoinis, 47.1 ov), 7-360 (Marnus Labuschagne, 48.3 ov), 8-363 (Mitchell Starc, 49.1 ov), 9-363 (Josh Hazlewood, 49.2 ov)

Fall of wickets: 1-134 (Abdullah Shafique, 21.1 ov), 2-154 (Imam-ul-Haq, 23.4 ov), 3-175 (Babar Azam, 26.2 ov), 4-232 (Saud Shakeel, 34.2 ov), 5-269 (Iftikhar Ahmed, 38.5 ov), 6-274 (Mohammad Rizwan, 40.5 ov), 7-277 (Usama Mir, 41.5 ov), 8-287 (Mohammad Nawaz, 42.6 ov), 9-301 (Hasan Ali, 44.5 ov), 10-305 (Shaheen Shah Afridi, 45.3 ov)

PAKISTAN	O	M	R	W	Wd	Nb
Shaheen Shah Afridi	10	1	54	5	3	0
Hasan Ali	8	0	57	0	3	0
Iftikhar Ahmed	8	0	37	0	2	0
Haris Rauf	8	0	83	3	3	0
Usama Mir	9	0	82	1	2	0
Mohammad Nawaz	7	0	43	0	0	0

AUSTRALIA	O	M	R	W	Wd	Nb
Mitchell Starc	8	0	65	1	6	0
Josh Hazlewood	10	1	37	1	1	0
Pat Cummins	7.3	0	62	2	0	0
Adam Zampa	10	0	53	4	1	0
Glenn Maxwell	5	0	40	0	0	0
Marcus Stoinis	5	0	40	2	3	0

the middle overs, snaring four wickets for the second game in a row as we went on to win by 56, bowling them out inside 46 overs. It hadn't been clinical from where we were early, but enough of our weapons were starting to fire. Internally, it gave us belief that we could get on a roll towards a semi-final and beyond.

Four free days were welcome, up north to Delhi before our hit-out against the Dutch. The Kotla was another of my home grounds, though not a successful one in my final season. But it wasn't the cricket I was focused on, it was Vini and Logan. It was emotional when we were reunited the day before the game, including the relief that they had reached me safely from Melbourne.

It had been so difficult kissing them goodbye when my newborn boy was not even a couple of weeks old. Of course I had monitored his development as closely as I could in the month since, but nothing in my life has compared to the bliss I felt holding him when he was so little. I knew having them for the rest of the tournament would make it all that much happier, no matter what happened on the field.

I had felt endlessly guilty being away while Vini was doing the parenting and the long nights. I was determined to do my bit from the moment they arrived. This meant a brutal bout of baby jetlag on night one – there was nothing we could do to stop Logan screaming the hotel down hour after hour. Of course I didn't begrudge my tiny boy but I was still aware of a World Cup game the next day. Welcome to parenting on the road.

Exhausted, I was grateful that Pat won the toss and decided to bat. For a time it looked like it might even be one of those days when I only had to do some fielding. Davey always steps up in big tournaments, and made it back-to-back tons up top. Smudge and Marnus got into a groove through the middle. But when Bas de Leede had Josh Inglis caught on the rope with 10 overs to go, it was my turn.

Based on tournament trends, going from 266 to 360 felt realistic, though the mess I'd made against Pakistan was playing on my mind. It's my job to lift the tempo whenever I go in, but I made a decision here to give myself just a little time. I wanted to start by playing the gaps, down the ground or reversing. Convention says that the latter is risky, but that's long since stopped being the case in my game. It's now as routine as easing one to long off. If the Dutch response was to bowl away from my stumps, I would be ready to launch.

I did hit three fours in my first six balls, but they were conventional drives. I wasn't trying to smash anything as I had against Shaheen. It felt good, I was calm. Cam Green got run out in the 43rd when we took on Sybrand Engelbrecht at deep midwicket for a second, not the best play given what a freakish fielder he is. With Patty joining me and seven overs to go, we were still at risk of being bowled out.

I suggested to the captain that it would make sense for me to farm the strike. On a small ground against a team that had been fielding in the heat all afternoon, I figured that if he and I made it to 45 overs, I could take up to 15 an over from the last five. We got to that point with 325 on the board, and I had 34 from 20. Then came the fun bit.

Anyone in cricket has to surrender to the reality that most of the time, you fail. You might run hot for a time, but the cold streaks are at least as long. Knowing I've hit the moment when I'm most dangerous is exhilarating. There's a confidence that I can hit any ball for four or six, with options all over the ground. I know, for that brief and precious time, that only the best deliveries can keep me quiet. Even faultless yorkers find a way of going the distance. I've only had this feeling a handful of times in my life. The star Dutch all-rounder Bas is a brisk seamer, so the point when I reversed him off middle stump for six, bringing up a 24-ball half century, I knew I was on for something special. I just had to make the most of it.

Patty was happy to come for the ride. My highlight was a reverse hook off Bas, a shot I didn't even know I had. In over 48, Logan van Beek overpitched his yorker and it went over long on into the crowd. He started losing accuracy, bowling extras outside off stump. When he finally landed one just inside the line, I leaned into a shot where I opened the face of the bat to drive behind point, carrying the ropes there too. That's difficult to play, but in the moment, it didn't feel like it in the slightest.

It was back to Bas for over 49, by which time we were past that 360 target and I was 75 from 35. Full and straight twice to begin, both back past him for four. I was trying to keep cool but my heart was pounding with excitement. Third ball: in the slot, six over midwicket. By this stage, any bowler would be struggling to keep it together, so the full toss that followed was almost to be expected, and I got inside the line to plonk it over backward square.

A couple of weeks earlier, at the same ground, Aiden Markram had broken the record for the fastest one-day World Cup ton, getting there in 49 deliveries to beat Kevin O'Brien's mark of 50 balls for Ireland. Given that Aiden had bumped me down to third spot after my 51-baller back in 2015, it came up in an interview, and I suggested that the mark might be lowered a few more times before the tournament was done. Well, here I was with 95 from 39 balls and poor old Bas in a world of pain. He repeated his full toss, I repeated my shot, and that was that: 101 not out from 40 balls.

I threw my bat to one side, took off my lid, and unfurled my arms, before making a baby-rocking gesture for Vini and Logan. It was a reminder to anyone who needed it, myself included, that I wasn't finished as a matchwinner yet.

One more boundary came in the final over before Engelbrecht pulled off a great take at deep midwicket. But my work was done with 106 from 44. Patty and I had put on 103 in 44 together, with the skipper adding eight. Neither of us could know how that would be echoed soon in the future. Most importantly, we had set the Dutch 399, a target they were never likely to chase against our attack.

The only man happier than me when we gathered in the dressing room was Zamps. Having suffered the indignity of having 113 taken from his 10 overs when Heinrich Klaasen blew up during our warm-up series in South Africa, our star leg spinner had joined Mick Lewis as having given up the most runs in an ODI innings. Well, I had pushed Bas de Leede to 115, meaning that record was broken too. The best bit was that Zamps didn't even realise I had scored a hundred with the same shot, he was too busy celebrating the other record.

It was Zamps who made certain of the result, four more wickets as we rolled the Dutch in 21 overs. If the Pakistan win was a sign that we should believe, a demolition job like this got the megaphone out to tell the whole competition. My no-sleep approach wasn't one to recommend, but it had somehow done the trick.

———

From Delhi to Dharamsala, and breathe. What a contrast, up into the Himalayas to one of the most serene places to play. It was what Vini and I needed with Logan settling in with both of us. This time it was a quick turnaround, three days before we played New Zealand, which meant there wasn't time to soak in the response to my century. I knew it would get attention, and my phone blew up as it does when something noteworthy for Australia comes along, but I was happy letting it wash over me. It was nice at least to have the public with me after my rough start, and it meant I could go on social media without being told repeatedly how shit I am.

As happy as my family was in Dharamsala, there was a new challenge on the field – the field itself. A Test there had been relocated six months earlier when the Australians toured because the ground staff couldn't get grass to grow. They had patched it

AUSTRALIA V NETHERLANDS

Venue: Arun Jaitley Stadium, Delhi
Toss: Australia, elected to bat first
Points: Australia 2, Netherlands 0
TV Umpire: Marais Erasmus (South Africa)
Referee: Andy Pycroft (Zimbabwe)

Date: October 25 2023
Result: Australia won by 309 runs
Umpires: Michael Gough (England), Sharfuddoula (Bangladesh)
Reserve Umpire: Nitin Menon (India)
Player of the Match: Glenn Maxwell, (Australia) 106 (44)

AUSTRALIA		R	B
Mitchell Marsh	c Ackermann b van Beek	9	15
David Warner	c Dutt b van Beek	104	93
Steven Smith	c van der Merwe b Dutt	71	68
Marnus Labuschagne	c Dutt b de Leede	62	47
Josh Inglis †	c Engelbrecht b de Leede	14	12
Glenn Maxwell	c Engelbrecht b van Beek	106	44
Cameron Green	run out (Engelbrecht)	8	11
Pat Cummins (c)	not out	12	9
Mitchell Starc	c Ackermann b van Beek	0	1
Adam Zampa	not out	1	1
Josh Hazlewood			
Extras	(nb 1, w 11)	12	
Total	(8 wickets, 50 overs)	399	

Fall of wickets: 1-28 (Mitchell Marsh, 3.5 ov), 2-160 (Steven Smith, 23.3 ov), 3-244 (Marnus Labuschagne, 36.1 ov), 4-266 (Josh Inglis, 38.6 ov), 5-267 (David Warner, 39.1 ov), 6-290 (Cameron Green, 42.2 ov), 7-393 (Glenn Maxwell, 49.3 ov), 8-393 (Mitchell Starc, 49.4 ov)

NETHERLANDS	O	M	R	W	Wd	Nb
Aryan Dutt	7	0	59	1	0	0
Colin Ackermann	4	0	19	0	0	0
Logan van Beek	10	0	74	4	5	0
Paul van Meekeren	10	0	64	0	3	0
Vikramjit Singh	4	0	27	0	1	0
Roelof van der Merwe	5	0	41	0	1	0
Bas de Leede	10	0	115	2	1	1

NETHERLANDS		R	B
Vikramjit Singh	run out (Maxwell)	25	25
Max O'Dowd	b Starc	6	9
Colin Ackermann	lbw b Hazlewood	10	11
Sybrand Engelbrecht	c Warner b Marsh	11	21
Bas de Leede	lbw b Cummins	4	7
Scott Edwards (c)†	not out	12	22
Teja Nidamanuru	c †Inglis b Marsh	14	18
Logan van Beek	c †Inglis b Zampa	0	3
Roelof van der Merwe	lbw b Zampa	0	1
Aryan Dutt	lbw b Zampa	1	8
Paul van Meekeren	st †Inglis b Zampa	0	1
Extras	(w 7)	7	
Total	(10 wickets, 21 overs)	90	

Fall of wickets: 1-28 (Max O'Dowd, 4.5 ov), 2-37 (Vikramjit Singh, 5.5 ov), 3-47 (Colin Ackermann, 9.2 ov), 4-53 (Bas de Leede, 10.5 ov), 5-62 (Sybrand Engelbrecht, 13.2 ov), 6-84 (Teja Nidamanuru, 17.5 ov), 7-86 (Logan van Beek, 18.3 ov), 8-86 (Roelof van der Merwe, 18.4 ov), 9-90 (Aryan Dutt, 20.5 ov), 10-90 (Paul van Meekeren, 20.6 ov)

AUSTRALIA	O	M	R	W	Wd	Nb
Mitchell Starc	4	0	22	1	2	0
Josh Hazlewood	6	0	27	1	2	0
Pat Cummins	4	0	14	1	0	0
Mitchell Marsh	4	0	19	2	3	0
Adam Zampa	3	0	8	4	0	0

up with sand for this World Cup, and the outfield was as ropey as you'll ever see at international level. This got into my head, knowing that going full speed on uneven ground, one slip could end my tournament.

We had a big inclusion against the Black Caps – Travis Head was back. He had been a chance for the Dutch but management played it safe with him returning from a broken hand. He still wasn't quite right in the nets, often yanking his hand off the bat, but that proved irrelevant as he propelled himself to a 59-ball century; seventh on that World Cup record list. It was awesome to watch him park length balls miles over the rope at midwicket, setting up our day alongside Davey, who backed up two tons with 81. The last thing we had expected on this ground was a high-scoring game, yet these two put on 175 in 19 overs.

Things slowed eventually, the Kiwi spinners getting it right through the middle. I was in during the 37th over with 264 on the board, a position from which we could touch 400 again. It was the same as Delhi: give myself time, get to the final five overs, and see what will be. It started as planned with a cover drive for four off Trent Boult, and after losing Marnus, I had Josh Inglis straight into his work. We both pulled Boult for boundaries along the floor. So far, so good.

Mitchell Santner has been a bad match-up for me over the years. A spinner with no front arm, I've found it hard to pick his changes of pace from an action that almost comes to a complete stop before he lets the ball go. He was in the attack starting the final 10 overs, so care was required. I backed myself against his fellow left-armer Rachin Ravindra, and nailed a reverse and a switch hit. Was I on again? It felt like it when getting hold of Santner, depositing him over his head onto the roof. That got projected at 104 metres, the biggest of the tournament. The ball after that, I stayed back for the over-correction, pulling six more.

As it was against the Dutch, everything I set out to do was working, I'd skipped out to 41 from 23 and it was happening on my terms. I could feel from the Black Caps' body language that they sensed this. Everyone except Jimmy Neesham, that is.

Jimmy and I knew each other before we met, sending DMs on Twitter to take the piss out of nonsense we had seen on there. When the 2020 IPL rolled around, he ended up with me at Kings XI. I've talked about that being a shocker of a season when nothing clicked. The exception was our friendship; we were inseparable. Having spent so much time in the nets together, he knows my game as well as anyone. So at a similar point to when the Dutch attack fell apart, Jimmy kept his cool when trying something different, angling wide across me from around the wicket and forcing an error, caught at long off. I wasn't thrilled, on the cusp of taking them down, but I can look back with respect that a very good cricketer and friend got the better of me that day.

Thankfully Patty stuck the landing to get 37 not out with four sixes, so we had 388 to defend. Like the Pakistan game, it was less than we should have got but it felt above par. At least until Ravindra started flaying us, in a classic and fluent way. When I was making my name it was all about risk-taking and power, but for him it was picking the right option with stunning footwork. His century put them in striking distance.

He was caught in the 41st over, just part of how influential Marnus was in the field in that frenetic final 10. But Jimmy picked up from where Ravindra left off, and was keeping them in touch with the 10 an over they needed.

That ask blew out to 19 from the final over, but with Jimmy there, they were a serious chance – even more so when Starcy sent five wides down the leg side. Needing seven runs from the last two balls, Jimmy forced it out to midwicket and came back for the second, which would have left them needing a boundary for a Super Over.

With so much riding on it, Marnus made a stunning play at full speed, preventing a four and returning the ball so accurately that it found Jimmy short. Five off the last ball was too much for their number eleven Lockie Ferguson. It was a reminder of how far Marnus has come. From not being in the initial World Cup squad to not missing a game, that's one story. But earlier, there was a time when he was so focused on his batting that he probably wouldn't have had the fine-tuning to nail this aspect of the game. The way he had worked deserved a defining fielding moment, and it showed what an asset he is to our best team.

———

So, we had got up in a tight finish, making four wins in a row. And now we had a week between games. How different it was to our last travel respite, after the South Africa belting in Lucknow with it

AUSTRALIA V NEW ZEALAND

Venue: Himachal Pradesh Cricket Association Stadium, Dharamsala
Toss: New Zealand, elected to field first
Points: Australia 2, New Zealand 0
TV Umpire: Nitin Menon (India)
Referee: Andy Pycroft (Zimbabwe)

Date: October 28 2023
Result: Australia won by 5 runs
Umpires: Marais Erasmus (South Africa), Sharfuddoula (Bangladesh)
Reserve Umpire: Michael Gough (England)
Player of the Match: Travis Head, (Australia) 109 (67)

AUSTRALIA

Batter		R	B
David Warner	c & b Phillips	81	65
Travis Head	b Phillips	109	67
Mitchell Marsh	b Santner	36	51
Steven Smith	c Boult b Phillips	18	17
Marnus Labuschagne	c Ravindra b Santner	18	26
Glenn Maxwell	c Boult b Neesham	41	24
Josh Inglis †	c Phillips b Boult	38	28
Pat Cummins (c)	lbw b Boult	37	14
Mitchell Starc	c Neesham b Henry	1	3
Adam Zampa	b Boult	0	3
Josh Hazlewood	not out	0	0
Extras	(b 1, nb 2, w 6)	9	
Total	(10 wickets, 49.2 overs)	388	

NEW ZEALAND	O	M	R	W	Wd	Nb
Matt Henry	6.2	0	67	1	2	2
Trent Boult	10	0	77	3	3	0
Lockie Ferguson	3	0	38	0	0	0
Mitchell Santner	10	0	80	2	1	0
Glenn Phillips	10	0	37	3	0	0
Rachin Ravindra	8	0	56	0	0	0
James Neesham	2	0	32	1	0	0

NEW ZEALAND

Batter		R	B
Devon Conway	c Starc b Hazlewood	28	17
Will Young	c Starc b Hazlewood	32	37
Rachin Ravindra	c Labuschagne b Cummins	116	89
Daryl Mitchell	c Starc b Zampa	54	51
Tom Latham (c)†	c Hazlewood b Zampa	21	22
Glenn Phillips	c Labuschagne b Maxwell	12	16
James Neesham	run out (Labuschagne/†Inglis)	58	39
Mitchell Santner	c Maxwell b Zampa	17	12
Matt Henry	c Hazlewood b Cummins	9	8
Trent Boult	not out	10	8
Lockie Ferguson	not out	0	1
Extras	(lb 4, w 22)	26	
Total	(9 wickets, 50 overs)	383	

AUSTRALIA	O	M	R	W	Wd	Nb
Mitchell Starc	9	0	89	0	9	0
Josh Hazlewood	9	0	70	2	1	0
Pat Cummins	10	0	66	2	3	0
Glenn Maxwell	10	0	62	1	0	0
Adam Zampa	10	0	74	3	0	0
Mitchell Marsh	2	0	18	0	1	0

Fall of wickets: 1-175 (David Warner, 19.1 ov), 2-200 (Travis Head, 23.2 ov), 3-228 (Steven Smith, 29.4 ov), 4-264 (Mitchell Marsh, 36.3 ov), 5-274 (Marnus Labuschagne, 38.1 ov), 6-325 (Glenn Maxwell, 44.3 ov), 7-387 (Josh Inglis, 48.1 ov), 8-388 (Pat Cummins, 48.3 ov), 9-388 (Adam Zampa, 48.6 ov), 10-388 (Mitchell Starc, 49.2 ov)

Fall of wickets: 1-61 (Devon Conway, 7.2 ov), 2-72 (Will Young, 9.4 ov), 3-168 (Daryl Mitchell, 23.6 ov), 4-222 (Tom Latham, 31.2 ov), 5-265 (Glenn Phillips, 36.6 ov), 6-293 (Rachin Ravindra, 40.2 ov), 7-320 (Mitchell Santner, 43.3 ov), 8-346 (Matt Henry, 46.4 ov), 9-383 (James Neesham, 49.5 ov) all on the line. Eventually we would take the field against England, who by now were were teetering on the edge of elimination, but on arriving in Ahmedabad, our first priority was downtime.

These pages have returned more than enough times to a love of golf across the Australian team. With a few days completely clear of cricket, the other sport was always going to feature prominently. Having noted this gap well in advance, it gave us time to plan something special: a two-day matchplay tournament among the group.

It was set to be Ryder Cup format with two teams named after players we watched as kids, Ernie Els and Colin Montgomerie. We had caps and shirts made up with the team names, one kit in white and the other red. I know this shouldn't be exciting for professionals who get to wear national uniforms, but we were buzzing at how cool this was when we arrived at the Kalhaar Blues & Greens Club for day one.

Starcy is the golf boss and had managed a draft, with Davey and me appointed captains as the players with the lowest handicaps. We picked through the squad, strategically selecting teammates. Way too much time went into this, but we loved it. Day one was set to include the first two rounds either side of lunch. With Bison, Stoin and Patty in my group it was a sensational day out.

For those who assume it was also a boozy day, Ahmedabad is in Gujrarat, and Gujarat is a dry state. This doesn't mean alcohol sales are banned, but they're very limited in quantity, and visitors need a permit. Most of us familiar with this had done the paperwork beforehand. We had followed up with local help to order some drinks for delivery at lunch on day one, and that volume would cover both days on the course and in the clubhouse.

However, the drinks were running late, and the first beer I saw all day was well into the back nine of our second round. I remember the round fondly because I made a monster putt for birdy on the 18th where a bit of a crowd had formed around the green, and I can assure you that I enjoyed the moment.

Back at the clubhouse, we stuck around for as long as you might after a day of cricket – a quick beer and debrief on the scores before heading back to the bus. We anticipated a few more drinks at the hotel but a fairly easy night because of the two further rounds on the course the next day. I couldn't wait because my guys were getting thumped and I was determined to lead us to a come-from-behind win.

Just before 6pm, the sun was setting as our bags were hauled to the bus. We piled into the golf carts, and with not many available that meant two passengers in the seats, two standing on the back. Our cart had Bison driving with Stoin up front, and Kez on the back with me, on a straight path from the club to the coach. When we were nearly to our destination, Bison pulled a u-turn. He and Stoin had some tunes going and were loving their singalong, so they wanted to buy themselves time to for their song to finish. There was nobody at fault. They were just having a good time and I guess I wasn't paying attention.

The reason I'm guessing is that I don't remember any of this myself. I remember everyone leaving the club and I remember the bus ride home. Everything in between has been relayed by other people. What I know is that the u-turn started, and I came straight off to smack my head and shoulders on the concrete path. Leigh Golding and Nick Jones, the team doctor and physio, were well placed in the cart behind us.

My next memory is Lee sitting in the row diagonal to me, monitoring my every move, even though it was obvious to him that I was concussed. I remember passing my hand through my hair and feeling the blood, plenty of it. I was confused, annoyed and couldn't work out why I was in this state. A traffic jam made things worse. My text history with Vini shows me repeating the same thing over and over, not realising that I had already told her.

After I got cleaned up at the hotel, the next job was glueing my scalp back together and tending to the grazes on my back. Once a concussion assessment was made there wasn't much I could do, other than head to bed and wait for the official process to run its course, and a shitstorm at home to begin.

When I woke up, the worry set in. I wasn't sick but I felt like a zombie – no emotions, just a throbbing head. Vini and Logan were there with me, but I had enough presence of mind to think that it might be tournament over. After everything I had done to rehab, rehab and rehab again, could something so ridiculous count me out? This was a lot to grapple with.

I also felt bad about accidentally ruining the golf day. It had been exceptional, and this was such a shit way to end it. Of course, I wouldn't be able to lead my team in the second part either.

Within our camp, there was love and support rather than a suggestion that anyone had done anything wrong. The coaches and teammates wanted me to be okay, get into recovery, and make sure I could return when fit. Concussion protocols meant there was no way I would make the England game in five days, but Afghanistan would be nine days after the fall.

Externally, however, it couldn't have been more different. It didn't take long to realise that I was getting carved up by the media at home, with the assumption that I was blind drunk. I've been around long enough to know how this type of story gets legs, but I was disappointed that it turned into common assumption when the truth was the opposite. I spoke to Mum, who confirmed how it was being discussed on talkback radio.

It's important to say here that I love a night out. It's also true that it only happens once in a while. That wasn't always the case; in earlier days I would jump at dinner or drinks with teammates. These days I mostly prefer to stay home on the couch. So when I do get the chance to head out, occasionally I get too excited about finally getting to spend time with good mates outside work. Those experiences are important, my brain is better for them, so if I'm around good people and good stories, I'm not volunteering to go home first.

This means I also accept that the loose-unit narrative about me is impossible to disperse. I can't put the genie back in the bottle. There have been times where I've been pinged for staying out too late, like on tour in Sri Lanka in 2016, and times when I've made headlines, like in Adelaide in 2024 when I got the beer to water ratio wrong during a hot day on the golf course. It looked more dramatic than it was, but I own that one.

Usually I shrug off criticism about it, because I know that when I play for Australia, I give myself every chance to be my best. We aren't robots, and I know that socialising helps me rather than compromises me. But in this case, despite it not involving a night out, the news cycle assumed that it had. Short of telling the full story as I have here, which wasn't viable with me in recovery and the team trying to concentrate on a World Cup, there was no setting the record straight.

Within two days my concussion symptoms has passed, which started the clock on my recovery. The headache subsided and I could function like a normal human. There would be no exercise permitted for a couple more days, but it was one step at a time.

For the England game I was allowed to wear the high-vis vest for twelfth man duties, something I was keen to do. As badly as England were going, they were defending champions and we didn't have a good recent record against them, so this would be a terrible time to slip up with a spot in the semis not yet certain. After our start, we had to keep winning.

We were hard held for most of our innings, 8 for 247 in the 45th over and a decent chance of getting rolled. Enter Adam Zampa. He'd been on fire with the ball and now it was his turn with the bat, smacking 29 in 19 balls. On a pitch that looked two-paced from the sidelines, 286 felt like a good score, but with England you can never be certain. My absence meant no overs from a second spinner, which was on my mind between innings.

But when Starcy nicked off Jonny Bairstow first ball, we were all able to take a deep breath. Zamps was superb with 3 for 21, not giving up a boundary in his 10 overs. And when it looked like England might have a late chance with David Willey's hitting, it was Zamps again dragging in a ridiculous diving catch at deep backward square to make sure we got it done.

Had my concussion been followed by a loss in the game I missed, it doesn't take much imagination to guess how that would have played with the audience back home. Instead we dodged that risk, and fielded perfectly on a night when batting was hard. We were one win away from the serious stuff. At the same time, I was one bit of bad luck away from going home early. I had carried that risk with my ankle, but now there was the danger of another knock to the head. A bad bounce, a slip, a top edge, a nets mishap; I was vulnerable head and toe, feeling in a place of precarious balance as we packed our bags for Afghanistan in Mumbai.

AUSTRALIA V ENGLAND

Venue: Narendra Modi Stadium, Ahmedabad
Toss: England, elected to field first
Points: Australia 2, England 0
TV Umpire: Adrian Holdstock (South Africa)
Referee: Jeff Crowe (New Zealand)

Date: November 4 2023
Result: Australia won by 33 runs
Umpires: Chris Gaffaney (New Zealand), Marais Erasmus (South Africa)
Reserve Umpire: Ahsan Raza (Pakistan)
Player of the Match: Adam Zampa, (Australia) 29 (19) & 3/21

AUSTRALIA		R	B
Travis Head	c Root b Woakes	11	10
David Warner	c Willey b Woakes	15	16
Steven Smith	c Ali b Rashid	44	52
Marnus Labuschagne	lbw b Wood	71	83
Josh Inglis †	c Ali b Rashid	3	6
Cameron Green	b Willey	47	52
Marcus Stoinis	c Bairstow b Livingstone	35	32
Pat Cummins (c)	c Malan b Wood	10	13
Mitchell Starc	c Ali b Woakes	10	13
Adam Zampa	c †Buttler b Woakes	29	19
Josh Hazlewood	not out	1	1
Extras	(lb 6, w 4)	10	
Total	(10 wickets, 49.3 overs)	286	

ENGLAND	O	M	R	W	Wd	Nb
David Willey	10	1	48	1	1	0
Chris Woakes	9.3	0	54	4	4	0
Mark Wood	10	0	70	2	3	0
Liam Livingstone	6	0	42	1	0	0
Moeen Ali	4	0	28	0	0	0
Adil Rashid	10	0	38	2	0	0

Fall of wickets: 1-11 (Travis Head, 1.4 ov), 2-38 (David Warner, 5.4 ov), 3-113 (Steven Smith, 21.4 ov), 4-117 (Josh Inglis, 23.1 ov), 5-178 (Marnus Labuschagne, 32.6 ov), 6-223 (Cameron Green, 40.4 ov), 7-241 (Marcus Stoinis, 43.4 ov), 8-247 (Pat Cummins, 44.2 ov), 9-285 (Adam Zampa, 49.1 ov), 10-286 (Mitchell Starc, 49.3 ov),

ENGLAND		R	B
Jonny Bairstow	c †Inglis b Starc	0	1
David Malan	c Head b Cummins	50	64
Joe Root	c †Inglis b Starc	13	17
Ben Stokes	c Stoinis b Zampa	64	90
Jos Buttler (c)†	c Green b Zampa	1	7
Moeen Ali	c Warner b Zampa	42	43
Liam Livingstone	c sub (SA Abbott) b Cummins	2	5
Chris Woakes	c Labuschagne b Stoinis	32	33
David Willey	c Zampa b Hazlewood	15	14
Adil Rashid	c †Inglis b Hazlewood	20	15
Mark Wood	not out	0	0
Extras	(lb 6, w 8)	14	
Total	(10 wickets, 48.1 overs)	253	

AUSTRALIA	O	M	R	W	Wd	Nb
Mitchell Starc	10	0	66	2	4	0
Josh Hazlewood	9.1	1	49	2	2	0
Pat Cummins	10	1	49	2	0	0
Adam Zampa	10	0	21	3	2	0
Travis Head	5	0	28	0	0	0
Marcus Stoinis	4	0	34	1	0	0

Fall of wickets: 1-0 (Jonny Bairstow, 0.1 ov), 2-19 (Joe Root, 4.3 ov), 3-103 (Dawid Malan, 22.3 ov), 4-106 (Jos Buttler, 25.1 ov), 5-169 (Ben Stokes, 35.3 ov), 6-174 (Liam Livingstone, 36.6 ov), 7-186 (Moeen Ali, 39.1 ov), 8-216 (David Willey, 43.2 ov), 9-253 (Chris Woakes, 47.6 ov), 10-253 (Adil Rashid, 48.1 ov)

12

The Impossible Dream

I don't know why the ball travels further in Mumbai, but it does. That's what I've always believed, ever, since coming to the Wankhede early in my IPL journey to join Sachin Tendulkar a decade earlier. By 2023 so much had changed, but it's still the case that balls getting hit here seem to wear the damage more than most places.

It felt that way in the nets the day before we faced Afghanistan. While the guys had taken care of England at Ahmedabad, I had been allowed my first bat since my concussion. This tune-up in Mumbai was my last box to tick. It was important that I had a long session to make up ground, but I didn't want to leave the net anyway, the way the ball was pinging off my bat.

It almost felt like range hitting. For me, those drills are about committing to not hitting the ball as hard as I can, but as far as I need to. My rule of thumb is that 80 to 85 percent of my swing should get the ball 80 to 85 metres. It's about tempo and rhythm rather than relying on muscle.

The purest swing I ever saw belonged to Jimmy Faulkner at the peak of his powers around the 2015 World Cup. As Big Bash teammates with the Stars, we would set up for range hitting at the MCG, which is a cool thing to do in an empty 100,000-seat stadium. He had such flow as he reached the ball, which meant he didn't often lose it. The times when I've struggled have been when I've forgotten that ball-to-ball consistency is more important than occasionally dinging it 100 metres.

On the morning of the game, I tried to focus on how well I was hitting the ball. Since my leg break, my preparation to get out the door begins at 8am even for day-nighters. A gym routine of 25 minutes to get my foot and ankle loose. A physio and massage session. A swim. Then to the ground for team warm-ups.

The home rooms at the Wankhede have been renovated since my first IPL but they aren't huge once you account for all our cricket bags, with every player wanting room to lay out bats and spikes and kit. I tucked myself in around the corner nearest the door to the steps to get a bit of extra space.

The first thing I noticed on getting to ground level for the bat-and-ball part of my warm-up was that it was so much hotter than the day before. After hitting into a net, I had to go back inside. After catching and fielding drills, I retreated again. I was drenched in sweat, and now we knew we were fielding first. I was scheduled for a bowling warm-up but thought I'd be better off inside. I already felt dehydrated.

Afghanistan were on a roll, having knocked off England, Pakistan, Sri Lanka, and the Dutch, all with some ease. When I first played them, my international debut in 2012, they were seen as the team you rack up net run rate against – we had done that in the 2015 World Cup when we made 417. By the present day, they're serious contenders. Their world-class spin crew developed first, but it increasingly feels like they have all bases covered.

Having lost the toss, we had the mission of keeping it together in the heat. Our final chat before taking the field was to make sure we played it smart by giving our quicks as much time as we could on the shady side of the ground. There wasn't a helpful cloud in the sky.

I knew early that I was in strife. I'd taken on as much fluid as possible but couldn't stay ahead of the dehydration curve. My light duties through concussion had caught up with me – it's telling how quickly you can lose your conditioning at the elite level. Pat got me on to bowl in the seventh over, sending down four in a row. Conceding 19 runs was a win, as I was already struggling at the top of my mark. I can't remember ever doing it tougher in the field than those 13 overs.

The moment my spell was done, I was up the stairs to drop my core temperature. It was a race against time: in order to bowl, you need to return to the field for as many overs as you were away, and Patty was going to need me. It was dramatic, the support crew stripping me down, draping ice collars over my head and neck, pumping me with as much water and electrolyte drink as possible. After four overs, I had to get back on the ground for part two.

Mercifully, the lengthening afternoon put more of the ground in shade. I had a job to do, and their first drop Rahmat Shah lifted the tenth ball of my spell to Hoff at long off. Halfway through the innings, they were 2 for 122 – solid but not running away with it. Patty got me out of the attack after my eighth over, with 1 for 34.

There's a book to be written on Patty as Australian captain, with his evolution in this tournament a study in how well he solves problems. Through these games in the middle he trusted his bowlers to send down short spells, working through match-ups like a bloke who had been doing this his whole life rather than for a handful of ODIs. Figuring out each contest with Ronnie and Dan Vettori, it was a reminder that they were the right people to run this team.

I bowled the 39th and 47th, getting smacked in the last, but 1 for 55 was on trend with Afghanistan's 5 for 291. They had taken 96 off the final 10 overs, but our consensus was that we'd kept it together in the heat on a pitch that had given little. As well as Ibrahim Zadran had played to bat through for 129, he hadn't put us to the sword.

Ever since Under-12s, no matter how many times I've gone through the ritual of getting ready to bat, I'm still too nervous to eat. But given the sapping day, I forced something down. Then it was time to get my leg replaced, as I describe it: tape off, a full massage from hip to foot, tape up again. I noticed that my back wasn't feeling good, the occasional spasm. Little did I know how many more were coming.

On the physio bench to watch the innings start, Naveen-ul-Haq nicked off Trav right away, and when he trapped Bison in front by the sixth over, I had to get my shit together, get into my playing clothes and pad up. That left one job: pick a stick.

I'll bring five bats to a ground, but only two might ever be in the frame for selection. They're forever in a grading system, and they know it – I don't think it's weird to think of them as living beings. A shiny new one gets delivered? Earn your stripes, pretty thing. There'll always be an old favourite knocking around from five years ago, re-stickered time and again.

At this World Cup, an unexpected favourite had emerged. I used it in the Netherlands warm-up game and didn't enjoy how it felt, immediately consigned to practice days only. But before the tournament proper, Josh Inglis next door in the Hyderabad nets said it sounded unbelievable. Maybe I'd been superficial? It wasn't a glamorous blade, with stains all over the wood and a toe that wasn't quite right. But it won the race in time for the group games and had reaped that 40-ball ton. The Beast, as Kookaburra branded it, was going with me this night in Mumbai.

In the middle, Davey was being tested by the seam of all-rounder Azmatullah Omarzai. It brought back the South Africa game, where the ball didn't move by day but hooped by night. If we lost Davey here, the game would speed up. Sure enough, Azmatullah castled him to start the next over as I took my seat.

I wanted to stay calm, sit on the sidelines, and take some time to pay close attention. I wanted at least an hour from the fourth-wicket partnership. But no. Not tonight. Ingo, first ball, edged a beauty to first slip. The Wankhede had been with Afghanistan all day, and now it was pumping. We were 4 for 49, Azmatullah was on a hat-trick, and I was on my way to face the music.

Only the day before, Angelo Mathews had been timed out in Sri Lanka's game against Bangladesh, so I didn't muck around. Generally, a bowler like Azmatullah is a nice pace for me to ease in, but he was bending his back like never before, a 23-year-old making a name for himself on a night that could open up a semi-final berth for his country.

Guard taken, fielders behind me. And what a hat-trick ball. As a bowler you want to give yourself a chance, and he sent down something practically unplayable for me. Angling in, shaping away, kissing my outside edge. Shit. But hang on, it doesn't carry to the keeper. They're appealing anyway, giving their all for leg before. Alex Wharf keeps his finger down.

I could see how emotionally involved they were, how badly they wanted to send it upstairs. After a second to digest my luck, I thought I should try to look as guilty as possible to encourage them. Head down, darting my eyes all over the place to look shifty. They took the bait, and as far behind the game as we were, I did think that it might come in handy later to have made them blow a review. Even better, the break gave me time to stop my heart beating out of my chest. I got off the mark with a push past mid off, out of the middle of my new favourite bat.

Marnus loves situations like this; he was picked in this squad to get us out of the shit. Even more so given Smudge was missing this game after a bout of vertigo a couple of days earlier. So it was

Marnus who took most of the early strike, building into his work to pull Azmatullah for four. I clipped a boundary to reach double figures. We were miles away but playing with confidence.

Rashid Khan's time at the crease was destined to be a major part of the plot, and he came on for over 15. I was glad to see spin at both ends given how well Azmatullah had been going – even the final ball of his spell did plenty and nearly bowled me. Still, I'd say the overall challenge presented by Afghanistan's spinners is unrivalled in this form of the game. I've seen Rashid get on a roll so often, and if it happened tonight we were gone.

I was happy with my positioning to his first ball, controlling it in front of square, calling for a quick single. Marnus came through, but for an instant thought about going back. Rahmat's throw wasn't forceful but was accurate, and the dive wasn't enough with the bat turned the wrong way, centimetres short. That hesitation was the difference.

I had to put it behind me before Stoin arrived, but there were soon other distractions. We were straight upstairs when Rashid beat him with a mesmerising leg break, saved by umpire's call. No such luck in Rashid's next over, my teammate looking to reverse and missing a wrong 'un. He had started well but we were 6 for 87.

Nor did I have much time with Starcy, next to fall to Rashid in bizarre circumstances that only I'm responsible for. Another wrong'un, with our big quick defending deep in his crease, and wicketkeeper Ikram Alikhil took a catch diving out in front of silly point after a deflection off his own gloves. Starcy came up and said he hadn't hit it, but down the other end I had heard a noise and seen the deviation. Don't waste a review on that. Until the replay showed that the ball had nicked the stump. Fuck.

We were 7 for 91, it was the 19th over, and we needed 201 more runs. Big trouble. Huge trouble. The emotion from Rashid was something else, lifting his teammates, their energy sending them surging on the way to annihilating us, having never defeated Australia in any format.

Tournament ramifications loomed. Afghanistan would be in the hunt for a semi-final, which could mean one less spot for us. Our remaining game would become must-win, and while most people would expect us to beat Bangladesh, they would have said the same about Afghanistan. Confidence would be knocked; weather could play a part. Basically, lose here and we would lose full control of our campaign.

I was even thinking about the bigger picture: net run rate. We had recovered ours after the big loss to South Africa, but if we lost badly here it would blow out the wrong way again. Going conservative to lose by a smaller margin would limit the damage.

When Patty arrived in the middle, we didn't talk much to start with, certainly not to that level of detail. He got moving right away, turning Rashid fine for four from his third ball. Little did we know that would be the only boundary he would hit across our whole partnership. In situations like this, all you can do is forget the scoreboard and deal with each delivery.

We began that way. Rashid swarmed me in his fourth over, beating my outside edge twice, but getting through six balls from him was a marginal gain. Then came the 22nd over, and bedlam. Somehow, looking back, it also became the moment when the tide began to turn.

Noor Ahmad was ripping down his left-arm wrist spin. For a young fella of 18, he was a handful – the heir to Rashid's throne. Second ball, his leggie hit me on the shin. Oh no. Yep, given out by Michael Gough. We had to review, no matter how plumb it felt, and I had some hope that it could have pitched outside leg.

Patty saw it differently, saying after the first replay that it would clear the stumps. As soon as ball tracking showed it pitching in line with leg stump, I accepted my fate and prepared to walk off, but the captain was right, as he always seems to be. The projection had it going over by the width of a bail. Noor's extra top spin had saved me.

I knew then and there that I had to change the record against their wrist spinners. I was a sitting duck if I didn't put pressure back onto them, playing the way I'm most effective. If that got me out, so be it. This early in the chase, with only four fielders outside the circle for another 18 overs, I had to make use of the restrictions. Fourth ball of the over, I got low for my first reverse sweep of the innings, four. As per my script, that sent backward point to the deep and brought up mid off.

It turned out I needed a second piece of good fortune. I tried the conventional sweep next, and this time Noor's extra bounce was my enemy. The top edge went gently towards the other Afghan spinner, Mujeeb Ur Rahman, at short fine leg.

As time stood still with the ball floating to the fielder, I was already turning to the dressing room again, facing the reality of a scoreboard that would soon read 8 for 112. The only thing going for me in that endless moment was that Mujeeb was never quite still, and given how much work I had put on the ball by chopping down, it was fizzing with spin. A little curve can be enough for a ball to miss the middle of a catcher's fingers, and this is exactly what happened. It hit his hands hard and bounced straight out, no chance of a juggle.

Twice in the over, Afghanistan thought I was finished, only to see me spared. It shouldn't have cost them – I was committed to a high-risk game, and I've got a lousy track record of making the most of chances. But the fielding energy changed immediately from exhilarated to volatile. Patty and I spoke about what might be possible if we found a way to shift the game more onto our terms. Might they self-combust?

I wasn't motoring yet: I'd been out there for 17 overs by the time I reached my fifty in the 26th. I got there hitting over mid off, the fielder who came into the circle as soon as I swept Noor. Midwicket was up to tempt an error, but I was seeing it well enough to pump a few in that direction. I did start to feel they were playing into my hands, letting my batting dictate their field.

Patty kept playing his roles to perfection. One was to keep me talking and relaxed, showing how well he understands his players.

When a wide went down the leg side he deadpanned to me, 'We'll get them in extras.' We didn't think we were a genuine chance of winning, so the pressure was off. But it must have been annoying for Afghanistan in their dominant position to see us smiling and chatting like two blokes at the pub.

In the 29th over I hit my first two sixes, taking Noor over long on and midwicket, and getting my strike rate beyond a run a ball when entering the 70s. Mujeeb was next, a bowler I know well from a season together at Punjab. He's talented but I feel at ease picking him, which is so much of the struggle against spinners with mystery about them.

I had already hit him for consecutive boundaries before Stoin got out, and now I took another of his overs for 11. That included four from a genuine outside edge that would have gone straight to slip. Looking at the situation, it beggars belief that they no longer had one. It showed they were feeling the pinch.

At this stage I felt like I was on autopilot, having Patty knock out dot balls to end overs, allowing me to start the next. Looking for boundaries, settling for singles when that didn't work, still scoring from almost every ball. Mujeeb's eighth over gave me the chance to back away to cut four, then stand still to await the overpitched response, over long on for another six.

That got me to 97, my swing feeling as trustworthy as it had in the nets the day before. I hadn't thought at all about another World Cup ton, two in three innings, but there was that natural satisfaction when cutting Noor to get to there in 76 balls. With our score around 200, we had avoided a calamity on net run rate.

We weren't quite daring to dream, but we had put on a century partnership too.

But with that milestone came the start of my body shutting down. I had already felt my back seizing up – it was fine when facing, but this was the time to call for the physio, trying to loosen the muscles down my back to the glute. When some jabbed elbows into the glute didn't do much to help, I turned back to the game for a new challenge. Naveen was returning, and my plan was to play their quicks watchfully.

I hoped we could make a dent when the warhorse Mohammad Nabi came on for some flat off-breaks – my favourite kind. Of course, he was going to set his boundary riders back to cover the leg side. Before the over Patty and I discussed that I had to watch out for that, and the safe bet would be to play the gaps and try to keep him in the attack for a bigger crack later. That plan evaporated when I smacked my biggest six of the night so far over deep midwicket.

The skipper came down with a laugh rather than a telling-off. 'Not going to take on the boundary riders then, Maxi?' Sometimes instinct takes over, as it did with a shot somewhere between a ramp and a pull for four. The required contortion hurt me badly enough to suggest that things were going to get a lot harder, as my dehydrated body increased its signals that it was about to stop me batting properly, if at all.

We needed 81 from 84 balls when Pat blocked out Rashid's eighth over, then blocked another from Naveen after I hobbled an early single. I got another physio visit but nothing was changing.

I had to stop Rashid before his next set, my right toes curling back in my boot. I had been using the footmarks to try to straighten my foot, but it was no good, much to the opposition's understandable amusement.

I figured that time was running out and I had to make the most of every ball. Helpfully, Rashid gave me a half-volley to start over 39, letting me hit over long on for six without having to move. Right then I started cramping in both legs. I got two more balls away for four while standing still in Naveen's next over. From there, zero footwork became my Plan A.

It was a strange and sudden journey back to the start of my career. Before the days of range-hitting at the MCG, my batting coach Richard Clifton had me do what he called no-foot drills. He has been such a big part of my life since I was 13, someone I have so much faith in, and right now, I was full of gratitude that he had set me up with that skill as a younger bloke, facing 10 balls before each net with no footwork to show what my upper body could do with the timing of a rhythmical swing.

I needed every trick in the book to compete from here, and being able to draw on this one was entirely down to Richard. The 20 years of work he had put into my game paid off like never before in the hour that followed. I know how much pride we both take from that.

With 10 overs to go and 60 runs to collect, it was now that Pat and I allowed ourselves to think about the finish line. It was also when the going got toughest. To this point, even with my impaired state, we were having a great time out there. In the

41st over it got serious. Noor gave me space to free my arms and wrist down the ground for four. But when trying for a single next ball, my legs gave way. I literally hopped to the non-striker's end and hit the deck. Lying flat on my back – doing the full salmon, as it was later dubbed – I was screaming for help.

Umpire Gough was first on the scene, seeing that I was distressed and struggling for breath. This wasn't a back spasm or a cramp anymore, it was full body. I needed my right leg pulled towards me to stretch that calf while at the same time lifting my left leg to relieve that hamstring. When I realised I couldn't reach either leg, I started to have a panic attack on the turf. Nick Jones, the physio, got both legs in the directions they needed to go, then focused on getting my breathing under control. After that he tried to get me drinking anything that would help – I'm sceptical of pickle juice but I was ready to try anything.

I suggested retiring hurt to get patched up, so I could return at the next wicket. Nick thought it wasn't realistic: if I stopped, my body would shut down and I wouldn't be able to get it moving again. I wasn't having that, so the only option was to keep swinging, staying put at one end as much as possible. Patty was up for that. Between times, Zamps made his second trip down the stairs to replace me, as he had earlier when I reviewed that lbw. Once more, he climbed back to the top.

Azmatullah, not spotted for two hours since his electric opening spell, was back for over 42. From the third ball I got him where I wanted him, full and straight, the chance for a no-feet lift for a boundary. Passing 150 was an irrelevant marker by this point. I'd worked out that my best technique involved rocking back and forth to build momentum as the bowler arrived, which helped get my hands where they needed to be faster. It was adaptation on the fly but it was working. Another four came from a similar back-and-forth, but I lowered myself at the last moment into a reverse tuck, letting me play a lap shot from in front of middle stump. I might get out any ball batting this way, but I was still fighting.

With under a run a ball to win, Patty did what we needed, absorbing over 43 from Noor. That maiden lifted the required rate but it meant the left-arm spinner was done. I decided that Azmatullah had to go – we were close enough to break the back of it, which meant we might win even if I fell. Riding my luck, an inside edge ran away first ball. But there was nothing scrappy about the reverse that followed, inspired by my shot off him the previous over. This time it went all the way over third man for six. It felt incredible. Next ball, slap, four. The cherry on top was hobbling a single to keep strike.

With 32 to win from 36, drinks were coming out every over. I had joked to Greeny with 60 to go that we could do it in 10 balls. Now, somehow going as well as I was, a quick finish felt realistic. For the first time all night, the game was ours to lose. Naveen's ninth over helped, starting with a standstill pull over midwicket.

Behind all these boundaries was my belief that swinging too hard would be my downfall, so it was back to that mantra of swinging at 80 percent to hit it 80 metres. I nearly chopped on later in the over, but again I was able to haul myself to the other end to keep strike.

Needing 25 from 30, the remaining player who could change the script was Rashid, with six balls left. Trying my audacious shots against him was laden with risk, so the percentage play was to leave him to Pat. In the end I got back on strike with three balls to go, instinct taking over again to attempt the run. But I saw him off, and for the third consecutive over, found a way to retain strike from the final delivery.

Afghanistan turned to Mujeeb. We got permission for a change of gloves and another gulp of sugar-water. I felt the best I had in an hour. Patty asked my plan. 'It's ending this over. We'll get it done now.' That sounds arrogant but I knew we had the short leg-side boundary, and I saw my chances as better against Mujeeb than the wrist spinners.

Perhaps the cricket gods sent me a reminder from the first ball, which I smashed into my ankle from a filthy swipe. I reminded myself of the process for standing still. When I saw Mujeeb go full, I was able to move into the ball and pick it up over long on. Into the crowd, who had long since jumped off Afghanistan and were with me every step of the way. Everyone loves a miracle comeback.

He went shorter with his third ball but I was in the zone with anything I could plonk over long on. Clearing the ropes. I couldn't believe my luck that so many balls were in my reduced swinging arc. The thought of a double ton hadn't even crossed my mind.

218

At last, Mujeeb changed the play and went wide of the off-stump, but he wasn't to know about my days as a Division 4 junior tennis player on cold winter mornings at the Belgrave Heights Tennis Club, nor that my favourite shot was the down-the-line forehand winner. That's how this shot turned out, just reaching it to bisect the gap between cover in the ring and long off at the fence. Maybe my favourite shot of the night, it put us within five runs of victory.

It was clear from his body language that I'd broken Mujeeb, and I expected one more ball that I could get hold off. So it was, quicker on leg stump, there to hit over deep midwicket. It sailed all the way. The chase was over. We had won. The relief kicked in immediately – I could finally stop. The first thing I saw was Patty's big, beautiful smile beaming down at me. We had put on 202 together, and I'd finished on 201 not out.

So many stats were thrown around in the aftermath, but they blew right by me. So much had taken place even in the week and a half since the golf cart, let alone the previous 360 days since my leg snapped. For it all to come together like that, so dramatically, it's still difficult to process.

All that was left was one final trip up those stairs. I had no earthly idea how I was meant to make it to the top, but I got there. Back to the sanctuary of the Australian dressing room, the best place in the world to be after a good day on the field. The guys were so exhilarated; we had a guaranteed semi-final. I was delirious as I sat back in my spot, but the unconditional affection from this team meant I didn't want that little window of time to end. It made everything worth it.

As we sat in a circle to debrief, the run out with Marnus felt so long ago, but not for him. He declared that if not for that, we would have knocked off those runs together for sure – I love that about his personality. We were also able to laugh about Starcy's non-review. The only serious point I tried to make was that I hoped this would be the night that turbocharged our campaign, and we would go on to win the whole thing.

Finally back to the hotel, there was no point going to bed. It was going to take hours to come down from that rush. There was a nice moment when everyone in the hotel bar saw me come in and gave me a standing ovation. A lot of friends were there, and a lot more love. My celebrations totalled a huge bottle of water with electrolytes and a solitary whiskey sour. I had that sitting around a table with Finchy and Neroli, long part of my inner sanctum.

Watto was there, so crucial to my first World Cup ton in 2015. Ian Smith came over for a chat. On the bus someone had shown me his awesome call of the final moments: 'The most remarkable thing you'll ever see in cricket!' We got to exchange pleasantries about each other's work. It was the perfect balance of euphoria and the quiet you can only have with true friends, before it was time to sneak upstairs.

Vini and Logan were sound asleep. Getting our baby to the game that day had been impossible, but the fact they were with me on this trip was making all the difference. With my last minutes awake I sent a text to my parents, then put my phone into sleep mode. Anything else could wait for tomorrow. There would be plenty. From all my years loving cricket, I knew that a few fortunate players get a chance at a moment that will define them in everyone's memory from then on. I had just had mine. The most important day of my professional life was complete.

AFGHANISTAN V AUSTRALIA

Venue: Wankhede Stadium, Mumbai
Toss: Afghanistan, elected to bat first
Points: Australia 2, Afghanistan 0
TV Umpire: Chris Gaffaney (New Zealand)
Referee: Jeff Crowe (New Zealand)

Date: November 07 2023
Result: Australia won by 3 wickets (with 19 balls remaining)
Umpires: Alex Wharf (England), Michael Gough (England)
Reserve Umpire: Sharfuddoula (Bangladesh)
Player of the Match: Glenn Maxwell, (Australia) 201* (128) & 1/55

AFGHANISTAN		R	B
hmanullah Gurbaz	c Starc b Hazlewood	21	25
Ibrahim Zadran	not out	129	143
Rahmat Shah	c Hazlewood b Maxwell	30	44
Hashmatullah Shahidi (c)	b Starc	26	43
Azmatullah Omarzai	c Maxwell b Zampa	22	18
Mohammad Nabi	b Hazlewood	12	10
Rashid Khan	not out	35	18
Ikram Alikhil †			
Mujeeb Ur Rahman			
Noor Ahmad			
Naveen-ul-Haq			
Extras	(lb 5, nb 1, w 10)	16	
Total	(5 wickets, 50 overs)	291	

AUSTRALIA		R	B
David Warner	b Azmatullah Omarzai	18	29
Travis Head	c †Ikram Alikhil b Naveen-ul-Haq	0	2
Mitchell Marsh	lbw b Naveen-ul-Haq	24	11
Marnus Labuschagne	run out (Rahmat Shah)	14	28
Josh Inglis †	c Ibrahim Zadran b Azmatullah Omarzai	0	1
Glenn Maxwell	not out	201	128
Marcus Stoinis	lbw b Rashid Khan	6	7
Mitchell Starc	c †Ikram Alikhil b Rashid Khan	3	7
Pat Cummins (c)	not out	12	68
Adam Zampa			
Josh Hazlewood			
Extras	(b 4, lb 1, w 10)	15	
Total	(7 wickets, 46.5 overs)	293	

Fall of wickets: 1-38 (Rahmanullah Gurbaz, 7.6 ov), 2-121 (Rahmat Shah, 24.4 ov), 3-173 (Hashmatullah Shahidi, 37.2 ov), 4-210 (Azmatullah Omarzai, 42.3 ov), 5-233 (Mohammad Nabi, 45.3 ov)

Fall of wickets: 1-4 (Travis Head, 1.2 ov), 2-43 (Mitchell Marsh, 5.4 ov), 3-49 (David Warner, 8.1 ov), 4-49 (Josh Inglis, 8.2 ov), 5-69 (Marnus Labuschagne, 14.1 ov), 6-87 (Marcus Stoinis, 16.4 ov), 7-91 (Mitchell Starc, 18.3 ov)

AUSTRALIA	O	M	R	W	Wd	Nb
Mitchell Starc	9	0	70	1	5	0
Josh Hazlewood	9	0	39	2	1	0
Glenn Maxwell	10	0	55	1	0	1
Pat Cummins	8	0	47	0	1	0
Adam Zampa	10	0	58	1	2	0
Travis Head	3	0	15	0	0	0
Marcus Stoinis	1	0	2	0	0	0

AFGHANISTAN	O	M	R	W	Wd	Nb
Mujeeb Ur Rahman	8.5	1	72	0	0	0
Naveen-ul-Haq	9	0	47	2	1	0
Azmatullah Omarzai	7	1	52	2	1	0
Rashid Khan	10	0	44	2	3	0
Noor Ahmad	10	1	53	0	1	0
Mohammad Nabi	2	0	20	0	0	0

13

Live by the Sword

How does it feel, the morning after a night that will shape the rest of your life? It's a question I chewed over when preparing for this chapter. How to digest the knowledge that – even if this shouldn't be the case – for a lot of people my career would be divided into 'before Mumbai' and 'after'?

It felt like a miracle that my legs hadn't cramped again during the night. I was ginger, but intact. As soon as we woke up, I took Vini through it all. The brief version anyway: the next game in Pune was three days away, and we had a bus to catch.

It was overwhelming reconnecting with the world. Four hours on a coach from Mumbai was not exactly what my body was after, but it gave my mind time to process the scale of the response. There's a jolt of anxiety even now thinking about the number of messages sitting there, waiting for me to respond. I never take that love for granted; it's special that so many people can share in what I do, but it had never been as full on as this.

People from every stage of my life were chiming in, many who I hadn't heard from in years. There was celebrity interest online, like the actor Hugh Jackman riding the bumps of the game. And salutes from countless cricketers, including so many who I've played with or against, players I respect like Ben Stokes and Adam Gilchrist. Some of them called it the best one-day knock ever; even Virender Sehwag gave it the nod. So did Sachin Tendulkar, with a philosophical tweet about my restricted movement. "Sometimes," he concluded, "no footwork becomes great footwork."

Sure enough, that post exploded, with millions of people seeing it and apparently most of them forwarding it to me. Its audience was only second to Patty's own post, with his usual dry humour. 'A lot of credit should go to Maxi, he played his role beautifully.' The only funnier one was from Kevin Pietersen, who posted a photo of us batting together for the Melbourne Stars that turned out be mostly just a picture of him: classic KP.

I didn't know that a huge Optus outage at home meant millions of Australians couldn't get online, so they got news of our win from the radio or TV, like when I was a kid. It had been 1:37am on the east coast of Australia when we lost our seventh wicket, so it must have come as quite the shock to everyone who chose that moment to go to bed.

As it turned out, my poor Dad was one of them. I felt for him, because he hasn't missed many innings of mine. Mum kept reminding him of that! She had been at my sister's house that night, watching the game on her phone in bed, and she didn't dare to ring Dad in case it meant she lost her connection. It's a story that will live on in our family forever.

They were both so proud, though, and when we spoke from Pune, told me how this was the biggest story in the country. Foxtel helped by publishing a supercut of the innings as what they called a Maxi Mini. The posts I enjoyed most were of fans describing their marathon nights sticking with me and Pat until it was done, or the ones from people like my Dad who woke up, couldn't believe it, and had to watch it over and over.

It dawned on me that this was a moment, like Steve Waugh's Ashes ton last ball of the day, or Michael Bevan's final four to beat the Windies. One of those events that makes you ask 'Where were you when . . .' It was crazy to think that I now had one of these, a moment when Australia was all on board.

It was a strange feeling. Most of my best efforts in Aussie colours have been quick fifties. The people invested in my story, whether people who are close to me or cricket watchers who enjoy how I play, would have this innings as validation of what I can do. My career had always been so divisive, even in microcosm during this tournament with the golf cart incident so soon before.

I had long accepted that my style isn't for everyone, with some never willing to accept that a bloke who reverse-sweeps his way around the world is a serious player. On the other side of the ledger were those who embraced it and lamented that I'd never become the three-format regular that we both felt I was capable of being. I was not used to widespread approval. But on this day, at this moment, I was to everyone's taste.

If I risked an inflated head that day, there was a timely reality check just before Pune. We were comfortable on a bus with the families, with lots of space to set up and keep Logan comfortable. Until he woke up close to our destination, and bam! An explosion from his nappy the likes of which we had never seen. It was something else, me trying to catch the mess with my hands for want of better options. We had to change him right there on the seats, bombarding everyone else on the coach with the stench. I hope he likes books; I'm sure he'll appreciate reading this when he's older.

It was awkward getting off the bus, with so many people offering handshakes that I had to decline, for obvious reasons. But in a way the moment was helpful to get me back to earth, reminding me that the most important person in my life didn't care yet what I did on cricket fields, and that I had a bigger responsibility off them. It was time to park the night before and move on to what was next, and even cleaning up in the hotel room, I was so happy my little family was there with me.

———

Despite having woken up better than expected, of course my whole body was sore. I still had to make up a gap on dehydration, and as the day wore on I realised my left hamstring had a slight strain, given how many cramps had rippled through the muscle. Rather than recovering, time made the toll from

Mumbai clearer. I was still damaged a good few days later. I knew all about injury, but for the first time in my life, I just felt weathered and old.

Our semi-final was set, in Kolkata against South Africa, but there was no sense of taking our last group game less seriously. You don't want to mess with a good run during a World Cup. So we had a crack at getting me right for the night, but in the end the safest place for me was on the physio bench and in the pool, getting my body back to where it needed to be. It was another example of a healthy dressing room, making a measured decision with no pressure to counterproductively tough it out.

The fact that my ankle had held up was the best news – it was unlikely to get a test more intense than that marathon. If anything, all the work I had put into my leg to prepare for fielding had meant doing comparatively less batting before the World Cup, so now it was my hips and glutes screaming instead.

I was also gutted that my first round of golf since the concussion saga wouldn't be in Pune. The hamstring meant I couldn't justify anything but rehab. Even though Pune is one of the few cities I haven't formally represented in the IPL, it was a home ground when Kings XI played some games there. There's even a cocktail named after me at the rooftop bar we gravitate to. I was sad to be lying low this time.

Starcy also got a safety-first break for the Bangladesh game, so it gave Sean Abbott his chance. We were thrilled for him, as a player who is so often with our squad but less often on the team sheet. He knew the only way he could get ahead of our big three quicks was injury, but prepared for every game regardless. In most eras he would have played hundreds of times for Australia.

I've only been the professional tourist once, early days in England in 2013. I didn't get a game in the one-dayers that followed the Ashes, but it was rewarding because it was the first time I could bring my parents to be part of an Australia trip. Dad hadn't been back to the UK since leaving as an 18-year-old. He showed mum around Plymouth, where he grew up, and dropped into a golf course he had played at. Looking at the honour board in the pro shop, he was approached by someone who worked there, and they remembered each other from playing at the course when they were kids.

Against Bangladesh, my job was the same as against England – be helpful without being a distraction. As senior players we basically have the skillset of assistant coaches, and have those kind of discussions with each other. The key is gauging what each player requires: some want a discussion with detailed intelligence about the attack, some are better with a pat on the bum and a line about looking forward to them smacking the bowling. In the field, especially in the afternoon, it's about making sure everyone has the fluids they need to keep going.

Sean bowled so well, a reminder of how much depth we have in that department. He was the only quick who was called upon to bowl a full complement, and showed his bag of tricks in picking up a couple of wickets. Even though Bangladesh set us 307, I didn't detect any dressing-room nerves. We lost Trav early, but Mitch replaced him and stayed until the end, an unbeaten 177 from 133 balls.

Over the last few years Bison has made the most of his ridiculous ability, putting us at ease once he gets himself in. At the start of the tournament he was knackered after so much travel in the build-up, but the fifty against Sri Lanka when we were right on the edge, then the ton against Pakistan to get us a mile ahead, meant he was well placed to cash in with his technique against spin of getting to the pitch and pumping the shit out of it. For all the modern tricks, there's something to be said for keeping it simple, and when he's on it makes him feel impossible to bowl to.

Mitch was also dealing with the aftermath of a dash home a couple of weeks earlier, having also missed our England game. His grandfather, Ross, was in his final days, and Mitch wanted them to spend that time together. Their family is so close, and it says a lot about Mitch's heart that he put them first. He was back with us in Pune when the funeral took place, then went out and made that ton – his first innings for Australia that Ross wasn't there to see. It's another illustration of why Mitch is the heart and soul of our team.

What felt as important as the Bison's colossal hand was Smudge joining him for the last 175 runs of the chase. His vertigo attack in Mumbai had felt serious at the time, too dizzy to even consider playing. But having him back in his happy place, turning the board over, felt like we had checked another box. It gives players like me the confidence to take risks knowing he can be relied on in the engine room.

Our group stage was done. We had got on the roll we needed, racking up seven wins on the bounce. Now to claim the

World Cup, it was back to the start: South Africa, then India, the two teams that had beaten us over a month ago. But first came one of those precious breaks, with five days off as we flew to Kolkata for the first time in the tournament.

Of course we arranged a hit of golf at Royal Kolkata. Feeling fit again, I had my first round since the concussion, though I delighted everyone else by playing terribly and losing a few balls along the way. But back to training at Eden Gardens, my hamstring flared once more, a gentle warm-up run enough to send me back to the physio bench. It eventually came good before the semi-final, but as it had been for months, the anxiety was always there that my body was about to give way.

When our final training session got washed out, we had the chance to watch the other semi in Mumbai. Seeing how hot it looked gave me flashbacks to our afternoon in the field against Afghanistan. Virat got into his groove, hunting that precious 50th one-day ton that took him clear of Sachin's record into territory all his own. Shreyas Iyer got a century too, and they set New Zealand 398.

The intense focus on milestones for Indian batters did stand out to me. We had seen it when they knocked us off at Chennai, with KL Rahul disappointed to hit a six and win the game on 97 not out. A four would have tied the scores with him on 95, meaning he could then have tried for a six to reach a century. It was strange seeing a player gutted at having timed a shot better than intended, and you could sense disappointment in the ground despite having handed a rival a hefty beating.

BANGLADESH V AUSTRALIA

Venue: Maharashtra Cricket Association Stadium, Pune

Toss: Australia, elected to field first

Points: Australia 2, Bangladesh 0

TV Umpire: Richard Illingworth (England)

Referee: Andy Pycroft (Zimbabwe)

Date: November 11 2023

Result: Australia won by 8 wickets (with 32 balls remaining)

Umpires: Ahsan Raza (Pakistan), Marais Erasmus (South Africa)

Reserve Umpire: Richard Kettleborough (England)

Player of the Match: Mitchell Marsh, (Australia) 177* (132)

BANGLADESH		R	B
Tanzid Hasan	c & b Abbott	36	34
Litton Das	c Labuschagne b Zampa	36	45
Najmul Hossain Shanto (c)	run out (Labuschagne/†Inglis)	45	57
Towhid Hridoy	c Labuschagne b Stoinis	74	79
Mahmudullah	run out (Labuschagne)	32	28
Mushfiqur Rahim †	c Cummins b Zampa	21	24
Mehidy Hasan Miraz	c Cummins b Abbott	29	20
Nasum Ahmed	run out (Abbott)	7	11
Mahedi Hasan	not out	2	3
Taskin Ahmed	not out	0	1
Mustafizur Rahman			
Extras	(lb 10, nb 2, w 12)	24	
Total	(8 wickets, 50 overs)	306	

Fall of wickets: 1-76 (Tanzid Hasan, 11.2 ov), 2-106 (Litton Das, 16.4 ov), 3-170 (Najmul Hossain Shanto, 27.5 ov), 4-214 (Mahmudullah, 35.4 ov), 5-251 (Mushfiqur Rahim, 42.1 ov), 6-286 (Towhid Hridoy, 46.3 ov), 7-303 (Mehidy Hasan Miraz, 49.1 ov), 8-304 (Nasum Ahmed, 49.3 ov)

AUSTRALIA	O	M	R	W	Wd	Nb
Josh Hazlewood	7	1	21	0	0	0
Pat Cummins	8	0	56	0	4	0
Sean Abbott	10	0	61	2	0	1
Mitchell Marsh	4	0	48	0	2	1
Adam Zampa	10	0	32	2	0	0
Travis Head	6	0	33	0	0	0
Marcus Stoinis	5	0	45	1	2	0

AUSTRALIA		R	B
Travis Head	b Taskin Ahmed	10	11
David Warner	c N H Shanto b Mustafizur Rahman	53	61
Mitchell Marsh	not out	177	132
Steven Smith	not out	63	64
Marnus Labuschagne			
Josh Inglis †			
Marcus Stoinis			
Pat Cummins (c)			
Adam Zampa			
Josh Hazlewood			
Sean Abbott			
Extras	(w 4)	4	
Total	(2 wickets, 44.4 overs)	307	

Fall of wickets: 1-12 (Travis Head, 2.5 ov), 2-132 (David Warner, 22.1 ov)

BANGLADESH	O	M	R	W	Wd	Nb
Taskin Ahmed	10	0	61	1	1	0
Mahedi Hasan	9	0	38	0	1	0
Nasum Ahmed	10	0	85	0	1	0
Mehidy Hasan Miraz	6	0	47	0	0	0
Mustafizur Rahman	9.4	1	76	1	1	0

It reminded me of the 2014 IPL season. I smashed a few scores in the 80s and 90s with strike rates well over 200, having the time of my life in a winning team, yet there was still criticism from some quarters about me not turning two figures into three. It was never something I was worried about when the aim was to score as quickly as possible. I understand there is a cultural difference, but in hindsight I do wonder whether this focus might have been counterproductive for India.

For about five overs in the semi it looked like Daryl Mitchell might run them close, but India made it through comfortably in the end. It was the first time I let myself daydream about how good it would be to take them on and win in front of a massive crowd at Ahmedabad. But to get there, we had to switch on the next day.

And boy, did we ever. Upon arrival, we wanted to bowl. Nobody thought the track would be as lively as it turned out, but with the rain the previous day, it looked like there was enough there to try putting on pressure with our quicks right away. We thought Temba Bavuma would think the same, but he went the other way when the coin came down in his favour. For a few minutes, everyone had got what they wanted. But for South Africa, not for long.

What a start. This isn't fair on Starcy, but so much about our team's energy can be set by his first six balls. We lift with him when it works, and can feel flat when it doesn't. Because he's so dangerous, we crave seeing his best every time. And of course, I know as well as anyone that this is not how cricket works. Today, though, he was on. One of those overs, nicking off Bavuma with the sixth ball. And it only got better from there.

At the other end, Hoff was as unplayable as I've seen him. Floating between backward point and cover point, I couldn't see perfectly how much the ball was doing, but the way the South Africans were playing said that it was plenty. It was incredible that our blokes who have taken the new ball for so long could still take it to a new level.

The batters hung on for a few overs, but Hoff's pressure broke de Kock, caught from a lofted drive. Markram did something similar to point for Starcy's second, then Rassie van der Dussen edged Hoff to slip. The fact that we still had two slips in the 12th over says all you need to know. South Africa were 4 for 24 and nowhere.

Their record in knockout games always leads to pronouncements around the team psyche and so on. The history is there about stumbling at these hurdles. But this wasn't a case of their top order freezing, unable to play well when they normally would. This was a team being bossed by two sensational fast bowlers getting everything right. After their start, the South Africans might have folded completely. Instead, they found a way out of the hole.

I was thrown the ball in the 21st over, and bowled my ten straight aside from a change of ends. After the post-Mumbai aches and the fresh hamstring worry, it felt great to get through my work without pain and keep the pressure on with a boring return of 0 for 35. It was the best I bowled in the tournament.

Our other offie, Trav, was the one who got among them just when South Africa were nearing a century partnership for the fifth wicket. We might bowl the same category but we go about it very differently, with his stock delivery coming more out the front of his hand to impart as much side spin as possible, while I go over the top for dip and bounce.

Into the attack in the 31st, he did Klaasen on the outside edge and hit his middle stump, something that takes some doing. With Trav's reputation of ragging it, Klaasen played for too much spin. It'll go down in Aussie folklore that he went and did it again next ball when blowing Marco Jansen's pad off. Having barely bowled in the competition, he was on a hat-trick in the semi. He didn't get it, but those two balls defined the middle overs and kept our target low.

David Miller was sensational to get them above 200. We were close from our Kings XI days back in 2014, when the media called us the M&M show and we took the franchise to an IPL final. I've always believed he had the talent to match it with the best. He got to a century in the final over and dragged his team to 212. One, it was something for them to bowl to. Two, as immediately chimed in my mind, our target of 213 was the score Australia and South Africa tied on in the 1999 World Cup semi.

Memories of that tournament are seared on my mind, not yet 11 years old but obsessed with events in England. This was one of many nights that I snuck out of bed, past my parents' bedroom, down the hallway to the living room. The plan only worked if I closed the doors so the light wouldn't reflect, then came the tricky move of muting the TV as soon as it fired up. One mistake and I would be found out. I did manage to watch those final few overs, with Damien Fleming rolling the ball down the pitch to Adam Gilchrist after Lance Klusener and Allan Donald got mixed up. You don't forget these moments.

This time around, thoughts of a close finish vanished when Davey got motoring, getting after Kagiso Rabada especially while hitting four sixes in six overs. He was out in the seventh, but knocking off 60 runs so quickly made our path seem inevitable. The only thing is, in an elimination chase, the one thing you most want to avoid is letting the bowling team take wickets in a hurry.

That's what happened the following over when Bison smashed a drive, and Rassie in the covers put in a full-stretch perfect dive. A catch like that, defending a small total, can be the thing that makes teams start to believe. We were all grateful it was Smudge walking in at that point. Nor did the wickets bother Heady, who slog-swept Markram for six before crunching the pace of Gerald Coetzee for three fours in a row. His half century had taken 40 balls, and if South Africa had a window, Trav was shutting it.

Halfway to the target after 14 overs, the only variable left was Keshav Maharaj. I was shocked that South Africa hadn't turned to him earlier given how effective we had been with finger spin, and we know the left-armer is as good as anyone. A fast game came to a grinding halt when his first ball knocked over Trav through the gate. It was the kind of delivery you dream of bowling. We had lots of time for our next 107 runs, but their star had all of his overs to come.

Marnus and Smudge played the percentages and neutralised the threat, including the wrist spinner Tabraiz Shamsi down the other end. After the runs dried right up for half a dozen overs, Marnus found two boundaries, driving Shamsi then sweeping Maharaj. It felt like the finish line was in sight with 80 to get. But we should have known better than to think it would be simple.

Marnus has a quality reverse sweep, so he had the confidence to take it on, but was out leg before. My turn, then. Despite the match situation and how much was riding on it, I felt unusually calm walking down the stairs. I was in great nick, knew these bowlers, and backed my ability to put them under pressure. I wanted to apply my usual game plan and break the back of the chase.

A good ball first up, one that didn't spin and picked up pace off the surface, thankfully beat the edge. Maharaj was convinced in the next over when I missed my reverse, sending it upstairs, but I knew I hadn't nicked it.

My fifth delivery offered the chance to go for it. Shamsi dropped short. In that fraction of a second when a bowler misses their length, I have a choice. There's always a choice. My instinct is to punish that ball. If you strip it back, it's one of the main reasons I've had success: bowl badly to me and I'm able to cash in. I ignore the option to knock it out to midwicket for one. That makes life more difficult for the bowler, and more likely I'll get another bad ball. This was one of those opportunities, and I had no doubt I was hitting the drag-down for six.

Watching the replay, that ball is on its way downward by the time it hits my leg stump. Keeping lower than I thought, my swing goes over the top. It's a shit way to get out and it looks dreadful, not my first time. I was gutted not to be the guy to drive us to the finish line. But if I stopped trusting my instincts, and stopped pouncing on errors, I would change the dynamic between me and bowlers. They wouldn't give me as many overpitched balls to knock down the ground in fear of getting short. I just had to cop that this was one of the times that went wrong.

It was a different feeling watching before and after my wicket, unable now to influence the result. We had 76 to get, and plenty of overs. Ingo came in to reprise the Marnus role with Smudge, steady as she goes across nearly ten overs as they got the runs down to 39. Maharaj only had one over left, Shamsi two. For the second time in the chase, we had been tested with quick wickets and settled.

So it was time for another twist. Smudge had barely made a false move in 102 minutes, anchoring a tense chase as well as anyone can. With pace at both ends, it was a case of sticking to the task, needing less than 2.5 an over. But when Coetzee dropped short from around the wicket, Smudge went back in his crease and decided to smash him out of Kolkata.

I'm hardly one to judge, but when the top edge ballooned up and landed in Quinny's gloves, it opened the game back up. It was the most out-of-character shot I've ever seen from Smudge, the type of thing you might have caught me doing in a random state game a decade earlier. His innings had been vital, but the bench was stunned and he was furious. We left him well alone as he got back.

Of course the South Africans were up and about. They had been all night, in our faces, giving it to us. Even in my brief stay I had copped a barrage. Over the years we have felt like they only make noise when things are going their way, and we can shut them up quickly by getting things on our terms. But on this night they were going to keep the energy up to the bitter end. We don't buy into the choking nonsense, they're a team we respect a great deal.

They had to go bang-bang again though. With Ingo having Starcy for company, South Africa didn't have enough runs without something special. Our pair saw off Shamsi's last two overs in between finding boundaries from pace at the other end.

But Coetzee is the type of character who embodies complete aggression. He was going to keep charging in no matter what. With 20 runs to defend, he got it right to Ingo, a ball that felt like a full toss but became a yorker. Bang went the stumps. Like Smudge's hand, the 49 balls of that innings were vital. When you think that Ingo had started the tournament on the bench, it had been quite the ride for him. But like Smudge, he was walking off with work yet to do.

It's excruciating on the bench by this stage, riding every ball, cheering every single like a match-winning six. It was like the T20 World Cup semi-final, when it was Matty Wade batting with Stoin. It's awesome in hindsight, because I've already seen the ending, but at the time, knowing I was one of those who hadn't got the job done that night, my nerves were shot.

In contrast to 2021, though, we were watching two fast bowlers tackle the job. But that doesn't start to tell the story of these two across disciplines. Pat Cummins, the man for all seasons: willpower and self-belief combined with an understanding of his strengths. There he goes again, needing to do it with the bat having already done it with the ball, barely a week since our version in Mumbai.

It's always him doing the tough stuff. The Edgbaston Test months earlier with Nathan Lyon, putting on an unbeaten 55 when all was lost. Having been in the crowd on day two, by the final evening I was in the middle of a T20 game in Durham with the umpire talking me through every run in the Test. Patty hit the winning boundary as I was leaving the field, pumping my fists at the crowd and roaring 'The Ashes are coming home!' as they playfully booed me. In Pat we trust, from his debut Test when he hit the winning runs as a teenager.

Down the other end, Starcy. He'd already been out there for half an hour, navigating the difficult terrain with Ingo to get us so close. He had made everything that day possible with the way he sent down that first spell. He had stepped up for us then and was now. There's a prevailing belief that Australian teams find a way to win when it matters most, something deep in our DNA. If this were a bilateral, we might end up losing half the time from here, but with these two warhorses in a World Cup semi, different story.

It took them 46 balls across 32 minutes to collect those 20 runs. There were false strokes and anxious moments but they went about their work as diligently as Smudge and Ingo had.

When Patty steered Marco Jansen for four to seal it, the feeling on the bench was as good as any I've been involved in for Australia. Relief yes, but pride that we had held our nerve. South Africa were shattered, a whole range of emotions visible. But the fact that they were still in with a chance so deep into the game speaks to their resilience and ability. There's no reason they can't go on to win a major trophy.

This time, it was our team's opportunity. As soon as we had calmed down from the initial high, the experience in our dressing room said to keep things in check. We had reached our first goal, to make the final, and Ronnie and Patty wanted to acknowledge that. From where we had been, so close to elimination while barely out of the blocks, this was a fine achievement. Knowing the lead-up would be intense, the other message was to enjoy the experience and not let it overwhelm us; to lean into what was to come and enjoy the possibilities.

With that said and done, the only thing left was to get back to the hotel and enjoy a quiet beer. It was a lovely vibe. We had our usual crew of about 20 people, until I noticed an unexpected visitor floating around. Older bloke, stylish . . . was that Mick Jagger? I couldn't quite believe it was, but then he came over for a chat. It didn't take long to realise that he's as much of a cricket nut as I am, specifically arranging Rolling Stones tours to match up with cricket that he wants to watch, which is why he was here at this World Cup. That conversation was an unexpected perk of the job. But we had one more task ahead in Ahmedabad if we really wanted to get satisfaction.

SOUTH AFRICA V AUSTRALIA

Venue: Eden Gardens, Kolkata
Toss: South Africa, elected to bat first
Points: Australia advanced
TV Umpire: Chris Gaffaney (New Zealand)
Referee: Javagal Srinath (India)

Date: November 16 2023
Result: Australia won by 3 wickets (with 16 balls remaining)
Umpires: Nitin Menon (India), Richard Kettleborough (England)
Reserve Umpire: Michael Gough (Bangladesh)
Player of the Match: Travis Head, (Australia) 62 (48) & 2/21

SOUTH AFRICA		R	B
Quinton de Kock †	c Cummins b Hazlewood	3	14
Temba Bavuma (c)	c †Inglis b Starc	0	4
Rassie van der Dussen	c Smith b Hazlewood	6	31
Aiden Markram	c Warner b Starc	10	20
Heinrich Klaasen	b Head	47	48
David Miller	c Head b Cummins	101	116
Marco Jansen	lbw b Head	0	1
Gerald Coetzee	c †Inglis b Cummins	19	39
Keshav Maharaj	c Smith b Starc	4	8
Kagiso Rabada	c Maxwell b Cummins	10	12
Tabraiz Shamsi	not out	1	5
Extras	(lb 4, w 7)	11	
Total	(10 wickets, 49.4 overs)	212	

AUSTRALIA		R	B
Travis Head	b Maharaj	62	48
David Warner	b Markram	29	18
Mitchell Marsh	c van der Dussen b Rabada	0	6
Steven Smith	c †de Kock b Coetzee	30	62
Marnus Labuschagne	lbw b Shamsi	18	31
Glenn Maxwell	b Shamsi	1	5
Josh Inglis †	b Coetzee	28	49
Mitchell Starc	not out	16	38
Pat Cummins (c)	not out	14	29
Adam Zampa			
Josh Hazlewood			
Extras	(lb 3, nb 2, w 12)	17	
Total	(7 wickets, 47.2 overs)	215	

Fall of wickets: 1-1 (Temba Bavuma, 0.6 ov), 2-8 (Quinton de Kock, 5.4 ov), 3-22 (Aiden Markram, 10.5 ov), 4-24 (Rassie van der Dussen, 11.5 ov), 5-119 (Heinrich Klaasen, 30.4 ov), 6-119 (Marco Jansen, 30.5 ov), 7-172 (Gerald Coetzee, 43.3 ov), 8-191 (Keshav Maharaj, 46.2 ov), 9-203 (David Miller, 47.2 ov), 10-212 (Kagiso Rabada, 49.4 ov)

Fall of wickets: 1-60 (David Warner, 6.1 ov), 2-61 (Mitchell Marsh, 7.4 ov), 3-106 (Travis Head, 14.1 ov), 4-133 (Marnus Labuschagne, 21.5 ov), 5-137 (Glenn Maxwell, 23.4 ov), 6-174 (Steven Smith, 33.3 ov), 7-193 (Josh Inglis, 39.5 ov)

AUSTRALIA	O	M	R	W	Wd	Nb
Mitchell Starc	10	1	34	3	4	0
Josh Hazlewood	8	3	12	2	0	0
Pat Cummins	9.4	0	51	3	2	0
Adam Zampa	7	0	55	0	0	0
Glenn Maxwell	10	0	35	0	0	0
Travis Head	5	0	21	2	1	0

SOUTH AFRICA	O	M	R	W	Wd	Nb
Marco Jansen	4.2	0	35	0	4	0
Kagiso Rabada	6	0	41	1	1	1
Aiden Markram	8	1	23	1	1	0
Gerald Coetzee	9	0	47	2	1	1
Tabraiz Shamsi	10	0	42	2	5	0
Keshav Maharaj	10	0	24	1	0	0

14

Enjoy the Silence

The 14th, a par five. Melting a drive, the sexiest four-iron I've ever hit, to within ten feet of the flag. Downhill putt, left to right, never looked like missing. Eagle. It was then, the morning before the 2023 World Cup final, that I knew I was ready to roll. Three under on the back nine, shooting one under off the stick all up – I can remember the whole round.

I was back at the scene of the crime: the Kalhaar Blues & Greens Golf Club in Ahmedabad. The scene where I flew off the back of a buggy and nearly lost my tournament. 'You made us famous!' said the man greeting me on my arrival. He wanted to fill in the gaps – the last time he'd seen our team, we had been about to leave the course and all was well. I filled him in on the unlucky u-turn, joking that before my round today I had better go and retrieve a piece of my scalp.

We only had a couple of days after our semi against South Africa, travelling from Kolkata on the Friday with the decider on Sunday. By this stage every training session was optional and I thought that extra focus would be counter to my interests. The leadership trusts us to make those calls. There was no avoiding that our next game was different, but changing our preparation wouldn't help. Some guys need to hit cricket balls, others are happier to take a breath. I was fresh, calm and grateful for that trust.

Unfortunately for Patty, captains don't have the same flexibility. He had to trek across town for his pre-match formalities. He sets up the pins in media conferences, calming things for those trying to read into how the group is faring. He's like a good footy coach at finals time, presenting as though he's enjoying the ride rather than letting it get to him. He nailed his appearance with a sentence that made the headlines: 'There's nothing more satisfying than hearing a big crowd go silent, and that's the aim for us tomorrow.'

We didn't have a formal team meeting back at the hotel, but we did all want to check what the skipper had seen in the middle of the vast stadium. There had been so much attention on the pitch from India's semi, with reports that the ICC were unhappy that a different strip got used instead of the appointed one, as nothing was left to chance for the hosts. Without getting sidetracked into specifics, this felt like an example of the tournament being set up to be an Indian triumph. From the moment we arrived it had seemed different to other World Cups, where the host is just another competing nation. The home team were more than that in 2023.

Patty didn't have much to go on, but it was fair to assume the pitch was as flat as could be. A little later, word circulated that the ground staff were conducting tests by bouncing balls at both ends. It seemed that the end with more bounce then got the shit rolled out of it. This may not have been accurate, but it was how we interpreted it, and to be honest, we were pissing ourselves laughing. If the play was to neutralise our quicks after what they did in the semi, so be it. In its own way that was helpful in sharpening us up, knowing that especially if we bowled first, we had to be perfect. Maybe that crept into India's thinking too, increasing the pressure on them?

Back from golf, I spent my day with Vini and Logan. I had to stay on for a T20 series after the World Cup, so we decided they should head home to Melbourne, and the best connection meant going direct to the airport from the final. A couple of weeks away isn't bad on paper, but with Logan so small it felt like a lot. We savoured our time together, which took my mind off what was coming. Our month in India had been so special, arriving when my tournament went into turbodrive at the Netherlands game. I was so happy they would see me take the field in a World Cup final.

After one final swim with my little crew, at a pool Vini and I knew well from the same hotel during IPL quarantine, it was time to kiss them goodbye and board the bus. The guys did as we always do, which for me is to put in headphones and listen to familiar music while playing Candy Crush on my phone. It gets me into an almost meditative state while keeping my fingers busy, all of which keeps my mind as free as possible on arrival.

Given everyone is so connected to phones now, it's strange to be a cricketer having to hand it over for integrity reasons when reaching a venue. It's helpful though to untether us from the outside world. It's a cue for me to switch on. We were earlier than usual, thanks to World Cup formalities, so there was no rush in the rooms, slowly unpacking and changing.

I knew that the moment I opened that dressing room door, staying zen would be a lot more challenging. Stoin was the unlucky man to miss selection. There was media chat they he might replace Marnus to give us the best chance of pushing our score, but the call went the other way. It never occurred to me until the final XI was picked that he wouldn't be there, and having taken the field together for so long it was difficult seeing a great mate miss out. It also showed a lot of faith in my bowling. But nobody could fault the way he approached the day, a team man through and through.

My time came to grab bat and gloves and warm up. Off I went, down what feels like hundreds of steps to ground level, similar to Johannesburg's Bull Ring without the canopy over the top. An hour and a half before game time, it must have been two thirds full with noise to match. I'm used to IPL games in packed and passionate stadiums, but the sea of blue shirts was striking and the emotion palpable.

When it was time for Ravi Shastri to play ground announcer, he opened by calling the stadium the 'biggest colosseum in the world'. It was funny to learn later that the crowd had been bigger at my first World Cup final at the MCG, but there you go. 'Heads,' called Pat into the microphone. 'We're going to have a bowl first, thanks.'

The Indian crowd roared and Patty smiled. I hadn't known his plan, but liked the idea of chasing under lights with the help of dew, as we had been through the second half of the tournament. The common wisdom was that we had to bat and go gigantic, but this day was about confounding assumption. Of course it looked a bat-first day – flat pitch, 33 degrees. But this would put India in a situation where they didn't know what would be enough, something that could hurt them if they didn't fully extend themselves.

The previous evening Patty had asked if I felt comfortable bowling one-over spells. He and the brains trust had clearly spent a lot of time thinking about knocking India off their game, and one option was six-ball instalments rather than traditional spells. I was up for it. This was going to be fun.

Rev-ups are not Ronnie's style. He made his way around the room to give handshakes, half hugs, low fives, depending on each personality. With me, it's always a handshake with a look straight in the eye: 'Mannnnwellllllll, all the best.' That's a nickname from my early Victorian days, when I changed my Facebook name for privacy and randomly picked Manwell. Probably because of the spelling, it stuck. A generation of senior players still love using it: Brad Hodge, Dirk Nannes, Wadey, even Bison gets in on the act without knowing the back story. Manwell then became my alter ego on nights out – you can use your imagination.

I knew the Ahmedabad steps from running up and down them as a spare player during the England game, and I'd done a few more reps by the time we went down for the anthems. The noise, even by Indian standards, was something else. How were we going to silence this? We were roared at down that open-air tunnel, and the tone had changed. A lot of us might be IPL players, but right now we were the hunted.

We're all over the place when it comes to Advance Australia Fair. Most try to sing along, some prefer not to. Usually I'm trying to eyeball one of the support staff, lined up on the boundary rope, to get them to laugh. It's an honour to be there, but having fun keeps a lid on things rather than getting overawed. On a day like this, though, with barely anyone on our side, it was time to give it big. For the Indian anthem, Jana Gana Mana is so familiar to most of us that some of us automatically started singing along, doing our best with the 'Jaya jaya jaya jaya he!' at the end. It was another small example of keeping a smile on our faces before the daunting task ahead. Then we were off to our positions, with barely a huddle. It had all been said.

———

I wrote earlier about how Starcy's first spell can give an immediate glimpse of our fortunes. The first few balls made it clear that he would be getting no assistance from the pitch. When Rohit shouldered arms, the fifth ball of the match didn't come close to reaching Ingo's gloves. Instead of getting frustrated, we laughed about it. What did we expect, and what else could we do?

Hoff is just about the most difficult bowler in the world to walk at because he gets so much bounce, but Rohit was happy doing just that, flat-batting him through cover before pulling him for another four. Having conceded 12 runs in eight overs in the semi, Hoff now went for 10 from his first three balls. Though the lack of bounce also saw Rohit play over one and nearly lose his off stump.

My bigger concern was Shubman Gill. Rohit could make a mess of us, but would give chances along the way. His opening partner is more traditional in his dismissals, often edging early. When Starcy got one to tail away, the edge landed well short of slip. Our laughs were more nervous now. Rohit plonked Hoff into the crowd at midwicket like he was a net bowler, then drove him down the ground for four more.

With nothing happening, the temptation for Patty would have been to get Starcy out of the attack and instead use him as an impact bowler. But he waited one more over, and second ball Gill tried to pull like Rohit, off the front foot, but whipped it to Zamps at mid on. He wasn't the biggest star in their top six, but with so much against us this was a boost.

It still left Rohit, who can reach a ton before you've looked up, and with seven fielders inside the circle there was little to stop him taking them on. There was no consolation after the wicket: he finished the over by flaying over cover for six. Starcy got another over, Virat got the first three balls away for four. The second and third were stunning off-side strokeplay. With three tons already in the comp, he would take as much stopping as his captain.

With 54 scored by the end of the seventh, Patty sidled up. 'What do you reckon? One from you now?' I can't stress enough the extent to which I did *not* reckon! But we all had jobs to do. Getting Rohit out in a warm-up game felt like months ago. It almost was. I knew that with his record against finger spin, and only two fielders back, he might eat me alive. He'd shown that the length of the boundaries was irrelevant. And he was on strike.

Given how often Rohit hits me for six, I was pleasantly surprised that he was happy driving my first ball for a single. Kohli did the same, then Rohit again. Patty came up to ask for intel. Any spin? Any bounce? No, and no. There was absolutely nothing. When Virat worked out they weren't turning, he cut an easy four. Conceding seven from the over felt like an escape.

Realising I would bowl the 10th too, I rationalised it as best I could. They would attack the last over of fielding restrictions regardless, so it was better that they tonk me than one of our frontliners. So long as I wasn't lined up for multiple sixes, it could be seen as a decent result. The lining up happened second ball. Rohit, over long on, way back into the crowd. Thinking I spotted him charging again, I made the classic overcorrection. Short, he cut four. Patty started walking over but I didn't want to chat. It was a bad ball, I could pull things back on track.

Last gasp of the Powerplay, a track as dead as any, Rohit on 47 from 30. There was nothing more certain than him trying to hit my next three balls as far as possible, laying a big bruise on us before the middle overs. I went to my cross-seamer, the type of off-break that has a better chance to pick up pace or bounce instead of landing in the arc of a right hander. In theory. I saw him advancing but bowled what I'd planned anyway, full enough for him to have a crack. But he didn't hit it for six. He didn't get much at all. Instead of going over midwicket, it was a leading edge.

'Caaaatch!'

With the ball hanging in the air, I couldn't believe it was going to land safely towards deep cover. A false stroke, Rohit, those big bats, it was cruel. But then, racing out of the circle at full pace, really motoring, there was Trav. With the ball about to drop, he had made so much ground that he was close enough to dive back with the flight. The ball was coming over his right shoulder. The degree of difficulty was as high as it gets. He hit the turf, and when he emerged it was with the white ball in his hand. It was an instant classic. It fired us up like nothing else. I reckon wickets are more exciting than tons, and this felt like it might have saved us a century.

It had been Trav who replaced me when I was dropped from the one-day team in 2016. I knew it was coming. In the West Indies, playing a tri-series with South Africa, things weren't going my way. In St Kitts the confirmation arrived. Having enjoyed a great run for four years, this was the first time someone had a real claim on my spot: a young fella from South Australia doing everything right.

A prodigious talent with the bat, Trav hadn't been exposed to the level of fielding you need to reach for Australia. Especially as a batter, you can't be hidden. Nor did he want to be. Flat about being dropped, I knew the best thing I could do was help the team rather than sooking, so I took on Trav's fielding as a project. He put in the work time and again. Seven years on, what a payoff. He had turned a World Cup on its head.

My over still went for 14, with Shreyas lacing me through cover, but little did we know how long it would be until India would hit another four. We left the Powerplay in better shape than we expected at 2 for 80. Two balls later, Shreyas hung his bat and Patty found the edge, which miraculously carried to Ingo.

That was the opening Patty needed to try getting the innings played how he wanted. He knew this game was all about limiting boundaries, and on this pitch, thumping the ball in short was the best bet. Luckily there's nobody in the world better than him for that job. After nearly bouncing out Virat in the 15th over, Kohli and KL Rahul took a safety-first approach, allowing Zamps to cruise in for three tidy overs. In the 17th, Davey and Marnus threw themselves around to save boundaries as they had in the semi. One of those sneaking through might have grown India's confidence, but it didn't happen. Instead, within half an hour, the energy had changed entirely.

For over 18, I was called upon for six balls. I knew that's all I was getting, regardless of how it went. Three singles? Perfect. Hoff's turn, more singles. Fine. Mitch Marsh, come on down. Two singles there, Ingo straight up to the stumps for his fellow West Australian. The pace-off variations from our seamers might have been obvious, but there was no getting them away. Fields kept changing, stacking one side then the other. Nothing settled. Trav did just as Mitch had, two singles.

The nuffie in me was loving this, having a crack at something so unusual and saving it for the final. On it went: Starcy, Bison again, me: four runs, three, three. We'd made it to the bloody halfway mark! In 15 overs since the Powerplay, no boundaries and a run rate of 3.4 an over. It felt like minutes earlier that Rohit had been running at us like a man possessed.

Patty and the coaches happened upon this plan by deciding that business as usual would slant this game in India's favour. We had to change as many variables as we could to be unpredictable. The toss, fields, bowling changes were what we could control. The games during India's unbeaten run had begun to feel like simulations. We wanted to stop them switching on the autopilot. By trying to make this game feel so different, maybe their machine would break down.

One part functioning as normal was Virat. It had been a long time between boundaries but he's the ultimate accumulator, works the angles, and if he went deep his strike rate would tick up. Even while we all wanted to get him out, old friendships still showed through. At one stage when I pinged the ball at the stumps he was in the way and stuck up a glove to deflect it. We pretended to square up to one another but very quickly neither of us could hide a grin.

Virat passed his half-century, and an over later KL got down low to lap me for four, his first creative shot. It had been 97 balls between boundaries, but both these superstars had the game to shift up gears in a hurry and dismantle our hard work.

But soon, Patty had his influence on the game again. It was the third ball of the 29th over when Virat chopped on. The quintessential Cummins dismissal – into the pitch, just enough movement back off the seam to find the inside chunk. There are remarkable photos where Pat and Virat realise what has happened before any of the 92,453 people in attendance. For me at midwicket, it was one of those moments that was almost in slow motion.

Kohli had been stopped on 54, something so difficult to do once he's set. By far the biggest moment of the game to date, Patty had successfully silenced the crowd. The loudest noise was from our huddle, and we sounded like a football team: they had stopped, and we had them where we wanted them. Keep going!

Now we were up against Ravindra Jadeja, a man who has saved his best for Australia in all formats. But with short bursts from Pat, Zamps, Starcy, Trav, nothing changed. KL's fifty came from his 86th ball. We couldn't believe our luck that he wasn't pushing his innings. Losing Kohli might have hindered his ambition, but this is a guy with 50-ball tons to his name. We held our breath as we kept moving the target and Patty kept shifting the levers. But nothing changed. Another boundary drought was underway.

When Hoff came back in over 36, it started with overthrows from consecutive balls. Not a huge deal, but those sort of errors can grow legs. Josh wasn't having any of that. He found some reverse, a welcome development, to beat Jadeja. We blew a review thinking he had nicked it, but there was no doubt about the very next ball, closer to the stumps and shaping slightly away, catching the edge and carrying.

I had the next over and KL let me bowl to him. I nearly had him stumped, and gave up a single run. That was likely my bowling day done, as Mitch, Trav, and I had done our collective duty as the fifth bowler.

Suryakumar Yadav finally made the most of a chance to cut Zamps for four. With what he does in T20 cricket, we knew that if this guy got away for even a few overs they could still pump their score up to 300. But the same pattern picked up: right when they might have taken us on, they chose the safer option. It was like SKY caught the bug from KL. Two more quiet overs took us into the final ten.

Given that Hoff had found precious old-ball movement, Starcy was a chance to be very difficult. So it proved when he sent down the delivery of the match – angled into KL, standing up perfectly to sort him out and find an edge. This was a different mission to what was asked of our quicks in the semi but they were delivering again. I felt for Mohammed Shami, doing what nobody else had done by having a swing, but he got caught behind as well. Now every edge was making it to Ingo, who deserves credit for moving closer to where he thought the ball would carry.

Zamps hadn't grabbed wickets as he had through the group stage, but nailed Bumrah in front of middle with five overs to go. SKY was the hope of a late rally but Hoff's slower bouncer was too good, helped to Ingo – a record five catches in a World Cup final. With only the last pair left, the innings sputtered to a close.

It was fitting that Pat bowled his complement without conceding a boundary, an absurd achievement. Also fitting that we got the tenth wicket, Kuldeep run out from the final ball. All out 240. From 40 overs after the Powerplay, India had only made 160 runs – exactly four an over. We couldn't have dreamed of putting the brakes on for so long. It was an awesome feeling when we left the field. 'How the fuck have we just done that?' was my question to anyone who would listen. Through planning and execution, that's how.

Even so, we knew the most difficult time to bat would be against the new ball under lights. Five an over can feel like a lot more than that in a final. I remember hoping that having been so good with the ball, we wouldn't follow it with a poor batting effort. Outwardly we were upbeat but I'd be surprised if anyone didn't have underlying nerves. India's quicks had been brilliant for two months. But this had become our game to win, or to lose.

Davey and Trav didn't need any parting words to know what they needed to do – put the pressure on India as soon as they could. But that nearly came a cropper. I hadn't yet made it to the viewing room when Bumrah set off. But I could hear how the crowd experienced the moment: roaring him to the crease, an even bigger boom of sound and emotion, then nothing. What was going on? Bumrah had found Davey's edge only for the ball to split Virat at first slip and Gill at second. Can you imagine the noise had that gone straight into Kohli's hands? It would have been heard in outer space.

Heady got straight into the contest, lacing a cover drive playing with the swing – much harder than it looks against Bumrah with his late release point and ability to move it both ways with little change in his action. Trav then forced another drive past mid off. Despite the near calamity first up, we had knocked 15 off the target in six balls. But it couldn't keep being that easy. Davey's next nick did go straight to Kohli, Shami had the wicket, the joint was pumping, and Virat's body language made sure the whole crowd was ready to join him on the ride.

Bison isn't one to poke around, lofting over point for four right away. That takes some guts. Shami had been the Powerplay bowler of the tournament, but Mitch decided to launch him over long off for six. He hit that one so well it was audible from our dressing room, a reminder that his World Cup streak was a hot one too. However, our flyer came down to earth when he got a bottom edge through to KL trying to cut. A second wicket inside five overs, getting Bumrah into the book and fired up as anyone.

Having bossed most of the last 45 overs, we were under the pump. Everyone knew it. Smudge was the guy to navigate past the danger and help Heady do what he does best. But Shami was getting the ball to talk, beating both edges. I had my pads on watching every ball, two wickets away from needing to walk in while it felt way too early. It was like Afghanistan again, except this time there was no other hope beyond tonight.

Smudge versus Bumrah is as good as it gets in the modern game. Steve got the early points with a piercing drive, but two balls later India's genius got past his blade with the slower off-cutter he's perfected, crashing into the back pad. Our assumption was that our guy would review, as he usually does when given out leg before. But he walked off. It must have been stone dead.

Wait a minute, though. That first replay wasn't convincing. Was that impact outside the line? Oh no. That's precisely what it was. Watching the projection come up on the screens was a tough moment. Having got ourselves into such a great position, this mistake had given India a massive gift, the wicket of the man born for situations like this. Seven overs down, it was 3 for 47, and I would be next after Marnus.

India's opening pair had ushered in India's moment. With three overs left in the Powerplay, it was only ever going to be those two bowling. The noise was like nothing you can imagine. A fourth wicket here and it would be a long journey to 241, the same score New Zealand and England both struggled to reach when they tied the 2019 World Cup final. Surely we weren't fated to have such a close one?

Heady and Marnus are both clever players. Seeing off maidens wasn't Plan A but it was necessary. Having our Test number three batting at five in this team was reassuring, as he defended and left Bumrah in the way he might on an opening morning with the red ball nipping around on a green seamer.

After India's lengthy quiet periods, we had just gone through 16 balls without a run while losing Steve Smith. It was time for a counterpunch, and who better than Trav? With Shami angling in at his off-stump, he had the touch required to steer where deep third had been taken out – a precious four. Per the plan for any batter, an overcorrection followed with Shami getting full, letting our gun opener smash him through mid-on. Times were tough, but those two balls did us the world of good. Heady had negotiated the early period that often looks tougher for him than for most, and now looked in rhythm. From there he takes some stopping.

I decided to get myself down the stairs one last time, to the dugout. As such a long journey, with distractions from the crowd on top of you, I wanted to get that out of the way before I had to bat. I was sitting with our sub fielders and support staff rather than the guys in the XI, who were glued to their seats in the viewing room. Padded up, cap on, helmet and gloves to one side, chewing the ear off anyone who would listen, up and down to stretch, ready to go. I don't think I've ever been so anxious waiting to bat, a contrast to the semi-final when I was at total peace. But – and what a relief it turned out this way – I had no idea just how long my wait would be.

In hindsight, the next passage of play showed that the two in the middle had it under control. Where we had thrown the ball around non-stop, India's play was quicks up top and spinners straight after. Jadeja and Kuldeep weren't doing much wrong but the pressure wasn't the same. Even with Marnus at one stage 9 from 27 balls, Trav took responsibility for finding gaps, then picked the perfect moment to assert himself. In over 16, his slog sweep off Kuldeep was hit so hard that it's still travelling.

They returned to pace: my RCB teammate Mohammed Siraj, another who prides himself on stepping up against Australia.

Trav carved four behind point, where he's always happiest, then climbed into a short ball, pulled to the gap at deep midwicket. His 50 from 58 balls was only a couple of deliveries slower than Kohli's half-century, but felt different with the number of release moments he gave the team. Six fours and a six, brutal shots too, hitting the ball so hard in a way that makes life tough for fielders.

The next ball should have been a chance, with Marnus edging Kuldeep, but with so few runs to protect there was no slip for either batter. It was becoming clear though that preserving runs would become redundant. India had to roll us. Back came Jadeja and Shami. With the required rate at 4.4, we had to avoiding overdoing it. In saying that, Trav deposited Shami's first ball back over his head to put us more than halfway there. At 25 overs, we had 106 to get. I must have played a hundred innings in my head, but if a wicket fell, this was now the kind of scenario for me.

More and more, though, it looked like I wouldn't be needed. Over 26 was the third in a row where we hit a boundary from the first ball. Marnus played a classical cover drive off Shami – again, that Test technique. It had taken him 53 balls to find a second four, but the only thing that mattered was Ahmedabad's silence. When Trav pulled a ball designed to rough him up, the runs required dropped to double digits.

Last roll of the dice for India was Bumrah. He had half his overs in hand, and everybody knows he can turn a game on its head. Nobody thought to tell Heady, though, who from the first ball of this spell flicked him over mid on, just short of a six. Such sweet contact, from a ball that was going to hit his middle stump. It's a fearless approach to play leg-side of the ball, giving the bowlers such a big target. Trav's welcoming party continued with a straight drive past Bumrah's boots. We were really believing now.

But Bumrah always finds something. His first look at Marnus in the new spell, he pinned him on the front pad from a full length. I was ready for Richard Kettleborough's finger to go up but it never came. Of course, India reviewed. The replay didn't look great for our number five. Where did I put my helmet? Ball tracking finally animated, nearly a minute later. Red, red . . . yellow! Umpire's call.

It must have been 49.9 percent of the ball hitting leg stump, but not enough. Saved by the angle. I sat back down. Good thing too, I hate coming in with one ball left in an over. Even though we were more than 40 runs ahead of the par score, a wicket there would have given Rohit ways to squeeze us. Instead, India's players and fans alike thought that may have been their last big chance. Plus Marnus had escaped strike with a leg bye. Their dread was heightened when Trav pulled the next ball for four. As it was with Bumrah's first over, we had been on the lucky side and this time taken 14.

With 79 runs to go, we could afford the five quiet overs that followed. But Heady doesn't stay quiet for long. Kuldeep bowling the 34th got lifted over mid on, then pulled the same way. Two more runs from a drive and Trav was 99. Being this close to a ton can do funny things, as he learned the hard way when getting out the previous Test summer in Perth.

This time, he pushed to cover and ran his legs off. A couple of issues: first, he was deep in the crease and off balance, not good for a quick single. Worse, here comes Jadeja, bounding in from backward point with a clean pick-up and throw. The only fielder I've seen better at nailing the stumps like this was Punter – Jaddu is that good. I don't think I've been as nervous for a teammate's milestone as I was in those moments, when it was clear that a hit would see him gone. Somehow, Jadeja missed. That really was India's last chance. Heady was home and it felt like we were too, as he got his goofy moustache out from under his helmet to celebrate.

He fits so well in our dressing room as a loved character. Like a lot of us, he's a bit odd. That's what separates us from other teams I've been in, not conforming to dressing room norms. Trav laughs so hard, often at himself, which is a great quality. From the moment we got him back for that New Zealand game, with his special century in Dharamsala, he was the final piece we needed to make our run. The love for him in that dugout when he made it through, with everyone down at ground level by this stage, was the moment of the night for us.

With 56 now to get, Heady could shift into his T20 gear. Sixes to start three of the next four overs – it didn't matter where the fielders were anymore, he was parking everyone into the stands. It wasn't reckless, it was calculated: to make sure of our situation, to keep the crowd seated, to finish it quickly. A slog sweep off Kuldeep was a replica of the shot he had played to get himself going.

With 20 to get came a half-century for Marnus. This was the ultimate in partnership batting, absorbing the pressure when needed, the awesome cover drive when called for. His flick off Bumrah was only his third boundary, but without him, Heady would not have been to able to do what he did. It was exactly why Marnus had been a fixture in our team, despite not having been in the original plan. Had you said before the tournament that he and Smudge would be picked throughout, we would have been accused of not being aggressive enough when 400-plus scores were predicted as the norm. It didn't turn out that way for any team, and his rock-solid technique stood up when it mattered. He celebrated his milestone by pulling another four, and we were rapt for him.

With ten runs to win, Heady started Siraj's over with one final signature shot, lifting him over mid off after moving to leg. That might be a long way from what you're taught as a kid, but who is going to tell him any different? His array of options make him what he is. Two to win, we lined up on the boundary ready for the team sprint to the middle. Trav tried to win it with a pull into the stands. And holed out to deep midwicket.

At the time, it didn't feel right that he missed the moment of winning it off his own bat. But with hindsight, it was special that he had the chance to depart the field on his own, to a reception just for him, like the way it played out for Michael Clarke in 2015. So much was made of silencing the crowd, but through their disappointment they applauded him all the way. It had been a masterpiece.

Oh shit, where's my helmet? Suddenly I remembered my immediate concern. Assuming I wouldn't need it, I'd put it down somewhere. Having scrambled to find it, I was off to the middle. I had been happy not being required, just like at the MCG in 2015, but now there was a chance to mirror the T20 World Cup final in 2021 and score the winning runs. As I entered the field I noticed that Ingo had taken his pads off, and told him to get them back on. I would be swinging hard and he might yet have to bat.

I wanted to give Marnus a huge hug of gratitude, but kept it cool with a quick hello before suggesting that I would smash whatever came at me. 'No worries,' he replied, casual as you like – it wasn't like he'd just been part of an epic 192-run stand or anything. When Siraj sent it down back of a length, I did as promised and gave it everything, a filthy slog square on the leg side. I hoped that my foot would wake up or I would be in strife coming back for a second run. But Kuldeep fumbled, we turned for two, and we had won the bloody World Cup! It was like a slow-motion montage as everyone sprinted to the middle, with Ingo and Zamps the first to leap into the pack. I get tingles even now thinking about that precious minute.

Amid our euphoria, it was impossible to avoid the desolation of the Indian team, having run the table only to be taken down at the last. I went and gave Virat a hug. We didn't need to say much, we both knew what it represented. I ended up with his playing shirt later, a kind gift. I wanted to win, I always want to win, but I also wished he could share in what we were experiencing.

Siraj was the other RCB teammate I consoled, as he sobbed with millions of others.

It must have been 45 minutes between the final ball and getting our hands on the trophy, which felt like four hours. To use the Warney line from our win in 2015, we were quite thirsty. So thirsty, in fact, that we dashed up for a quick beer during one of the ad breaks on the coverage, having said we were going to change into our runners. The perfect crime from Starcy and me.

Understandably, there wasn't much of a crowd left for the formalities. I know what it's like when your team gets done in the big one – I cried my eyes out when St Kilda couldn't get over the line in 2009 and 2010, both times a bounce of the ball away from a premiership. The last thing you want to do is watch the other mob hold up the trophy. We got our medals from dignitaries, including Sachin, who was kind in his greeting to me but was obviously heartbroken as well. At some level he's just an India fan, who wanted his team to win.

At last, it was time for Patty. It was a very odd moment when he was given the World Cup by the Indian prime minister and the Australian deputy prime minister, only to be left on stage on his own for what felt an eternity as a light show started behind him. None of it really mattered. Eventually we got our hands on what we came for, and could now get upstairs to celebrate.

In the privacy of the dressing room, with plenty of family, it was a time to take stock and smile. Cameras captured every group: the fast-bowling cartel, the batters, the coffee club, the golfers – you get the picture. I realised I had made a mistake with Vini and Logan going home, because it would have been wonderful having photos of them that night with the trophy, but you can't get everything right with a new baby. Trav did have that with his little girl Milla and his wife Jess, and of course, he was player of the final.

As the leader of the song in the white-ball teams, it's up to Zamps when and how we sing it. This was surely a night for it. When just the team was left, that was his moment to go back into the middle. Before getting into verse, though, he read through his Receipts File – the comments from former players who had written us off after two games. It was a reminder of how unpopular we had been only six weeks before, and how far we had come. Raised to fever pitch, we belted out the song.

On a Sunday night in a dry state, there was no hitting the town that evening, so we were straight back to the hotel. The bus trip was a beauty, our ritual singalong after a big win. I don't know why 'That's Amore' has become popular on those journeys, but we all gave it big. 'We Are the Champions' by Queen also naturally got a run.

In the absence of a bar, we had decided to make our own in Patty's room. He's well looked after with more space as captain, so we piled in. The alcohol licence situation means you can only access a couple of bottles per week, so we had stockpiled and brought them in like at a high-school house party. The bath was full of ice, the music blaring, every inch of the room taken up. Usually after a game you're racing for the shower, but when winning a trophy the goal becomes to stay in your kit as long as possible. We were all still in gold until calling it quits. Heady's ridiculous sunglasses got passed around, with the photo of him wearing them becoming as much of a classic as his century or his catch.

Despite staying up until sunrise, I was back at Patty's a few hours later for a quick beer before our celebration day. It won't surprise you to learn that it was another day at Kalhaar Blues & Greens – a course I'll never forget. It was a beautiful afternoon, nowhere to go, nothing to do. Heaps of food, a couple of drinks, hundreds of stories of the time we had shared together, all with our medals still on.

Being who we are, we naturally had to hit a few balls. We went out to the feature hole, a par three where we could play nearest-the-pin. Instead of a flag, we popped the World Cup on the green as target practice. Don't worry, there was never any danger of it copping a ding, with most of us struggling to get the ball off the tee box, let alone up to the green. Oh, and we did get taken to and from in those golf carts, and yes, a few of the boys were hanging off the back. Not me, though. I was up front cradling the Cup.

I sat there for a while with that trophy before we finished up that evening. Just a shiny object, but also a symbol of the work we had done. It was then that it started to sink in, what this represented. A bunch of us had won this as young lads, but to think how we had all changed and grown, the highs and the lows. One win secured in the comfort of home, another in the most confrontational environment. One triumph as favourites, another as underdogs. When I was a kid, I idolised that

1999 team who won it from nowhere. It felt like we had done something as special.

Earlier in the day, I'd made a point of going to the support staff – the doctor, physio, strength and conditioning, massage therapist – to thank them all personally. They had made it possible for me to be there in the first place. Without such intense care, there's no way I would have played again, let alone done what I was able to do in India.

A year before, my leg was in two and my foot was on the line. Even my cricket career was secondary. So many times since, I could barely see myself at this tournament, as much as I wanted to. In the previous month alone, I had gone from zero to hero to dickhead to world champion. Even by my action-packed standards, it had been an absurd ride. As I stared at that that trophy, thinking of the history it represented, thinking of the effort it embodied and the friendships it had solidified, looking at the inscriptions and markings that covered it, I noticed my face in the reflection. And smiled.

INDIA V AUSTRALIA

Venue: Narendra Modi Stadium, Ahmedabad

Toss: Australia, elected to field first

Points: Australia won the 2023/24 ICC Cricket World Cup

TV Umpire: Joel Wilson (West Indies)

Referee: Andy Pycroft (Zimbabwe)

Date: November 19 2023

Result: Australia won by 6 wickets (with 42 balls remaining)

Umpires: Richard Illingworth (England), Richard Kettleborough (England)

Reserve Umpire: Chris Gaffaney (New Zealand)

Player of the Match: Travis Head, (Australia) 137 (120)

INDIA		R	B
Rohit Sharma (c)	c Head b Maxwell	47	31
Shubman Gill	c Zampa b Starc	4	7
Virat Kohli	b Cummins	54	63
Shreyas Iyer	c †Inglis b Cummins	4	3
KL Rahul †	c †Inglis b Starc	66	107
Ravindra Jadeja	c †Inglis b Hazlewood	9	22
Suryakumar Yadav	c †Inglis b Hazlewood	18	28
Mohammed Shami	c †Inglis b Starc	6	10
Jasprit Bumrah	lbw b Zampa	1	3
Kuldeep Yadav	run out (Labuschagne/Cummins)	10	18
Mohammed Siraj	not out	9	8
Extras	(lb 3, w 9)	12	
Total	(10 wickets, 50 overs)	240	

AUSTRALIA		R	B
David Warner	c Kohli b Mohammed Shami	7	3
Travis Head	c Shubman Gill b Mohammed Siraj	137	120
Mitchell Marsh	c †Rahul b Bumrah	15	15
Steven Smith	lbw b Bumrah	4	9
Marnus Labuschagne	not out	58	110
Glenn Maxwell	not out	2	1
Josh Inglis †			
Mitchell Starc			
Pat Cummins (c)			
Adam Zampa			
Josh Hazlewood			
Extras	(b 5, lb 2, w 11)	18	
Total	(4 wickets, 43 overs)	241	

AUSTRALIA	O	M	R	W	Wd	Nb
Mitchell Starc	10	0	55	3	3	0
Josh Hazlewood	10	0	60	2	1	0
Glenn Maxwell	6	0	35	1	0	0
Pat Cummins	10	0	34	2	2	0
Adam Zampa	10	0	44	1	1	0
Mitchell Marsh	2	0	5	0	0	0
Travis Head	2	0	4	0	0	0

INDIA	O	M	R	W	Wd	Nb
Jasprit Bumrah	9	2	43	2	0	0
Mohammed Shami	7	1	47	1	3	0
Ravindra Jadeja	10	0	43	0	1	0
Kuldeep Yadav	10	0	56	0	0	0
Mohammed Siraj	7	0	45	1	0	0

Fall of wickets: 1-30 (Shubman Gill, 4.2 ov), 2-76 (Rohit Sharma, 9.4 ov), 3-81 (Shreyas Iyer, 10.2 ov), 4-148 (Virat Kohli, 28.3 ov), 5-178 (Ravindra Jadeja, 35.5 ov), 6-203 (KL Rahul, 41.3 ov), 7-211 (Mohammed Shami, 43.4 ov), 8-214 (Jasprit Bumrah, 44.5 ov), 9-226 (Suryakumar Yadav, 47.3 ov), 10-240 (Kuldeep Yadav, 49.6 ov)

Fall of wickets: 1-16 (David Warner, 1.1 ov), 2-41 (Mitchell Marsh, 4.3 ov), 3-47 (Steven Smith, 6.6 ov), 4-239 (Travis Head, 42.5 ov)

Epilogue

Remember the bat I told you about from the 201 not out? It got one more hit after the World Cup. I thought I would let it retire after serving me so well with the 40-ball ton against Netherlands, the Afghanistan night, then the winning runs in the final. But the international game is not very good at endings. Days after the high of holding that trophy in Ahmedabad, an Australian team and an Indian team were at it again in a five-match T20 series.

Some of the World Cup players were picked, and we didn't want to let Wadey down as the captain of that tour, so we compromised with an early leave pass. I would get home to Vini and Logan after three matches. The last of them happened to be my 100th in the format for Australia, at Guwahati. Treating myself to one more outing with that bat, I made an unbeaten ton as we chased 220, hitting the winning runs from the final ball after needing 21 in the last over. I'll always cherish that stick.

It was the ideal note on which to leave India, turning another game that looked out of grasp and getting it done with Wadey. But I couldn't have been happier boarding that flight. It was on arriving back to Melbourne that everything felt different.

I never mentioned The Big Show in this book, did I? Yeah, that's not an accident. It's a nickname that has been a problem for me ever since Wadey coined it on my first Australian tour in Dubai in 2012. No harm was meant, but when Pup mentioned it publicly, boy did it stick. It's a wrestling reference, but it made me sound like I drink my own bathwater. And whenever I missed out with the bat, it invariably got followed up with The Shit Show, The No Show, or something less printable.

Life as a public figure is volatile, and I've tried to come to terms with that. I know that the way I bat doesn't equate to a moral failing. Sporting failure isn't failure as a person. Even so, it's difficult to shut that out, and extra parody often hasn't helped.

So, what was it that I noticed when I got back to Australia? Well, nobody was calling me The Big Show anymore. Not in interviews, not in print, not in the street. Maybe I'm reading into this, but it felt like having followed my World Cup so closely, people understood me better than before. The judgemental negativity had been outshone by acceptance. I didn't feel divisive anymore.

There were lots of ways this revealed itself, the most extreme being the bloke who got a tattoo of my face on his arm. I don't think anyone was rushing out for one of those a few years ago. There were heartfelt chats, so many stories about watching the Afghanistan game overnight. At a Final Word podcast recording in Melbourne, the half-hour edit of my innings got shown during interval before I came on stage, and people gathered in front of the big screen roaring for every boundary even though they knew exactly what was going to happen. It was some wave to ride.

At my local cafe in Black Rock, getting a bite to eat and reading the paper, I went up to pay but the bill had been settled by someone who had spotted me, leaving a message to say thanks for the happiness the World Cup had brought him. I felt kind of guilty – I've had enough paydays out of the game. But I had to realise it was a kindness that someone wanted to express. I don't judge myself on being liked, but being appreciated without other baggage felt good.

It also felt different taking the field. All that pressure I'd put on myself over the years had gone. Instead, it felt like the hard work had paid off. Even though I'll never take fitness for granted again. Another T20 century for Australia in Adelaide was the highlight, all the more special with my parents being there. It was my last campaign leading the Stars in the Big Bash, a part of my life that hasn't featured heavily in this book because I wasn't able to play during the year in question. For those home games I had Vini and Logan there with me at the MCG.

In my first summer as a dad, there was more personal balance. Knowing that nothing as a player would be as intense as my journey to the World Cup, this was about family and the happiness of the routine. I read somewhere that you can never hug a baby enough, and I set about doing just that with the little fella in my arms as often as possible. There were challenging days, that's life. But the calm I'd found helped me enjoy the little things more.

Steve Waugh had a diary called *Never Satisfied* that went through what his team did after winning the 1999 World Cup. While I feel satisfaction for what 2023 turned out to be, there's also what I now see as positive tension as I think about what's left as a cricketer. Once you lose the drive to get better, you may as well give it away. There's no risk of that for me.

On the contrary, I do want to keep going for Australia. I know this book will come out before a Test summer, and each season carries a chance of playing Test cricket again. You already know I would jump at that, and if it came to pass, I'm confident I'd be better equipped than ever. The belief that the current management put in me is something I want to keep paying back however I can.

Then when the time comes for me to stop playing at the top level, that's only one part of the relationship with the game. Nurturing talent is so enjoyable, that's a logical place for me. But do I want to go on the formal coaching pathway and try to run the Aussie team? Probably not. I have a great time behind the mic, but don't expect me to end up following the sun commentating on every T20 competition. I'll play a lot of golf, but I don't have a pipedream of going professional.

All I'm certain of is that if Logan wants to play cricket himself, I'll be there volunteering to take the scorebook on a Saturday morning, or to stand at square leg brooming the pitch at the end of each over. Whatever I do, I'm always going to be a nuffie.

Beyond that, it feels like answering the question you get in high school. What do you want to do when you grow up? So far, I've been blessed with the chance to never have to find out. Cricket has given me years of play, so a big part of me is excited to find out what will happen once those years are done. I'll try to take on those challenges with the same energy and enthusiasm. You never know, I might not do them in exactly the same way as everyone else. And I think that's ok.

Acknowledgements

How do you thank everyone who has made a career like mine? There will be time for that when I retire, which is hopefully some distance away, so I won't try and fail to fit all those people in these pages. I hope that I've already told you who you are.

Here I want to recognise the people who were instrumental to the year covered in this book, from injury to World Cup.

The support staff from several teams gave a career's worth of treatment. With Cricket Australia, physio Nick Jones, doctor Leigh Goulding, and massage wizard Lou Murray. In Victoria, Adrian Mott's strength and conditioning support, physio with Nick Adcock. Everyone at Cricket Victoria had my back, not least coach Chris Rogers.

Behind the scenes, my beloved St Kilda Football Club opened their facilities for much of my rehab. Carn the Saints. In India, RCB's most important all-rounder Nav Gautum worked on me around the clock for each of our IPL games in 2023, along with Evan Speechley.

After the surgeon Iswadi Damasena put my leg back together, my case was handed to Andrew Oppy who provided me with the best care.

Professional sport needs a selfless support network at home. My mum, Joy, and dad, Neil, sacrificed so much to help me realise my dream. My siblings Daniel and Lisa, I'm so proud of. You can't choose your family, I just got lucky.

You can choose your friends, and I've been blessed with Rob Cockerell since we were kids – always my best mate. Then there's my personal coach Richard Clifton and his wife Ros, riding the bumps with me since I was a teenager and through 2023.

Australian coach Andrew McDonald and our old mate Aaron Finch worked so closely to help me become my best as a player in the Australian team.

Pat Cummins has been immense to play under. Sharing those partnerships in India means so much, as does his foreword to this book. Virat Kohli also put pen to paper, and I'm grateful not just for his kind words but for turning my IPL career around.

So many other teammates looked after me when my career was in the balance.

Getting on this rollercoaster in my early twenties with a lot to learn, I needed extra guidance. The late Tony Connolly, my manager, took me from being a young buck to an established player, steering me through every challenge. Ben Tippett has taken that role with immense patience, especially in my year of greatest need. He was instrumental in encouraging me to write this book, and getting it to completion. What a gem.

Adam Collins is my co-author on a project we had talked about in various forms, until the timing was clearly right. This book is the culmination of so many conversations and the trust in our friendship to tell my story. The same applies to Geoff Lemon, who was recruited as editor and did so with customary style and care.

The final words go to my little team at home, Vini and Logan, my wife and my baby boy. Becoming parents is our proudest achievement together. The love we share as a three is precious and fuels me every day. For your dedication and devotion, and for helping make me the best version of myself, I thank you and adore you forever.

About the Authors

Glenn Maxwell is a professional cricketer who debuted for the Victorian state team in 2010 and the Australian team in 2012. He is one of three Australians to score centuries in all three international formats, and has won the T20 World Cup once and the one-day World Cup twice. His career has taken him around the globe, most notably a dozen seasons in the Indian Premier League and another dozen in the Big Bash League, with half of those captaining the Melbourne Stars. He lives in Melbourne with his wife Vini and son Logan.

Adam Collins has written for cricket publications around the world including *The Guardian* and *Wisden Cricket Monthly*, and commentated for radio and television broadcasters such as SEN and Sky Cricket. A host of The Final Word cricket podcast for a decade, he is proudly from Melbourne but now lives in London with his young family.